"So I'm talkin' to this guy..."

Rob Borsellino at The Des Moines Register

Published by:
The Des Moines Register
Des Moines, Iowa

Printed by:

McMillen
Publishing.
A Sigler Company

Library of Congress Control Number: 2005927182
ISBN: 1-888223-66-9

Cover photo by Doug Wells, *The Des Moines Register*

Cover design by Mark Marturello, *The Des Moines Register*

Photo of Rekha, Raj and Romen
(pages iii & 201) by Crayola England

Photo of Mario Cuomo
(Page 53) by Fred R. Conrad/*The New York Times*

"So I'm talkin' to this guy . . ."

Dedication

This is for my soulmates — Raj, Rekha and Romen.

I think of our lives and I see the back streets of Calcutta and the beaches in Boca Raton.

I remember the family dinners — the lakeside shrimp in Italy and the curbside corndogs at the Iowa State Fair.

And I'm hearing that one line we kept laughing about:

"What's not to like?"

Thanks

I've got a lot of folks to thank.

My wife for insisting that it made perfect sense to pack up our lives, leave New York and move to Iowa in 1991. I'm about ready to admit she was right.

My mother for raising me in a public housing project in the Bronx. If we'd lived in some tony subdivision in Jersey or Long Island, I'd have missed out on all the cursing and drinking, the sick jokes and the lifelong love and friendship of Gene Gallo, Jerry Satriano and Ralph Bianca.

Thanks also to my in-laws, an interesting mix of Punjabi, Bengali and New York Jew. These folks — Romen, Rasil, Amrita, Mark, Ishan and Javed — have taught me that it's not just the Italian families that are over-the-top with their emotions.

I want to thank a couple of guys who took a chance and hired me for my first two jobs in the news business. Bob David was news director at WKNY radio in Kingston, New York, in the fall of 1974. Tom Geyer was editor of the Kingston Daily Freeman in 1976.

I have to thank Dennis Ryerson, my boss at the Register, who showed up at work one day and announced it was time for me to get off my ass and do something productive. It was time for me to stop being an editor and go out and write columns. He was sure the good people of Iowa were just dying to get a Bronx perspective on everything from loose-meat sandwiches to the Pella Tulip Festival.

I also want to thank Barb Henry — publisher at the time — who agreed this wasn't as ridiculous as it sounded.

For making this book happen I want to thank the current Register folks: Mary Stier, Paul Anger, Rick Tapscott, Gage Church, Tom Cooper, Deb Belt, Jacqui Biscobing and Mark Marturello.

And I want to thank my pal John Gaps, who decided this book would be a good idea, got things moving and then wouldn't get off my case until it came rolling off the presses.

Who is this guy?

Rob Borsellino was hired as Metro Editor of *The Des Moines Register* in 1994 and became a columnist at the paper in 1998.

He's a graduate of Bronx Community College and the State University of New York at New Paltz. He's worked in TV and radio- the ABC affiliate in Des Moines, WKNY in Kingston, New York.

He's been an editor and reporter at newspapers around New York state — including *Newsday*, the *Albany Times Union* and the *Kingston Daily Freeman* — and he was the Palm Beach County columnist for the *South Florida Sun-Sentinel*.

Borsellino is married to Register columnist Rekha Basu, and they have two sons — Raj, a student at Amherst College in Massachusetts, and Romen, a student at Roosevelt High School in Des Moines.

"So I'm talkin' to this guy . . ."

Introduction

One of the first people I met when I became president and publisher of *The Des Moines Register* was Rob Borsellino. He was thin, with a wavy shock of hair. He talked with his hands, dressed in black and smiled a lot. I didn't know what to make of this man. I went to the newsroom archives and read his columns to figure him out.

I learned quickly that he had a charming way of telling a story — staccato style, street-smarts advice — an interesting recipe of terse tabloid writing for the Heartland. His columns had grit, yet were laced with grace and compassion.

I say compassion, because while Rob Borsellino often deals with the most difficult topics, he understands that the people he writes about are his neighbors, his friends and his readers.

And believe me, Iowa readers connect with this animated writer from the Bronx.

Rob and his wife, Register columnist Rekha Basu, left the newspaper in December 2000, and moved to south Florida. After they left, readers would seek me out and say: "Please bring Rob and Rekha back. We miss them."

I did, too.

I kept in touch and in time they were ready to return to the land and the people they had come to love. Because underneath this New York persona is the heart of a Midwesterner.

He is fresh, he is honest, he knows how to weave a story.

And he does it with that Borsellino attitude.

> — *Mary Stier, publisher and president,*
> *The Des Moines Register*

Foreword
A journey from the Bronx to Iowa

Jan. 25, 1998

In the summer of '92, not long after moving to Iowa, I was in the men's room at a Des Moines coffeehouse and the wall behind the sink was thick with graffiti.

At a glance, no one seemed to be asking for a sex act or making an obscene comment that I hadn't read on other bathroom walls.

Then, as I reached for a paper towel, I noticed in the middle of all that scrawled nastiness someone had written — in handwriting worthy of Catholic school — E=MC2. Back then, I was still in my anthropology mode, on the lookout for signs of why the Midwest was different. I had lived in and around New York City for 43 years and I understood the mind-set. I knew that some things in the city were a given:

• Somebody accidentally bumps into you on the street, and the first thing you do is check your wallet.

• Someone is selling brand-name wide-screen TV sets for $50 apiece; you pay cash and don't ask questions.

• When someone invites you for dinner at 8 p.m., you aren't expected to show up before at least 9.

But now I was living not just in the Midwest, but in Iowa. Des Moines, in fact, where people invite you for dinner at 6 p.m., and if you're not there by 6:15 they call looking for you, concerned they might have said something to offend you.

My Line: Einstein

So now I needed new road markers. And I needed something to tell folks back home, like the woman who asked in that derisive tone particular to New Yorkers: "What the hell is it like living in that god-forsaken dump?"

Here was a little something I could use.

"Well," I'd tell them, "the coffee's weak, everybody's in bed by 10 and the best politicians don't have the chutzpah of Cuomo and D'Amato on a bad day. But it's a very literate, civil place. In fact, just the other day I saw Einstein quoted on a men's room wall. You don't see that sort of thing in Bensonhurst."

So far as I know, that Einstein anecdote has not encouraged even one New Yorker to move to Des Moines. But some things cannot be objectively measured.

How I came to be living in Iowa is not a particularly interesting story. Suffice to say I did it for love. My wife got a job with *The Des Moines Register*, packed up the kids, put the house on the market and turned to me on the way out and asked: "You coming, or what?"

I hesitated. "Uh, sure, babe. You know I'd love to move to Iowa," I said, trying not to act as if my entire world had come crashing down around me, "but I need time to, you know, deal with this. You go check it out and if you think I can live there, I'll come out."

I struggled with that one for about a year.

I took inventory. What did I know about Iowa? Hogs, corn, flat, caucuses. The obvious, the superficial — typical of what coast-dwellers know about the Midwest.

Friends I spoke with were sure the move would be a disaster.

One of the sports writers at the newspaper where I was working had lived in Wisconsin for a while. Close enough. I asked what he thought about my moving to Iowa.

He was a thoughtful man who considered my question carefully before passing judgment, saying finally: "Are you out of your friggin' mind? Iowa? Look at you. Listen to you. They're gonna hear you and think you're in the witness-protection program."

But I wanted to make it work.

So after my wife and kids moved in the fall of '91, I traveled to Des Moines about once a month to visit and I'd look around with an open mind.

There is, however, only so far my mind can open.

True story: My first trip to Des Moines, Christmas 1991. We're in a large, relatively new supermarket and there's an older woman giving away free samples of Weight Watchers food. She calls me over and tells me to wait because a fresh batch will be out of the microwave in a sec.

So I wait, casually asking her, "What are you making?" and she tells me with a straight face, "Enchiladas — just like the real Eye-tal-ians eat."

I look at my wife, figuring this was some sort of setup. I could not believe that would happen to me on day one. It was too perfect.

And it was no setup.

On that same trip, a native Iowan — an older man from a rural area near Waterloo — asked me: "So what do New Yorkers think about Iowa?" And the honest answer was: "They don't."

But I had anticipated that question. I knew someone was going to ask and I had my answer all ready. I told him: "New Yorkers see Iowa as a clean, friendly place; a place where people have a strong work ethic and good values. Where neighbors know when you're born and care when you die. Iowa, as we say in New York, is America the way it ought to be."

He thought about that for a second and then said: "But it's so (expletive) boring here. Don't people know that?"

What Counts As Exotic

Another guy I met on that first trip was a consultant, an African-American originally from Chicago. He was young, single and had been living in Des Moines for about 10 years. I asked him how he did it, how he managed to have a social life in a city that — at least out-wardly — was virtually all white.

He shrugged. "No problem, particularly with the ladies. You fig-ure, black guy from Chicago, born and raised in the 'hood. Right there, before I even open my mouth, I'm more interesting than 90 per-cent of the guys they meet at the bars in this town."

It was a good line and there was some truth to it. In Iowa, a little bit of exotic goes a long way. Even Italians — even second-and third-generation Italians — enjoy a certain cachet in Iowa. I heard more ref-erences to the Mafia on my first few trips to Des Moines than I'd heard since the first "Godfather" movie came out. Most comments were of the sophomoric "don't put a horse's head in my bed" variety, but some of it was actually funny.

One guy told me about a friend of his, a hotshot businessman who did time for price fixing, got out and fell in love with an Italian woman from the south side of Des Moines. "He was all nervous, because she had a huge family — grandparents, aunts, uncles, cousins — and she wanted him to meet them, you know, go over for a big Sunday dinner and he was really a wreck because he's just a farm boy from rural Iowa and he's telling me this and I'm thinking to myself, 'OK, so the guy's not Italian, but at least he's been to prison.' "

And I, of course, had to feed into the hype, casually mentioning that "every Italian family in New York has in some way been touched" by organized crime.

I made it sound as if my father was a lieutenant in the Gambino family, but the closest we came was a distant cousin — a plastic surgeon — who made millions giving fugitive mob guys new faces.

'Guinea Grinders'?

There was even a different language around ethnicity. On the two coasts, using the term "guinea" in reference to an Italian is akin to calling a black guy a "coon" or a Jew a "kike." In Des Moines, Italian hero sandwiches are called "guinea grinders," and no one seems bothered by that.

And there's a fast-food chain called "Godfather's Pizza," which — while not on par with "guinea grinders" — doesn't exactly conjure up warm feelings about Italians.

That nonsense aside, the 1,200-mile commute got real old real fast that first year. So one June morning in 1992, I moved to Iowa.

And I was miserable.

Keep in mind, I am not one of those New Yorkers who has to live on the corner of 42nd Street and Broadway in order to feel connected to the city. For 16 of my 43 years I did not even live within the city limits.

If I could avoid the subway for years at a time, that was OK with me. The last Broadway show I saw was "I'm Not Rappaport," in 1986. I've never been to the Metropolitan Opera or the Brooklyn Academy of Music.

And the first time I took a trip out to the Statue of Liberty and Ellis Island was the year after we'd moved to Iowa and we went back to New York to visit.

What I missed was the idea of New York, the access. Even if I didn't go to a game all season, I wanted Yankee Stadium close at hand. If I felt like having sushi at 2 in the morning, I knew where to find it. When a major concert tour was announced, it would not have occurred to me — or anyone I knew — to wonder whether the group was going to play New York.

As I said, when I moved to Iowa I was miserable.

I'm a journalist, and when I left New York I was covering the Cuomo administration. It was challenging work going head-to-head every day with a guy who thought nothing of taking your question on live TV, looking you in the face and saying: "Borsellino, that's a stupid question, even for you."

My first job in Iowa was at a weekly business newspaper that had the corporate community's major players on its advisory board.

But my family was whole again and I muddled through, working in TV for a while, freelancing, trying to plot my next move — and my escape from the Midwest.

And then my kid's soccer team needed a coach and one of the guys from the league called to see if I'd help out. I told him I knew very little about how the game was played and nothing at all about the rules. "That's OK," he said. "They're 7 years old. They just want to kick the ball around and have a good time."

By the time the season was over I began to feel like I was part of something.

I would run into folks at the supermarket or the mall and I was the guy from New York who coached this one's grandson or that one's nephew. They would thank me for taking the time and I would tell them the pleasure was mine.

And I knew that sounded like bull, but these people were basically strangers. I wasn't about to get into some long drawn-out story about how coaching had helped me get in touch with the Midwest.

A New Measure

After the soccer episode, I started measuring things, not only by how much I'd left behind, but also by how much I had been experiencing.

I started thinking about the things I would have missed had I stayed on the East Coast. A lot of it was practical stuff. As a newsman, covering the Flood of '93 was a sobering and exhilarating — at times frightening — experience.

There are two images from that summer I will never forget.

The first is the guy in the wheelchair among hundreds of other volunteers filling sandbags in the blistering heat in what they must have realized was a useless effort to stop an out-of-control river.

The second image is that of a family in one of the poorer sections of town as they watched their home burning. They prayed for the fire trucks to arrive and rejoiced when they did. But the heartache was even worse when they — mom, dad, two boys and a girl — realized the hydrants were empty and the water truck wasn't going to make it.

After almost 25 years in the news business, I pride myself on my ability to be a dispassionate observer of tragedy. But I cried that morning. It upsets me now, years later, just thinking about those kids.

Then beyond the practical stuff there are those "Iowa moments" — a term originally used around our house with sarcasm, but now a term of affection:

• The kindergarten teacher who called my nervous 5-year-old a few days before he started school, saying she looked forward to having him in her class.

• The kids who show up at the door on May Day and leave bags of candy.

• An August day at the Iowa State Fair.

And, maybe most telling, when I arrived in Iowa there was no way I'd have expected — or admitted — that I could get pleasure from what had seemed like such mundane events.

Now, reading back over those last few lines, my impulse is to take them out because it makes me wonder whether I'm losing my edge; whether I'd still notice if I saw E=MC2 on the bathroom wall; whether people would still think I was in the witness-protection program.

But instead, I think about a recent incident on the freeway when a guy cut me off and I chased him for about five miles — well past my exit — just to give him what my Uncle Domenick refers to as "the Italian salute." And I feel better. I feel secure enough to live with that stuff about the State Fair and the ball game.

I feel like myself: a New Yorker living somewhere else.

Table of Contents

"So I'm talkin' to this guy . . ."

"So I'm talkin' to this guy . . ."

Chapter 1: Struggles

By Ako Abdul-Samad
CEO/Founder Creative Visions
Human Development Institute

A woman loses her son, there's a tearful moment at the Holocaust Museum, a mother is serving time for the murder of her baby.

For years Rob Borsellino has given a voice to those who have struggled. He has taken us readers out of our comfort zone and helped us find solace from our own struggles and woes.

As the woman who lost her son told me, "He felt my pain." That is four stars for Rob. He has set the bar high for other reporters because he writes with his heart, soul and mind.

And readers come away with the feeling that they are sharing a struggle with someone they've never even met.

It has been my blessing to have befriended a man who has told so many stories without being judgmental.

1

Lovelady's parents struggle to deal with his death

March 9, 2000

Three weeks ago, her son was killed and she couldn't find out how it happened or who did it. Now JoAnn Hughes is hearing it'll be months before it's decided if the killers will even be charged with anything.

She spends every day at the kitchen table of her south-side duplex, sipping water, staring straight ahead, looking at pictures of her son, crying. Sleep is not an option and eating is something she does because her family forces the food on her. Her body aches and so does her mind.

The story is that her son, Charles Lovelady, died in a fight with two bouncers, whom lawyers have identified as Tom Dueber and Jeff Portman. Investigators say the bouncers are 6-foot-4 and about 275 pounds. Charles was 5-foot-7, 210 pounds.

He was just months away from his Grand View graduation. There was going to be a big family celebration. And then he was killed, leaving his mother with memories, confusion, pain. She can't seem to understand how life can go on around her when one of her babies is dead.

She knows there have been rallies and marches, meetings and press conferences. She's heard that radio shows are top-heavy with talk about her 26-year-old son's death. But JoAnn Hughes ignores it all. She says a public display won't bring Charles back. She just wants justice.

So she sits at the table and dabs at her eyes with tissues. On a chair next to her is her ex-husband, Lamont Lovelady. On the chair next to him is a catalog of tombstones. They've got to buy one for their son.

JoAnn's voice is shaky, low and tired. She talks a lot about her son's early years, when he was at Greenwood Elementary and Callanan Middle School. He played Little League at Raccoon Valley and the whole family would go, bring a picnic and make a day of it. He played football at Dowling and Valley, and he loved to speed-skate out at Skate West.

In those days, life was built around the kids — around Charles' ball games and his sister LaToya's dance recitals.

But from where JoAnn Hughes now sits, that looks like somebody else's life. It's hard to imagine she was ever that happy.

"I have to live the rest of my life like this and I don't know how I'm gonna do that. I'm just so hurt that someone would kill my son. I brought him here into this world and now they took him away."

The last time she saw her son alive was the night he died — Wednesday, Feb. 16. He came by her place around 8 to do his laundry and hang out. He left about 10, but said he'd see her in the morning for breakfast.

She settled in for the night, watched TV for a while, took a shower. Then she got a call from a friend of Charles' telling her to go to Mercy Medical Center. Not long after midnight JoAnn Hughes was being told her son was dead.

She got the news from her ex-husband.

Lamont Lovelady is a Des Moines firefighter, and five months ago his other son, Lamont Jr., was killed in a Minnesota car crash. After that, Charles kept a close eye on his dad. He'd come by the fire station and hang out with Lamont and the other guys. There was even talk about Charles joining up.

On the night of the homicide, Lamont was at the firehouse on Douglas and 48th. He heard the call for an ambulance and a pumper at Graffiti's dance club on Merle Hay Road. But he was working the ladder truck that night. Later there was more talk on the police scanner and he realized his son was hurt. He went to Mercy.

"I got there and looked at my son's eyes and I saw they strangled him. I walked next door to where JoAnn was and I said 'He's dead.' And nothing's been right since that moment. I can't understand what's happening here."

Lamont and JoAnn talk about their son, and faint smiles come across their faces. They remember how angry Charles would get because Lamont was so strict.

"He's this big high-school football star, a teen-ager, and I made him be home by midnight, no later. He said the other guys used to call him Cinderella."

They look across the table at each other and they almost laugh.

Maybe Mom needed him with her

November 13, 2002

Joe Tumea went through one of those ordeals, one of those personal traumas that leave you wondering where you go next. His wife died last month after a year-long fight with cancer, a brain tumor. Joe and Lucretia — Lou — were close. They worked together for years — six days a week, about 12 hours a day, baking bread, making deserts, cooking pasta, mixing salads at Tumea and Sons, their southside restaurant. The menu has a little blurb about how they met. He came over from Sicily in 1960 and she came from Calabria a year later. They met in Des Moines and got married in '67.

So Lou died and there was the wake, with friends and family filing past the flower-draped coffin, hugs and tears all around. There was that soft background music — Bocelli, Lanza, Pavarotti — mingling in with the rosary.

Then the funeral — the church service, more tears and memories and the graveside prayers.

It was probably the toughest thing Tumea has had to live through. The toughest he'd ever expected to live through.

But he had his four sons around him and they got through it together, propping each other up, telling each other that Mom wouldn't want to see them this sad.

And the friends came through. The other south-siders and the paisanos from around the city — the Laconas and the Barattas, the Grazianos and the Tursis, the Formaros. One of their own was hurting and they brought food and drink and comfort.

It was tough, but within days of the burial Tumea was back working at the restaurant. And the sons were with him. Salvatore was tending bar. Mario, Joe Joe, and Luigi were working in the kitchen, waiting tables, doing what they've always done. They were in pain, but they kept going. Tumea kept pushing, telling folks, "I just got to get on with it."

That was last month.

Then things got worse. Yesterday, Joe Tumea buried his oldest son, 33-year-old Salvatore, the bartender, the one they called Sammy. The one who worked as a reserve cop for the Des Moines PD, one of only 55. Sammy was the one with diabetes and the one they all say was Mom's favorite, one of the perks of being the first-born.

After she died, Sammy's health degenerated. His diabetes got worse every day and by last Wednesday he was in a coma. Thursday he died. Tuesday was the funeral.

It was one of those services thick with tears, a testament to the lives Sammy Tumea touched — 3 1/2 miles of cars in the procession, 1,600 names in the guest book.

Look around the church and it was sprinkled with politicians and some of the heaviest hitters in the business community. There were dozens and dozens of Des Moines cops — from the chief on down.

And hundreds of family and friends, other folks he met along the way. People he knew from Lincoln High and from his Little League days, folks like Frank Chiodo, the state rep. Some were from his days working the bar and the door at Jukebox — the club that's now Papa's Planet. Some were from his brief stint driving a limo.

But whatever the period, the time frame, they all talked about a driven guy. They remembered a man who was close to his mother, devoted to his dad, tight and protective of his brothers. They had a few laughs about his obsession with his hair — never a strand out of place. They shed a few tears when they remembered that every year his mom's birthday wish was that her Sammy didn't have diabetes.

There was one thing everybody who knew him mentioned. They all said the proudest day of Sammy Tumea's life was the day he became a Des Moines police officer. He was back in college now to get the 15 hours of credit he needed to qualify for full-time police work.

Then his mother died. Then he died.

And last night, Joe Tumea was trying to get his mind around all that's happened to his family.

"There are no words. I just don't know what to say except maybe his mother called him because she wanted him to be with her."

Camp lets kids be kids,
at least for one week
August 16, 2004

They're called "at-risk children," and for 51 weeks a year they go through hell.

These are the kids you read about. The ones who are sexually and physically abused. They're the ones with nothing resembling a family life. The ones with the meth-addicted mother and the father behind bars.

These particular kids are between the ages of 8 and 12, and 70 percent of them are on medication — mostly anti-depressants.

Maybe the worst part is that they don't know any better, so these kids blame themselves for everything they're going through.

But for one week a year they catch a break.

They get to spend five days at a place called Wildwood Hills Ranch in Madison County.

It's the first time a lot of them have been in a swimming pool, gone fishing or horseback riding.

Instead of watching a drunk father beat up a drunk mother, they get to go on treasure hunts and find candy.

Instead of sitting in a bedroom and crying, they get to go play in the woods with the other kids or take the slide into the lake. They learn how to make ice cream. They don't have to worry where their next meal is coming from, and they can enjoy an afternoon snack of soda and cookies. They don't have to go to bed worrying that the cops will be knocking at the door at 4 in the morning.

The idea of the camp is to give these kids a chance to see another side of life.

It's a nonprofit started four years ago by Mike Whalen, who owns the Machine Shed restaurants. He modeled it after a Wisconsin program he'd heard about.

Whalen has come up with a lot of the cash, and he's gone out and raised money. But his biggest contribution was MaryLou Garcia. For years, she worked at his restaurants — ran some of them — and then three years ago moved to Texas. Last year, Whalen brought her back to run the program.

She's focused on the kids. She knows how she wants this to play out.

"We just want to give them a chance to have some fun. They're children. They should be laughing and playing, not crying."

These kids come from all over the state, mostly from inner-city neighborhoods in Davenport, Des Moines, Cedar Rapids, Sioux City. Some are from rural areas.

Garcia finds them through churches, schools, the state Department of Human Services office, and groups like Big Brothers and Big Sisters.

There's a weekly pattern that she's come to recognize.

They arrive on Monday, about 100 kids, and about a dozen get sent home because of head lice.

On that first day the walls are up, most of the kids are in their "don't come near me" mode. A lot of them are just scared. Garcia and her staff know better than to get in their faces.

The kids are split into teams of about 10 — boys and girls separate. The first stop is the pool, where their swimming skills are assessed. By then it's lunch time.

It's a chance for Garcia and her staff to see what these kids are about.

"So many of them know nothing about things like table manners. They grab as much food as they can for themselves. It's sad."

By Tuesday the kids are connecting, feeling comfortable with one another. Each little group has gone through these team-building exercises, little games where they have to rely on each other to make things happen. Ten kids get together, and the idea is to climb a 10-foot wall, to help each other make it to the top.

They learn arts and crafts, they sing and dance. For one week they forget all the clutter in their lives.

But by Thursday night that starts to fade. These kids know they'll be heading home the next day, and the walls are going back up.

Garcia says Fridays are a heartbreaker. There are tears all around — from the kids, the staff, the college-age volunteers and from Garcia.

"You can imagine what it's like when a little girl comes up and says, 'Can't I stay? Please. Don't make me leave.' We try to stay in touch. We send them Christmas cards, birthday cards. But it's tough."

To make the point, Garcia points to a note on the board in the counselors' meeting room. It's from a kid named Jenny:

"Dear Staff, I miss you. I wish I was there right now. I had so much fun at camp. Please write me back."

Without a kitchen
this mother can't do her job
November 2, 1999

Debra Wardlow works as a housekeeper at Broadlawns Medical Center, making beds, vacuuming, sweeping, scrubbing floors. These days she's been putting in extra hours to raise the $600 deposit and the first month's rent on her new place, a four-bedroom house with a yard, not far from the intersection of M.L. King and Hickman.

By this morning, she was hoping to be in that house and have her family back together — her five kids, her 16-month old granddaughter, and the nephew she's raising.

She was hoping to have her own kitchen again, because, she says, it's a mother's job to cook for her kids.

But Wardlow's two sons and her nephew are still living with the family pastor. Two of her daughters are still living with their uncle, Wardlow's brother. The third daughter, the 12-year-old, is living with Wardlow in the basement of a friend's' house.

Home these days is a small room with a mattress on the floor. Whatever clothes Wardlow has are stuffed into a green garbage bag at the foot of the mattress. That's pretty much all she has left. Everything else Wardlow owned — from her furniture and housewares to the family photos and her kids' birth certificates — is gone.

"Everything. My father died in May and I had his hat and his harmonica and — I know this sounds silly — his driver's license. It's all gone. The bracelet he gave me when I graduated from high school is gone. It's a nightmare."

This nightmare began in late September, when Wardlow had to move out of the house she'd rented for five years. The place was in the path of the freeway revamp and she had to leave. She farmed her kids out to her brother and her pastor and put everything she owned in a U-Haul storage facility at Southeast 14th and Watrous. Then she moved into her girlfriend's basement — directly across the street from the U-Haul place.

When she needed something, she'd go over, sign in, get the key from the desk, go halfway down a long hall to the 10-by-15-foot room and get what she wanted.

The room was full. Six kids can generate a lot of stuff — clothes, books, games. She says there was a dining room set, a washer and dryer, TV, stereo, the entire contents of a four-bedroom house.

Then one day just about all of it was gone. The only things left in the room were two mattresses and her granddaughter's walker. Wardlow — who still had a few weeks left on her contract with the storage company — says she was told there was a mix-up with some paperwork and they thought she'd abandoned her belongings. They put it all out in the hall and told folks they could help themselves to what they wanted.

They apologized and offered her a month's free rent — $97. Then they offered to replace what she lost. But, she says, when she told them what was missing "they acted like I was lying. I don't want no more and no less than what I lost. All I want is my stuff back."

As Wardlow describes it, what followed was the runaround: a cycle of unreturned phone calls from the facility, from the corporate headquarters, the company president and from their insurance carrier. When she did manage to get someone to talk to her, she says they made her feel like she was the culprit and not the victim.

I phoned around to check out Wardlow's story. The storage facility referred questions to Randy Dixon, president of U-Haul Company of Iowa, here in Des Moines. Dixon intimated Wardlow was responsible for the problem, that she may have left the door open. Then he said he was too busy to talk about it. He told me to call his insurance company.

The woman at the insurance company said they're trying to work with Wardlow to get things straightened out.

Wardlow, meanwhile, is continuing to pay her brother and her pastor a few dollars each week for food and for shuttling the kids from their west-side homes to school on the east side.

She's trying to keep her spirits up.

"I'm trying to be there for my kids. I keep telling them I'm sorry, but they're kids. You know how that is. I'm their mom and I can't even cook my family a meal."

This week, with no furniture and little more than the clothes they're wearing, Debra Wardlow and her kids are moving into their new place. Just being together, she said, will help.

Family greets news with tears, anger

September 9, 1999

Sofie Ochoa had just gotten home from her daughter's volleyball game at Goodrell Middle School. It was a long day at the office. Ochoa's been a state worker for the past five years. She graduated from East and went to DMACC. These days, she works for Chet Culver in the secretary of state's office.

She was looking forward to taking it easy Monday night. Then the phone rang. It was her brother. Santos, her great-nephew, had been shot. He was at Mercy. She put on her coat, told her daughter to get ready, and within minutes she was making her way toward the emergency room. She stopped outside the hospital to talk with other family members, trading what little information they had.

Some of it was rumor, some second-and third-hand. They tried to piece together the scraps of what they'd heard. All they knew for sure was that one of their own was hurt — critically wounded in a shootout with police. Maybe dying.

Santos Vidal Rodriquez is Sofie Ochoa's great-nephew, one of her niece Lupe's sons. Ochoa doesn't have a lot to do with that end of the family. There's a lot of trouble there, and Ochoa wants to keep her daughter away from that.

One of Rodriguez's brothers — Ted Severeid, 17 — was arrested last month and accused of trying to rape a female worker at Eldora's state training school for delinquent boys.

At the time, Severeid was waiting to be sentenced for another sexual assault.

A sister, Luisa, is locked up, and Ochoa doesn't know where and can't even remember what she did.

"This is not a good situation. Not something I want to be involved in."

But when there's a problem, Ochoa goes. That's the way it is with family. You do what you have to do. So Monday night, Ochoa was the strong one. The pillar. She and her daughter sat outside the hospital and tried to comfort other relatives. There were tears, and there was anger.

And there was a lot of confusion about what happened between

"So I'm talkin' to this guy . . ."

Rodriguez and the cops.

No one in the small circle of relatives seemed surprised at what happened. Ochoa least of all. She was sad but not shocked when she heard her great-nephew had been shot by police.

"They're trouble. This one especially. In and out of trouble, guns, drugs, in and out of treatment. He doesn't go to school. It's always something. He's bad, and the system is bad. It just doesn't work. They arrest him and a few days later he's out again. They say he's too young to do anything with. He should have gotten help years ago."

Ochoa says Rodriguez's father hasn't been in the picture for years. His mother — Lupe Gomez — was born in Des Moines. She's in her late 20s, has six kids — three at home — and, as far as Ochoa knows, doesn't work.

Ochoa couldn't talk any more. She had to go inside and try to comfort her niece, who was sitting in the hospital chapel, praying for her son.

Ochoa motioned to her own daughter — a teen-ager.

"She sees this stuff, and she gets scared. I'm not trying to scare her, but she's got to understand what happens if you behave like that. She's a good kid. If I say 'no,' it means 'no.' She understands that. Too many of these parents have no control over their kids and this is how they end up.

"Santos needed help long ago. The system failed him."

If nothing else, Ochoa was going to make sure her daughter was spared a similar fate.

If you're white, you're not sitting there wondering

November 18, 1999

About a dozen years ago I went into a Manhattan restaurant with my wife and mother-in-law. Only three or four other people were in the room and the waiter was all over those folks — taking drink orders, filling the water glasses, bringing them bread, chatting them up.

We sat down and waited. And waited.

Finally I flagged the guy and he brought us menus. I had to flag him again when we decided what we wanted. He took the order without even looking at us. We had to ask for water and for bread.

I figured it was just bad service. My wife and her mother — the only two people in the room who weren't white — thought maybe something else was going on. They mentioned the possibility of racism and I did the mental equivalent of rolling my eyes.

A few months later we were in the Paris airport and I walked through the security gate and into the boarding area. My wife — walking behind me and carrying a year-old baby — was pulled over and her bag was searched by hand. While they were picking through her stuff, other white people were walking through the gate.

Pulled over alongside my wife were several other Asians, a few Arabs and a couple of black men and women. Racism? Maybe not. But when you aren't white, you just never know.

To most folks in this country, racism is still the obvious stuff — a water fountain with a "Whites Only" sign on it or black folks getting shuttled to the back of the bus.

But this is subtle. A gray area. Hard to see and hard to prove.

It takes a keen eye to recognize it and a cool head to deal with it.

Surge Kobsa seems like he's up to the task. Kobsa is a 19-year-old Drake student, a Croatian in the United States for only three years. He's a white guy who feels some black students at Drake deserve an apology from the school newspaper.

Last month at the Homecoming celebration they had a song and dance contest called "Yell Like Hell." The first-place winners were women from the Coalition of Black Students. A sorority came in second. When the school paper came out a few days later there was a front-page photo of the second-place winners — all white women.

Racism? Probably not. But the folks from the newspaper weren't saying. There was no editor's note explaining why they didn't have a picture of the winners.

Kobsa wrote the paper, accusing the staff of being culturally insensitive and wondering if there was some racial undertone at play.

The other morning, talking about his little crusade, Kobsa said the whole race issue is new to him and he's fascinated by it.

"Eastern Europe, Croatia, we only have white people. There's no box to even check on the census form for 'other.' But people always find something not to like about each other — religion, nationality. I've always had Serb friends and you wouldn't believe how cruel kids were to them, and to me sometimes. Here it's based on skin."

Kobsa says his background sets him apart from a lot of his classmates. So he joined the Coalition of Black Students and that's how he ended up writing to the newspaper.

The letter was e-mailed around and it got a lot of attention on campus — from students, faculty, administrators. That led to a forum this week on "The Role of Race in Media Coverage." About 120 people showed up to hash over what happened at Drake and to talk about the media in general.

The forum gave folks from the school paper a chance to talk about what happened. They said the problem was technical: The photos of the black students did not come out, so they used what they had. They apologized and said they've learned a lot in the past few weeks.

There was general agreement that if the first-place winners had been white and no photos had been used, it wouldn't have seemed like anything sinister was going on.

It's sort of like getting bad service in a restaurant. If you're white, you're not sitting there wondering why.

Anfinson's husband understands, but won't believe
February 17, 2000

His baby is dead, his wife is serving time for murder, and Mike Anfinson isn't sure he can take much more. He sat in his living room on the north side of Des Moines late Wednesday, a Bible on the table in front of him, a statue of the Blessed Mother on the bookshelf nearby. He looked like he hadn't slept in weeks.

"I just don't know where you go from here. I might not survive it."

Anfinson cried softly, shook his head and said: "I blame myself for this. I should have been home with her that day. I was selfish and stupid. If I was with her, this wouldn't have happened."

Mike Anfinson was out with friends that Sunday in September 1998. Heidi was home with their 2-week-old son, Jacob. When Mike got back at around 3 in the afternoon, Heidi first told him she didn't know what happened to the baby. Then she said someone came in and took him. Then she said the baby drowned in the tub during a bath, she panicked, drove to Saylorville Lake and dumped the body.

A Davenport jury believed she killed the baby, drowned him in the lake. Tuesday she was convicted of second-degree murder, and the law says she has to spend at least the next 42 years in prison.

Mike understands the verdict — she changed her story, it didn't look good — but he says, "I'll go to my grave maintaining her innocence."

Mike Anfinson met Heidi Hoffbauer in 1988 when they were living next to each other in a Windsor Heights apartment complex. She was a Valley grad, raised in West Des Moines, working as a waitress at Jimmy's. He was a computer programmer, from Des Moines. He went to Hoover and graduated in '77. They started seeing each other, and within months they were living together.

"I knew, and she knew. We were right for each. We were born on the same day, April 2, 1959. I just always liked being around her. It was about companionship. We could just sit around and do nothing — read the paper, whatever. That was OK. We just want to be together."

For 10 years they lived together, and when Heidi got pregnant at the end of '97, they married and bought a house a few blocks north of Hickman. Heidi continued to wait tables into her eighth month.

Mike remembers that period as the best time of their lives. Friends and family were all around them. Heidi had never been happier. There was a baby shower, and not long after that — on a Saturday — Heidi woke up feeling the time had come. He remembers every detail of Sept. 5, 1998, the day his son was born. They went for a ride in the morning, ate lunch at Wendy's, visited friends, watched the Iowa football game. Then just hung around the house and waited.

"She kept smiling, saying, 'It's going to happen. I just know it.' That night we went to Des Moines General. At 10:20 Jacob was born. I cut the umbilical cord. I did all that stuff."

Again he tears up. Through the tears, he talks about the two weeks of his baby's life.

It's tough to hear him talk about what it felt like to hold his son.

And then he came home that day, and Jacob was gone. Dead, he later realized.

Looking back, he sees that her story — that somebody took the baby — didn't seem right. He should have questioned her more. He admits that over the past 18 months he's had moments when he's wondered if his wife murdered their baby. They've talked about it, cried about it.

But he doesn't believe she intentionally hurt Jacob.

"We may never know. Maybe she was guilty of neglect or endangerment, but not murder. Not Heidi."

For the past 10 years Mike Anfinson has worked as a systems engineer at Norwest Bank — now Wells Fargo. At some point soon he's got to get back to his job, back to his life. But for now, he says, "I just want to be alone." He talks, and the phone rings. He reaches for it saying: "I don't want to answer, but it might be Heidi."

It was Heidi. She was in the Polk County Jail. Mike Anfinson asked for some privacy. He wanted a few minutes alone with his wife. And later he was thinking about taking a ride out to Glendale Cemetery, to the children's section. He wanted to spend a few minutes alone with his son.

Continue to celebrate black history beyond February

February 29, 2000

Back in the late '60s, when Don Graves was in fifth grade, there was no Black History Month. There was Negro History Week. And it was right around Valentine's Day. So the bulletin board outside Graves' class at Woodlawn Elementary was covered with hearts and flowers.

He decided to do something about it. The 11-year-old took down the fluff and put up photos of Angela Davis and Lew Alcindor. He stuck in a shot of Ramsey Lewis and one of John Carlos and Tommie Smith — the two '68 Olympians making the black-power salute.

Then he waited for the fallout. The next morning the teacher wanted to know who was responsible. Thirty years later and Graves still laughs at that question.

"I was the only black kid in the class. Who did he think did it?"

The teacher seemed to understand and the display stayed up.

"That was the important thing," Graves said. "I accomplished what I wanted. I got us some recognition. Back then, the only thing you'd get was a paragraph and that would include Nat Turner, Harriet Tubman and Frederick Douglass. That was it for the accomplishments of the entire race."

These days Graves, 41, runs a group that works with inner-city businesses. Today, as we close out another Black History Month, he's wondering if maybe this annual event is too much of a throwback. He's wondering if there's some way to retool it for the 21st century because, he says, there is recognition.

The birthday of Martin Luther King Jr. is a holiday, and Malcolm X is on a U.S. postage stamp. Those are things Graves never thought he'd live to see.

"The problem with Black History Month is that it's like saying, 'OK, you got your month. Now let's get back to business as usual.' We're buying into it. It's the only time we get out and push our history. We should be celebrating every day."

Frances Hawthorne does celebrate just about every day. She writes about black history, she talks to civic and political groups, she visits schools and churches. She's out there spreading the word.

She believes this month of recognition is important and necessary. She has a hard time understanding why anyone would think otherwise.

"In the best of worlds we wouldn't need it, but we don't live in that world. Not yet."

The other morning Hawthorne, a retired Des Moines school administrator, was in front of an African-American history class at East High, telling the 15 or so black students that they've got opportunities she wouldn't have dared dream about.

She talks of times when the only job a black could get was in a factory or running an elevator. She remembers making $25 a week and thinking that was good money. When she was in school, she learned plenty about Greek and Roman history and plenty about the history of this country. Little was said about what African-Americans brought to the table.

"I remember thinking, 'We must have done something.' But I heard nothing. Then I went to Lincoln University (in Missouri) and Dr. Lorenzo Greene had books on African-American history. I don't ever want to go back to those days when these things weren't taught."

Melanie Posey is 26, went to integrated schools in Kansas and doesn't remember the days Hawthorne is talking about. But she's just as committed to keeping Black History Month in the public eye. Posey, a reporter at Channel 13, made the case throughout February in a series of Wednesday-night pieces on blacks in Iowa — from Jack Trice and George Washington Carver to Edna Griffin and John Bibbs.

Then there was the piece she did two weeks ago on Buxton, a turn-of-the-century Monroe County mining town that was 85 percent black. That got a lot of attention — phone calls, mail, invitations to speak at schools.

"The impressive thing is that I'm hearing from blacks, whites, everybody. There's a lot of positive feedback from all around the community. People just didn't know how much of a history African-Americans have here."

So now she's thinking about keeping her series going, continuing the celebration beyond February — something that would speak to both Don Graves and Frances Hawthorne.

There's new life in a young man and an old corner

April 4, 2000

For all of his 22 years, D.J. Morris has lived, worked, played and gone to school within walking distance of the corner of Forest and M.L. King.

He's heard the gunfire, he's watched the fights and the other violence. He's gotten to know the drug dealers and the hookers, folks he grew up next to, went to school and played ball with.

When he was a kid of about 7, when his 5-year-old sister slipped into a coma and died, Morris walked the streets for hours and passed that corner a number of times. And when his older brother was gunned down at an east-side video arcade in the summer of '94, 17-year-old Morris went to the TNT Lounge on the northwest corner to have a few drinks and try to forget.

There was even a time, he says, when he sold crack near that corner.

Morris still lives in the neighborhood, and his travels still take him past the intersection of MLK and Forest. But these days he goes past there as a man of God, a deacon at the Amazing Grace Church. He's a husband, a father, a young businessman. He's met the vice president of the United States and the federal drug czar. He's talked with the governor of Iowa and the mayor of Des Moines.

He's gotten all kinds of recognition for his work with kids. He's cleaned up his act and so has the corner of MLK and Forest. The entire area is looking better.

A block off the corner there's the How to Eat to Live cafe, Muhammad Mosque and the Constance Kitchen Bakery. On the southwest corner, across from the old TNT, a bar called the Cloud has been replaced by an empty lot.

And as of Friday, the building that used to house the TNT is the state headquarters for Citizens for Community Improvement. This is one of those groups that's in the fight on everything from urban issues like redlining, crime and bringing sewers to the east side to rural issues like factory farms and urban sprawl.

They've been at it for 25 years, and Morris is glad to have CCI in his part of town. He's dealt with them through a group called Youth

Working for Positive Change.

"That old building brought a lot of violence," Morris said Sunday. "This place brings life, hope, peace. It certainly makes the inner-city look better."

Over the weekend CCI had its grand opening at the site and they say about 350 people showed up. A bluegrass band — not something you hear much of at MLK and Forest — did the music. Farm families from the group's chapters in Hardin, Humboldt and Carroll counties were hanging out and partying with folks from Des Moines' inner-city.

The farmers brought the meat and the vegetables. The city folks were giving neighborhood tours to their new-found country friends. A lot of the rural folks have lived in this state their entire lives and knew nothing about Des Moines beyond downtown, the malls, the fairgrounds and whatever you see off I-80.

There was a lot of talk about the devastation and the work that needs to be done in that part of town. But mostly there was talk about what this revamped building means to that corner of the city.

CCI's Mary Welsh was in on this from the beginning. She was there in the early stages when there was talk about finding space in that neighborhood. And Welsh was there when the talk turned to rounding up the usual suspects — Knapp, Kruidenier, Pioneer, Polk County — and getting them to kick in some big money and help with the fund raising. They came through.

CCI ended up needing about $750,000 for the TNT and the place next door. Welsh is still traumatized by what they found inside the buildings.

"We filled 28 dumpsters. I heard it was like 20 tons of junk. There was everything from dead cats to old refrigerators and toilets. But the important thing was to be in this neighborhood. We're about organizing low-and moderate-income people to do it for themselves. We didn't want to be in West Des Moines." She and others said they've been getting calls from business types around the city wanting to know what kind of space is available in that area.

D.J. Morris said that's good to hear. And, in a strange way, it's good they didn't knock down the old TNT Lounge.

"They've turned it into something positive. I go by there and think about what it used to be and I feel real good about how things turned out."

Des Moines man escaped Hitler's pogrom in 1938

May 30, 2000

He's 76 and, like a lot of guys his age, Fred Lorber's got war stories. But his stories go beyond the bullets and the blood. This is a guy who was there the day Adolf Hitler pulled into Vienna.

It was March of '38, a Sunday. Lorber was 14. Just a day earlier the German army had stormed into that city of 2 million. He saw the tanks and the trucks and the steel-helmeted soldiers with their guns. To a high school kid, this was hot.

Then, 24 hours later, Hitler showed up.

Lorber remembers the streets were thick with cheering crowds, folks waving Nazi flags. There were swastikas on the sides of the buildings. It was something of a homecoming for the Austrian-born German leader. Lorber was on the street with his friends, and he remembers seeing Hitler in the back of an open Mercedes.

"He just ignited that crowd. There was this incredible energy, excitement." And then he pauses, shakes his head and says: "Nobody in their wildest nightmare could imagine what was coming."

The Lorbers were Jews and within months Fred could no longer go to school, take books out of the library, ride the bus, see a movie or sit on a park bench. He got beat up a few times; nothing serious. His friends — non-Jews — stayed away. Jewish businesses were shut down. His father lost his job. The Nazi propaganda machine was cranked. Storm troopers made those once-friendly streets a scary place for a kid.

Then, in the summer of '38, a Polish Jew killed a German Embassy official in Paris and the crackdown in Vienna was absolute. Synagogues were burned, Jewish men and boys were arrested. The Lorbers — Fred and his parents — didn't leave their apartment for days.

Late one night they heard the knock.

"The Nazi storm troopers came to our house and took my father. They wanted to take me also, but my mother begged them. I was so young. I can still see them — brown uniforms, black boots. They came into my room and looked over my books."

Months passed. One day a card arrived from Dachau. The card

said, "I'm fine," and was signed by Lorber's father.

"The next months were hazy. I ran into a friend on the street and told him about my father. His uncle was a big shot. The uncle made some calls for us. He said if we could leave (Austria) in a month or two he could get something done. In April of '39 my father got out. In September the war started and in October we got our (U.S.) visas.

"It still boggles my mind how lucky we were. We lost everything, but we were the lucky ones."

They started over on New York's Lower East Side. Lorber's father would buy men's socks wholesale, then sell them door to door out of a small suitcase. He wouldn't come home at night until the suitcase was empty.

Fred Lorber graduated from high school, was drafted into the Army and sent to North Africa. At the end of the war he was one of the first GIs to enter Vienna. It was in the summer of '45. The Russians had already cleaned out the city, looting, raping.

With another GI along for the ride, Lorber drove a Jeep over to his old building. He was sitting there when a woman came out and saw the two soldiers.

"She looked at me, realized who I was and screamed my name, rushed to hug me. Heads were poking out of every window in the building. Old friends of mine were around me. All of a sudden there were like 200 people in the street, and I didn't know how to handle it. I had terrible mixed feelings. I knew these people hadn't lifted a finger to help us. Such bad memories."

Lorber got out of the service, went back to New York, married and in 1950 took a job with a Des Moines textile company. He became president of that company, then bought and sold several other businesses.

He's made a lot of money and had a good life. But there's a darkness to it all. You look at Fred Lorber, and you see a successful man of 76. Then you spend some time with him, listen to his story. Now you're in the company of a 14-year-old boy who's watching Adolf Hitler roll into Vienna.

Homeless youth has no desire
to live any other way
August 3, 2000

Not that long ago, James Cory was playing ball at Grand View Little League. He was with the East Des Moines Wrestling Club, played golf at North. Home was the house he shared with his parents, an older brother and a younger sister.

"But even back then I always felt different from everybody else. Can't explain it."

He's 20 now and hasn't lived at home since he was about 15 — right around the time he started shooting heroin.

These days he goes by the street name Sic. It's short for Sick Boy. He's wrestling with his drug problem — heroin, sometimes meth — and he faces charges for stabbing his friend, something he doesn't remember.

"I was blacked out from drinking. They say I stabbed him twice in the stomach. He doesn't remember it. We were both trashed. But we're still friends."

He says that like he says everything else — low-key, in a bloodless way, a blank look in his eyes. He's been in and out of the county jail on burglary and assault charges, for violating probation. The folks at Broadlawns are telling him alcohol has pretty much destroyed his liver.

Home these days is a makeshift camp under a graffiti-strewn bridge in the shadow of Sec Taylor Stadium. He keeps the place neat. There are a few empty liquor bottles and some half-eaten boxes of cereal and crackers.

The remnants of a campfire are not far from a mattress and dirt-covered blanket. He's proud of the place.

"Right now I like being on the streets. I'm having fun living free. I don't look down on people who work 9 to 5. But is that supposed to be for everybody? My 9 to 5 is survival, and I'm good at it. Maybe I won't do this my whole life. But this is what I choose for now."

Howard Matalba listens and nods along. Matalba works with homeless kids and he figures Sic is one of maybe 400 between 13 and 21 who are living on the streets in and around Des Moines. He said about 30 more hit town every month, some by train from the east and west, most from rural Iowa.

But Matalba says Sic is unique.

"He's actually homeless. He has no desire to live any other way. A lot of them are out there doing it because they think it's cool."

Matalba spends his days and nights tracking kids down, trying to get them food, medical help, maybe get them into the few shelter beds available to the homeless under 18.

His job is getting tougher. A lot of these kids were living in abandoned buildings along Grand and Locust, places that have been leveled to make way for the Gateway project. Now Matalba spends his time looking under bridges, in the woods on the west and south sides, in the east-side railyards.

On a recent morning he was looking for Sic. When he couldn't find him at his camp, he hit some of the other hangouts, like the abandoned garages near Southwest Ninth.

Matalba approached slowly. Nobody was around, but there were signs of life: 17 empty liquor bottles, used condoms, a copy of Hustler and a copy of Watch Tower. There were audio tapes — Fats Waller, Buddy Guy, Paul Simon — and several empty spray cans.

"Not a good sign," said Matalba. "Kids must have been huffing."

From there he hit three south-side bridges and the woods near Meredith. Lots of porn, graffiti, empty bottles, but no Sic.

Late in the afternoon he found him along Third near Court. They agreed to meet later at Matalba's downtown office. The deal is that Matalba wants to take Sic to D.C. in February for a conference on homeless youth.

"I want to get his story out there," said Matalba. "He's rare because he's willing to talk about what he's going through." On the down side, said Matalba, "I don't think he's going to make it. The way he drinks. His liver. It's life-threatening." He shakes his head. His voice trails off.

Sic hears that and shrugs. "I just don't want to be sober right now. Maybe that'll change. For now, this is who I want to be."

But he wants to tell his story. He says it might help some kid out there who feels different, who thinks he's alone.

Grief grips parents of teen charged in child's death

August 8, 2000

Dean Newman sat on the porch of his Valley Junction home Monday and cried for the 5-year-old killed the night before. He cried for Cassidy Mahedy, and he cried for her parents.

"My heart goes out to that little girl and her family. I just wish there were something I could do or say."

He has asked his minister at West Des Moines Christian Church to help him compose a letter to the family.

Like the Mahedy family, Dean and his wife, Nancy, may have also lost a child in that fatal wreck. But they don't expect much sympathy. Their 18-year-old daughter — their middle kid — is accused of getting drunk, driving and then running down Cassidy on a sidewalk.

Dean Newman didn't even know about the early-evening accident until his brother called late Sunday.

"It was about 10, and he called and said, 'I'm so sorry,' and I didn't know what he was talking about. When he told me, I couldn't believe it. I'm still stunned. You cannot imagine."

It was about 1 in the morning when Newman finally got in touch with his daughter. He didn't get to see her until after her court appearance Monday morning. At that point, the child had died, and Melissa Newman had been charged with vehicular homicide. Until then, Dean Newman said, she hadn't realized the child had died. The last she'd heard, Cassidy was still breathing.

The charges didn't register until she left the courtroom and got back to the county jail.

Her father says there wasn't much he could do to comfort her.

"I know Melissa is at fault. She knows she screwed up, and she's just devastated. Devastated. She loves children. She's still a kid herself."

About that point in our conversation, Dean Newman mentioned that his own father had died two weeks ago and that he was still struggling with that death. He said Melissa has helped him get through.

Newman said his daughter graduated from Valley two months ago and has been working with him at CIGNA Health Care, learning to process claims. He said she'd never been in trouble, but later —

when his wife joined him on the porch — they remembered an incident about six months ago after a spring break party.

Nancy Newman said her daughter was stopped for a bad headlight and police found an empty container that smelled of alcohol. Melissa was arrested and ordered to do community service with the understanding that staying out of trouble for a year would make the matter disappear from her record.

While Newman talked, the phone kept ringing. Friends saw the TV news and were calling to express sympathy, saying — according to Nancy — "This could have happened to any one of their kids."

And then folks started showing up at the house, friends, relatives, including Nancy's father, who was in town visiting from St. Louis. As more folks arrived, there was a continuing struggle to hold back the tears.

A few miles to the north and a couple of blocks east, a pink wreath on a white cross marked the spot where Cassidy Mahedy was killed. There was a picture of the child among the yellow flowers.

Tire marks bit deeply into the lawn, and a piece of a taillight was on the sidewalk. Orange paint, sprayed by the police, marked various spots around the crime scene.

Neighbors — with tears in their eyes, hands shaking — came by and placed flowers and notes on the Mahedy porch. Other folks drove by, slowed down and took it all in.

And from a back yard a few doors away, a child could be heard laughing, blowing on a whistle, enjoying a summer afternoon in a safe, quiet part of town.

Activist stands by city's Latinos
February 22, 2002

To get to the Lopez apartment, Felipe Gallardo takes you through a parking lot loaded with broken beer bottles and bike parts. He takes you up a shaky staircase with a rotting banister.

Once inside you're looking at a family of five — two parents, three little boys — jammed into a one-bedroom. The kitchen table bumps up against the living room couch. The cracked and peeling walls frame a large picture of the Virgin Mary.

The kids are watching cartoons on a tiny TV with bad reception. Mom's in the kitchen chopping vegetables for the gravy. Dad — decked out in an ISU sweat shirt and a Cyclones cap — is getting ready to go to his day job. He cooks at a West Des Moines restaurant. At night he cooks at a place on the east side.

If you want to talk to the Lopezes, you've got to go through Gallardo, the guy from Citizens for Community Improvement. Gallardo keeps an eye on the Lopez family and dozens of other Latinos around this part of town. He works the neighborhood near Forest and Sixth to see if anybody needs help — dealing with the landlord, finding a doctor, getting the kids in school.

They need him because most of these folks don't speak English, and most — as Gallardo puts it — are here without papers. He calls them "undocumented" and gets testy when you call them illegal immigrants.

Ask why these folks shouldn't be rounded up and sent home and Gallardo hits you with all kinds of facts, figures and government reports that show this state would pretty much collapse without these people. In Des Moines — where growth was flat during the '90s — the Latino population was up about 185 percent.

"The Latinos went from about 4,629 to 13,138. They are doing the work others won't do and they are living in very difficult conditions. They're easily intimidated because they don't have papers."

He talks about families that wrap duct tape around the crib so the roaches don't get at the baby. And he talks about folks who have to walk miles to work because they can't get a license — some of them working two and three jobs.

But Gallardo is not some wide-eyed do-gooder who just doesn't get it. He grew up in East L.A., raised by an aunt after his father split and his mother decided she couldn't handle him. He spent his teens drinking and drugging with the other guys in his gang — The Crazy Boys.

He quit high school at 18 and within weeks he was in the Ventura County Jail on assault charges. He would have rotted there if he hadn't gotten into a work-release program, finished high school and joined the Army. He was posted in Korea, got into the Airborne Rangers at Fort Benning, got his girlfriend pregnant and — when she left him and moved back to her native Iowa — he followed her to be near their son.

He's been around here for about two years and he's worked for the National Guard, the Wapello County sheriff, the Des Moines schools, and now CCI. He's 27 and he doesn't pretend that his street years are behind him. He's still struggling.

"I've still got a lot of hate and anger inside me. I still have to catch myself sometimes. About six months ago I was at a party and some guy hit me in the face with a beer bottle. I got a black eye. But I held back. That was a big deal for me."

So he's trying to channel that energy and use that anger. He tries to deal with landlords, get them to provide clean, safe housing. More than once he's had to get confrontational. But — unlike the old days — he doesn't punch the guy out.

"We get the tenants together — maybe 30, 40 people — and we go to the landlord's house and stand outside and let him know we mean business. That usually works."

Sometimes he'll corner a politician or some corporado and get them to hear him out about some injustice. Then he goes home at night and shakes his head in disbelief. He has a hard time understanding how this L.A. street kid is going up against these major players and getting results. But you see him connect with the Lopez family — talking their language, laughing with the kids, asking dad about work, telling mom the gravy smells good — and Gallardo's ongoing journey makes perfect sense.

Des Moines woman is taking war personally

April 2, 2003

Janet Fink figures some of her friends and neighbors are against the war, but they're not about to tell her that.

Not when her husband is living in a tent near Najaf, Iraq, about 90 miles south of Baghdad. Not when her 18-month-old daughter sits on the couch every night and waits for her father to get home from work, yelling "Daddy, Daddy" every time there's a knock on the door.

Not when her 4-year-old son knows his dad won't be in the stands this week when the T-ball season starts.

And not when Janet spends her nights and early mornings watching TV, sometimes crying, waiting for any scrap of news about the 3rd Infantry Division, the unit her husband's been attached to.

For Janet, this war is not political. It's personal. You can see it when you pass the Fink house — the American flag, the yellow ribbon on the tree, the blue star in the window. You can hear it in Janet's voice when she talks about her husband.

"I've known Alex for 14 years and we spoke every single day. Then the war started and I didn't hear from him for 10 days. I've gotten some e-mail and two phone calls since then, and I missed one of the calls because I was on the phone. He said he's fine and then he laughed and said the accommodations are not very good. It's unreal how they're living. He gets five hours of sleep, and Handi Wipes are as close as he gets to a shower. He's eating MREs, those are meals ready to eat. He talked about all that and then he got teary eyed talking about the kids."

Then Janet — still smiling — gets a bit teary eyed.

"I can't say enough good things about him. He's an honest man with a lot of integrity. He's not the type who couldn't wait for a war to start. Not at all. He was very reluctant to leave his family, but he's in the reserves and this is part of his responsibility."

Janet met Alex Fink in college in Missouri, dated him for four years, married him and followed him around the country until five years ago when he got a job at Kemin Foods, where he's now sales director. They settled on the west side of Des Moines, a small street with about a dozen houses, one of those tight-knit neighborhoods where everybody looks out for the kids on the block. That's helped Janet.

"The neighbors come over now and then, the kids come by and that's wonderful. They've all been very supportive in a good way. It's not like they feel sorry for us. That's not something Alex would like."

Alex was in the Army for three years and stayed in the reserves, rising to the rank of major. In late January he was in Florida on business and he got the call. He had three days to get things together and ship out to Germany. Then three weeks later he was in Kuwait. And for the past two weeks he's been in Iraq, in the desert, using a truck as his office and a card table as his desk. He's the company commander of a logistics unit, making sure supplies and equipment get to the right places.

So he's not exactly in the line of fire, but he's close. Suicide bombers have taken out men he's worked with.

When he called Janet, he told her about the sandstorms that turned his world bright orange. He told her how he sits in his tent thinking about her and the kids, watching the nighttime sky light up with bombs, praying they don't come down on him.

And Janet sits thousands of miles away and prays for her husband, hoping he doesn't get hurt, hoping he doesn't even see the death and destruction, the war images that have been known to cause a lifetime of trauma and pain.

She tries to keep up her routine, working two days a week as a nurse, taking the kids to preschool and day care. The family ends each day in front of a picture of Alex. They pray and then the kids drop red, white and blue beads into a jar — one for each day their father's gone.

Once the kids are in bed, Janet turns on the TV and watches the news. She prays, checks her e-mail, waits for the phone to ring.

Shoes bring flood of memories
April 16, 2003

The other morning I was staring at a picture of a woman who was cut in half, her breasts sliced off. Next to that was a picture of dead children, blood coming out of their stomachs and heads. Then there were photos of body parts — arms, legs, skulls — piled a few feet high.

I wanted to look away but I didn't, I couldn't. This is what I'd come to see at the Holocaust Museum in Washington, D.C. I was looking at a photo spread showing how the Nazis used Jews for medical research. There were hundreds of other photos, just about every one of them powerful and painful to look at.

There were grainy films showing Hitler's rise and fall. There were sound bites of survivors talking about what they'd seen and lived through. They had a box car that carried people to their deaths, and they had the little bunks where dozens of people were stuffed in for the night. They had the bowls that carried whatever scraps of food these people were given — a small piece of bread, soup that was all water.

And then there were the shoes. Thousands and thousands of dirty, worn-out shoes in these large bins. For all the blood and destruction, the tears and the violence, the shoes had the most impact on me. They were real, you could touch them. I just kept thinking about the people who wore those shoes.

Then my mind went back to those years when the war was still a part of everybody's life. I thought back to the apartment building we lived in during the 1950s, early '60s and how every floor had at least one family with a personal tie to the war — from veterans to Holocaust survivors.

I thought about Mrs. Auslander alone in her apartment on the sixth floor. The place was always dark — shades drawn — except for the candle she kept burning in front of her daughter's photo. She hadn't seen her daughter Sarah since that night near Warsaw when they were held at gunpoint, sent off in different directions. Sarah was about 16.

I thought about the Sapersteins, Charlotte and Will Figman, the Tischler family. They all had these old photos around their apartments

— pictures of uncles and aunts, parents and cousins. But nobody from the family ever came to visit. Only a few of the Jewish kids had grandparents.

I kept looking at the shoes, and my mind drifted from the apartment building to the ugly incident at Zimmerman's, the candy store we passed on the way to school every morning. There were two guys behind the counter — let's call them Sam and Max. Sam was married to Max's sister, and the three of them lived in a back room behind the shop, a thin curtain the only thing between them and their customers.

For a kid, that store was a great place. The candy and gum, the baseball cards and soda, comic books. But there was something else going on. There was a heaviness, a sadness that — even at age 9 or 10 — you could feel. Day after day we were in and out of that place, and Max and Sam never smiled, never said a word. After a while, some of us started to wonder if maybe those numbers tattooed on their arms had something to do with them not smiling, never saying hello or thank you.

It's not the kind of thing you talk about at that age, but it was there in the background. Then one day after school — maybe fifth grade — I was in there with Gene Gallo, and I called him from across the store. For reasons he was never able to explain, he raised his arm in my direction and yelled, "Heil Hitler."

I started to laugh and Sam lost it. He came over the counter screaming — "DIDN'T HE CAUSE ENOUGH TROUBLE." Before he could get to Gallo, Max was on his brother-in-law, holding him back. Sam's wife came out to see what was happening. The two of them hugged him and tried to calm him down. Sam kept screaming and then crying. I looked over at Gallo, and the two of us ran out the door and didn't go back again for about a year — a lifetime at that age.

Now it's been about 40 years, and I've never forgotten that day, that look of pain and anger in Sam's eyes. It's something I thought about the other morning when I was staring at those shoes.

Friendship survives tragedies
May 23, 2003

Adam Duerfeldt looks like a pretty tough kid. He's well-built, a college ballplayer — baseball at Central. He's got the earrings, the knee-length shorts, even a bit of an attitude.

But he isn't shy about getting emotional. He talks about Tim Heggen, and he has to keep stopping himself to let the tears flow. Sometimes they're tears of sadness, talking about the hard times, the pain and the death.

And sometimes Adam cries when he remembers the good times, the days when they were little kids playing catch out at Raccoon Valley.

Adam met Tim about 10 years ago when they were on the same Little League team. Tim's dad was the coach. Adam's dad was in the hospital with a brain aneurysm. Adam couldn't understand what that was about, so Tim's dad — Rick Heggen — stepped in. He explained the illness in a way that an 8-year-old could make sense of it. He went further, helping Adam with his baseball game and just being there for him.

Adam remembers those days.

"At that age, you're vulnerable to peer pressure, looking for someone to look up to. I was in bad shape, and he understood that. He made me feel like family. They all did. They surrounded me and made me feel like another one of their sons. I got to be good friends with Tim, having sleepovers, watching videos, playing games, doing all that kid stuff."

Adam talks about those times and smiles through the tears.

He keeps going. After the aneurysm, Adam's father recovered; things were pretty normal.

By then, the two guys were really close, things were going well, the families got to know each other.

Tim's family moved from Des Moines to Ankeny, and Adam's family moved from Windsor Heights to Urbandale. The kids stayed in touch, and Adam still felt like he was part of Tim's family.

Then more pain, more trouble. Tim's dad was badly hurt in a fire: third-degree burns. It was Adam's turn to step in and comfort Tim and his kid brother, Matt. It was his turn to be there for the Heggen family

— "the strongest people I've ever met."

And he came through.

"By that time we were older, sophomores. Me and Tim talked a lot, leaned on each other. It was tough times again."

Rick Heggen eventually recovered and, as Adam puts it, "We were 2 and 0."

But the good feelings were short-lived. In spring 2001 it all fell apart. Ankeny High played Urbandale in a baseball game. At the end, the two teams lined up to shake hands. A mutual friend pulled Adam aside and told him Tim had pancreatic cancer. It was terminal — six months, maybe nine, not much more.

That was followed by a year of all kinds of medical procedures. Tim spent a lot of his time in the hospital. Adam spent a lot of time visiting. It was uplifting for both of them.

"I don't know how he did it, but every time I walked into that room he was smiling, laughing, joking around. I didn't know how long he'd live, so every visit was important, precious."

Things continued to get worse, but there was a high point. Last May, Tim Heggen had a wish come true. He got to walk across the stage at the Ankeny High School graduation and accept his diploma. He got a standing ovation.

Two months later — July 3 — he died. Adam Duerfeldt was one of the pallbearers. Now he's on a mission to raise money for pancreatic cancer in Tim's memory, and every time he suits up for a game he has Tim's initials on his wristband. He's trying to be a big brother to Matt, and he stays in touch with the rest of the family.

And he thinks about Tim every day.

"I'd give anything to play catch with him again just once. Just once."

Adam says that and then he just can't say another word.

Prison robbed him of 10 years
June 6, 2003

Rick Daye has been out of work for two years, needed a place to stay, and his sister took him in. So home these days is a modest little house on a dead-end street out near the fairgrounds. Pull onto the block and there are shiny new SUVs parked next to rusted-out cars from the '80s. A few of the lawns look like something you'd see in a gardening magazine. Others are an overgrown mess.

Some of the houses are well-kept, freshly painted, cheerful looking. Others are tired, worn, ready to collapse.

It's a curious mix. It's the kind of street where you'd expect to find Rick Daye, who's also a curious mix.

He's a guy who's been on "Oprah," "Good Morning America," "Frontline." And he's a guy with a police record that goes back to the '70s, when he was a teenager — robbery, possession of pot, underage drinking. He's been married and divorced, married again and separated. He can't hold a job.

One day he's sitting around the house struggling with his drug problems — crack, other things — and a few days later he jets off to New York to give some lawyers his input for a program they're putting together.

He's devoutly religious, peppering his talk with references to God. And he was in California's Folsom Prison — a convicted rapist and kidnapper.

And he was one of the first people in this country to be exonerated by DNA testing. But that mistake by the system cost Daye 10 years — '84 to '94.

"The worst thing was being thrown into that world with thousands of lifers, killers. Prison is about punishment. It makes you hard-hearted. You know what I'm saying? I was 26, a Des Moines guy. I didn't know about gangs and Crips and Bloods. First week I was in there I made a knife out of a sardine can. I had to stab a few people, crack a few people in the head to protect myself. I was in and out of solitary. You can't understand how angry I was. I didn't do it. Never touched that woman. You know what I'm saying?"

Daye grew up in Des Moines, graduated from North High in '75.

In the '80s he moved to San Diego with his girlfriend and in January of '84 he was arrested and charged with rape, kidnapping and robbery. This case involved a woman who was carjacked by two guys, robbed and raped. One of the guys had long straight hair and a gold cap on his left-front tooth. Daye had that same type of hair and a silver cap on his right-front tooth. Daye also had an alibi and a bunch of witnesses — he was at a birthday party at the time of the rape.

The guy who was supposed to be Daye's accomplice — David Pringle — was tried separately, convicted of rape and took the Fifth in Daye's trial. Daye was convicted and got a life sentence. A few years later, Pringle admitted Daye was not involved. But that went nowhere, no one investigated and Daye sat in prison until DNA tests were conducted in '94. Daye remembers the morning he got the call with the results.

"The prison was locked down because some guy got killed. I was playing dominoes and listening to music and an officer handed me the phone and I thought it was a death in the family. But it was a watch commander, and he said, 'Mr. Daye, you're getting out in the morning.' I started jumping around and screaming, 'I told you I didn't do it.' It's been almost 10 years and I'm still pumped, but I'm struggling. You know what I'm saying?"

His story got the attention of some lawyers who are putting together a program to help ex-cons, folks who were wrongly convicted. They want to offer job training, help with housing and mental health services. So Daye was in New York last month meeting with other folks cleared after DNA testing — about 125 since Daye was released.

Now he's back in Des Moines, still trying to get his life together. Still struggling.

"You have no idea how much things can change in 10 years. When I got out I couldn't even work a remote control or things like a VCR, cell phone. Things everybody else could do. I've been so angry. You know what I'm saying?"

I can't imagine.

Pageant has plenty of victories, both big and small

July 25, 2003

Deb Scharf was on the sidewalk getting ready to go over the curb and onto the street. A couple of folks watching told her not to do it. She might not make it, and she could get hurt. Scharf said, "I'm going," put her wheelchair in gear and made it safely to the street. She got a round of applause.

Scharf raised her right arm, said "YES!" and smiled like she'd just scored the game-winning run.

There was a time when getting from the sidewalk to the street wouldn't have been a problem. But in the summer of '93, Scharf was driving home from Big Creek, hit a railroad track, the car was airborne, landed and broke her back. She hasn't walked since. So this curb move was a big deal. And the folks with Scharf understood that. Most of them were in wheelchairs. They're in town this week for the Ms. Wheelchair America contest.

Scharf — Ms. Iowa — was getting off on the whole thing.

"This is so cool, very uplifting to be with all these other women. We can talk about things, personal problems that you would never talk about with other people."

The women were hanging out at the Botanical Center. They were telling their stories, comparing notes, comparing wheelchairs — Who's got the best spokes and shock absorbers, who's got lights on their wheels. They were talking about dealing with doctors, about driving, how tough it is to buy clothes and shoes, how tough it can be to raise kids. And how those same kids were the inspiration for some of these women to stay alive, the only thing that kept them going.

But no tears, nothing heavy. They were laughing, teasing each other, creating bonds that'll last long after a Ms. Wheelchair America is crowned tomorrow night.

These women go from 21 to 60, and they come from 24 states. Some of them were able to stand on their own but couldn't walk. Others couldn't lift their head or move their arms. Some of them wore neck braces. Some wore finger splints so they could use their hands. Some could barely speak.

But they all have a message. That's part of the competition. And they've all got a story.

Catherine Gugala — the reining Ms. Wheelchair — is from Wisconsin. She got a blood clot on her spine when she was 5 and hasn't been able to walk for 27 years. But she's had two kids, and she's traveled the country talking at companies and schools, telling people "to focus on their abilities, not their disabilities."

It's simple stuff, but coming from her it means something.

Jennifer Rechsteiner is Ms. Maryland. She was born with cerebral palsy. She's got a degree in sociology, a master's in psychology and she's a career counselor with Homeland Security. She's 36, has two daughters and talks at various schools and clubs "telling kids not to be afraid of people in wheelchairs. You'd be surprised how frightened they can be."

Lisa Wartchow is Ms. Wisconsin. She has MS, and she's been in a wheelchair for eight years. She says the important thing is to make sure her kids have a normal life. And — asked how she gets by — she says "90 percent of it is your attitude toward your circumstances. It took me a long time to realize that."

But there's a lot more to this gathering than just talk. Every night there's a theme dinner — country and western, the '50s, "Moonlight Dreams." You haven't lived until you've seen these women rocking to Elvis singing "Burning Love," out on the dance floor doing wheelies, clapping, locking arms and doing 360-degree turns. Wednesday they rolled from the Embassy Suites to the Botanical Center, where they ate lunch and just hung out and fooled around, took pictures. Saturday they're doing a whole hair and makeup thing for the big night. Every day they're going through interviews with the judges, letting them know what they've accomplished while in a wheelchair, telling what they'll do if crowned, what their particular issue is and how they'll get the word out.

Then Saturday night one of them wins, and Sunday they head home. But that won't be the end of it.

Deb Scharf puts it this way: "Being with these women validates me as a person. It's the first time I was able to celebrate being in a wheelchair. It feels wonderful."

So there's no way she can lose this contest.

Nowhere to go
October 29, 2003

Susan Crabb is scared and she can't stop crying. She's in her late 50s, on disability, and she can barely pay her $245-a-month rent. She has a heart condition and bone problems. She has an '80 Chevy and she lives alone in a 40-year-old trailer. Parts of the place are held together by tape. The windows are covered with plastic, the siding is falling off, the driveway is a muddy mess.

"But it's my home and I don't have any place else to go. I can't believe this is happening to me."

That's the same thing you hear from Crabb's neighbor, Mindy Whiteaker. She's 26 and works the counter at a fast-food place. Her three kids are being raised by relatives and she's been living in her trailer for about nine years. An ex-boyfriend gave it to her when they split up.

Whiteaker hasn't been able to sleep since a week ago when she got the eviction notice.

"I'm just sick to my stomach. It's going to cost me about $2,000 to move this trailer and I just don't have that kind of money. It's incredible. I don't know where I'm going to go."

It's like that in just about all of the 75 trailers in the Highview Mobile Home Park.

The place — off Southeast 14th — is closing and the 400 or so folks who live there have to be out by the end of the year. They don't have the money to move their trailers and if they don't move them, they have to pay the landlord to have them moved or demolished. The trailers are old — from the '60s and '70s — and most parks won't take them. Those that will take them have a six-or seven-month waiting period.

And it's a particularly tough time to find low-income housing around here. Mike Matthes heads up city housing and he says the public programs have waiting lists that could go on for at least a year.

So these folks are on edge, waiting to see where they'll be living in two months. For some — like Merle Ragan — this park has been home for 25 or 30 years.

"I got carpal tunnel, my back is shot, I got other problems and now this. I got nowhere to turn."

For others — like Gabriela Amaro — it's been home for only a year or two. But it's the only home Amaro's had in this country. And for her and her husband, the problems get even more complicated than just money. They're trying to learn the language, keep jobs, raise a family. The Amaros have two sons at Jackson Elementary and Gabriela's worried about moving them when they're adjusting, learning English, making friends.

"They like it here," she says. "They're happy and they don't understand why this is happening."

Norman Forget can answer that. He's the manager of Forget Properties, owners of the park. They bought Highview about two years ago and he says they didn't know there were problems.

Forget says they're closing it on short notice — in winter — because this all gets worse in cold weather. The big problem is getting water to these trailers.

"It's mostly the plumbing lines that are breaking and leaking and it's just too costly to fix. We're losing money on this. It's a sad story and I know we look like the devil in disguise, but that's not the case."

Forget says it's an old park and if it were reopened under current city codes, you could only put about 25 trailers in there.

He says he doesn't know what'll happen with the property. He says he has no plans to sell it.

The park's streets, yards and driveways are littered with garbage, rusted out car parts, broken bikes. Most of the trailers could use a paint job. A lot of them need new glass in the windows.

About a half-dozen of them don't have front steps so folks use what they've got. A pile of concrete blocks is standard. One place has a few lawn chairs of different sizes that create a ladder effect. Another has an old air conditioner turned on its side.

Since the eviction notices went out, the physical problems are overshadowed by a sense of desperation. Walk around the park and you feel it.

But tucked in with all the tears, anger and sense of loss, there's some hope. These folks are starting to be heard. Meetings are going on and drawing the usual crowd of activists, but also business types, school administrators, legal aid lawyers, state and city housing officials, cops, nuns, politicians — Chris Hensley and Ed Fallon, Archie Brooks, a rep from Tom Harkin's office.

They're looking at all the angles, first trying to figure out if this whole deal is legal. If it is, then where do they go. They're trying to set up housing options, trying to keep the kids in school, trying to lower the level of anxiety.

It's going to be tough. But depending on how this plays out, it'll say a lot about this community and the folks who live here.

A bond they'd rather not share

November 14, 2003

Peggy was one of 10 kids being raised by a single mom in a small Iowa town. It was an ugly scene. Her mother drank and ran around. A lot of nights she didn't come home. Sometimes things got violent — fists flew, bottles were thrown. Her uncles drank, and they'd come by the house screaming and yelling, banging on the door, looking for trouble. Peggy would wake up in the morning and there'd be strangers sleeping on the couch, on the porch, in a pickup out front.

"I'd have friends sleep over and they'd see all this, and you can imagine how it feels to an 8-year-old. It was all screaming and violence and rage, and whoever was left standing was the winner."

Peggy grew up, became an alcoholic and then married one. After a while she got divorced and sobered up. But she's got a kid with a drinking problem.

That's her story.

Kim's family was solid, upper-middle class. Her father was an optometrist in southern Iowa. The family belonged to the country club. Her parents were polite, respectful and respected people. They never argued, no voices were raised. But behind closed doors, her father was an alcoholic. He'd come home from work and knock off a half-gallon of wine — just about every night. Years went by, things got worse, and eventually the marriage and family fell apart.

Kim didn't see it coming.

"It wasn't the stereotypical situation. In my mind the alcoholic was the guy in the gutter with a wine bottle. This was different, but it got to the point where I couldn't even look at my father. I thought he was disgusting."

Then Kim married "a loud, blue-collar, in-your-face type. He was the opposite of my father, so I thought it would be different."

But it wasn't different. Her husband was a drunk, and Kim got to the point where she was so crippled by grief and anger that she couldn't leave the house.

Now Kim and Peggy both get out a few nights a week. They go to Al-Anon meetings. These meetings are for families and friends of alcoholics. Every one of them has a story about growing up or living with an alcoholic, becoming one or marrying one, even raising one.

Some of them have done it all.

So they get together and lean on each other. It's a chance to connect with people and not have to explain things. These folks get it.

Jim knows what it feels like to have to throw your 20-year-old son out because he gets drunk and abuses his mother, trashes the house, and threatens his father. And he knows what it's like to lie awake nights wondering where his son is — if he's dead or alive.

Bruce knows what it feels like to hold hands with his wife and take a long, slow walk around Gray's Lake, talking and reminding each other why they fell in love and got married. And he knows what it feels like to come home a night later and find her drunk again, lying on the couch, cradling an empty vodka bottle.

"She's a smart, beautiful woman. I just wish God would smack her upside the head, and she'd see what she's doing to herself."

And Joanne knows what it feels like to get the call telling you your husband is behind bars again — another drunken-driving arrest. She bails him out and he blames her for his problems.

"That's after all I've been through with him. I just had to get out and come here tonight and escape the insanity or I'd be home breaking windows."

Cindy is too upset to talk. The others in the room don't push her. They understand. They just move on to the next story and then the one after that.

At the end of the evening there are prayers and hugs, words of thanks and comfort. Even a few laughs. Then these folks get back to their lives.

Jim heads home wondering where his son is.

Joanne is hoping her husband didn't spend the night at a bar and then get behind the wheel.

Bruce wonders if his wife will be waiting with a smile and open arms, or if she'll be drunk on the couch.

Boy who lost it all finds a dream life
April 12, 2004

It's sixth period and this kid — a junior — is sitting in the library at Perry High School, talking about his life, what it was like growing up. He remembers back about a dozen years ago when he was 6 or 7 and his family was on the run, going from their jungle village on the Sudanese border over into Ethiopia. It took them about a month.

He was with his mother, three brothers, two sisters and an uncle. Food and water were hard to find. He remembers one three-day stretch with nothing to eat and little to drink.

"It was difficult to keep walking when you're that thirsty and hungry. I was a little boy. But we had to keep going or we would die. There was always gunfire. Very scary. We walked all day and then lay down at night and rested. Just stop and lay down."

Doboul Koat is one of the countless Sudanese children who fled the country during the decades-long civil war, a fight that's still going on. His family is from the south; they're Christians. The northern part of the country is Muslim. The bloodshed has been nonstop.

So there came a point when the Koat family left everything and ran.

"My grandfather was considered rich. He had a lot of cows."

Doboul grew up in an Ethiopian refugee camp. He lived in a little shack built by his family. They put it together from whatever random pieces of wood they could scrounge up. They had no electricity or running water. They slept on the ground. They ate when folks from the United Nations showed up with food. They cooked over an open fire. There was a school — a roped-off area where he could go and learn to speak English. But most days he was too tired and hungry to get it together and go.

This went on for 11 years. Then one day his mother said the U.N. had found him and his uncle a sponsor in America, a Sudanese guy living in San Diego.

"I always hear people talk about America, but I had no idea what to think about it. I couldn't even dream about it. I just didn't know."

This was in November 2000, and things moved fast. Within weeks he was bused out of the camp and put up in a hotel in the Ethiopian capital of Addis Ababa. It was the first time Doboul had seen a phone or a radio or TV or anything like that: "I kept wondering, 'What is all this?' I had no idea. You hear about TV and all that, but until you see it and hear it, you don't know what to think."

For a week he went through all kinds of tests, medical exams and, because he had no papers, he was given a birthday — June 7, 1983. He was put through something called "cultural orientation."

"They taught us how to use a bathroom and how to use a phone, how to call 911 in an emergency. They talked to us about American law and how to follow it. How to find a job."

And at the end of seven days he was on a plane for the first time — another life-altering experience. He spent a few months in San Diego, and then in April 2001 he heard from a relative, an uncle who was living in Iowa, working at the Tyson Foods plant in Perry. Doboul came here and started school the following August.

Folks around Perry heard his story, met him, and were impressed. Cathy Stone, a Perry Middle School teacher, is his biggest advocate, making sure folks in town know he's there.

"I wanted our students and their parents to realize we have this treasure in our midst. Somebody who walked three days to find food. It's amazing the effect he's had on the other students. They have so much respect for him. He is so gracious and polite."

Doboul works hard, and he takes nothing for granted. Every day after school he goes to the Tyson factory and works. If he's got a lot of homework, he leaves early — at 9. If not, he works until midnight. He's missed only two days of school in three years.

He's getting with the program, the good and the bad. He's eating a lot of pizza and hamburgers, drinking orange soda, and trying to figure out "why it's called football?" He listens to country music on the radio — "I like Alan Jackson on KJJY" — and he watches TV.

"I have cable, so I can see movies, but not too much. I like to read and do my homework. I want to get skills and go to college."

Not long ago his mother and the rest of the family came to the United States and settled in Des Moines. Doboul stayed with his uncle in Perry and sees the family on weekends. He says he's happier than he could have ever imagined, but he still thinks about where he came from.

"Everything is good, a dream. But I think about Africa a lot. I miss my people. I can't go back because I would be killed."

So he keeps looking forward, working hard and reaching out. He knows what he wants, and he's going after it.

"College is so important. I want a good education. And this summer I really want to get a cell phone."

Given all Doboul Koat has overcome, you've got to believe he'll make that happen.

Principal's lessons go far beyond reading, writing, arithmetic
May 24, 2004

Al Graziano learned a lot in school this year, but it wasn't about math and science and history.

It was about watching teenagers deal with pain and tragedy — the deaths of friends in car crashes and suicide, arrests, gay bashing, all kinds of threats and harassment, arson charges.

It was about realizing how these high school kids can pull together and help each other keep going.

And it was about Graziano realizing how deep inside himself he could dig when he had to. He talks about finding the strength to walk into a home and try to comfort a woman whose 14-year-old son was just killed in a car wreck.

"This year has reminded me about the role we play in the lives of young people. The responsibility we have even in normal times."

He talks slowly, chooses each word.

"How we have to be there for them. And how extraordinary it is that they can be there for us."

Graziano is the principal at Lincoln, a south Des Moines high school with about 2,000 students. It's the place he graduated from in 1960.

He took over last spring, and the problems started within weeks. Last May's graduation was marred by anti-gay protesters. Families and friends showing up to celebrate a defining moment in their children's lives were greeted with signs about how "God hates fags" and "God hates America."

Then — after the summer break, during Homecoming week — there was the devastating blow that stained the rest of the year.

Four Lincoln students were in a speeding car when the driver lost control and hit a utility pole. Three died and the fourth — the driver — was charged with homicide. Friends from school got together and set up a candlelight vigil at the crash site. It was powerful event, and Graziano keeps a photo of it in his office. He says he looks at it a few times a week. It gives him strength.

He's needed it. Just weeks after the triple fatality, a Lincoln student hanged himself in a closet at his home. Then a week later police were investigating a suicide pact involving nine other Lincoln students — friends of the boy who killed himself.

The next month, in November, the cops broke a four-month case where a Des Moines family was haunted by harassing phone calls and pornographic notes. Dead mice were thrown on their lawn, nails placed in their driveway, and a gasoline-soaked pumpkin set on fire outside their house. In a related case, a Lincoln senior's car was vandalized, her tires slashed. Five Lincoln students were busted and charged with criminal mischief. Four of them also faced harassment charges. Three were also charged with arson.

Even when things were quiet, there were daily reminders — like birthdays and anniversaries.

Graziano was in on all of it. That was only a small piece of his job.

"We had to keep the school going. That was the toughest part. We had sports, music programs, dance teams, drama presentations. They had to study and take tests. This is an important time for these kids. These years will stay with them forever. You want them to have wonderful memories."

It would have been easy for Graziano to just hang back in his office, sit on the couch, read, do paperwork and stare at the pictures of the loves of his life — his two granddaughters. He could have focused on the academics and left the hand-holding to the professionals — the grief counselors.

But that's not what this guy is about. He starts his day at around 7 in the school cafeteria. A few hundred students show up for breakfast, and it's a chance for Graziano to connect in a fairly loose environment. It's also a chance for him to get a sense of where things are at, figure out which kids are hurting, who needs some one-on-one time.

"It's a good place to pick up on how things are going. I've found that if I'm out there and visible, they will come up and speak to me. At that hour I'm not the principal. I'm just another person."

He spends time walking the halls and sitting in the classrooms. He goes to the games, the plays and the parties.

This year he spent time at funerals and in court. Al Graziano goes where his job takes him.

Unity's value to workers hasn't changed
September 9, 2004

I got caught in traffic from the Labor Day parade on Monday, and sitting there watching float after float, I got to thinking about unions and how they seem like something out of the dark ages, something your grandfather would be involved with.

Ironworkers, steelworkers and autoworkers in the age of high tech just don't seem to fit.

Then I started thinking about Martino's dress shop, the place my mother labored for most of her adult life.

It was a factory, rows and rows of women at sewing machines. They were called "operators." There were maybe a half-dozen guys in the place working at the ironing boards. They were called "pressers."

They all worked with their heads down, leaning over. Don't even think about talking to the person next to you, unless it has something to do with the job.

These folks were more than happy to have the work. They were in the place Monday through Friday, from 8:30 to 5, a half-hour lunch break.

This was in the late 1950s and early '60s, and they were making 75 cents an hour, about $30 a week.

Some of the women — younger ones in their 30s and 40s, the ones with a lot of energy — were "pieceworkers," and they were making about $1.50 a dress. If they worked through lunch, they could take home as much as $45. That was a good deal for a single parent.

It was a joyless atmosphere, with only the hum of the machines filling the air.

But every once in a while, somebody would screw up and the grim silence was broken by the shop owner, Michael Martino.

He was in his 50s, short and stocky, thick Italian accent, always wearing a white shirt and tie, always sweating, never smiling.

Most of the time he'd just walk the floor looking around, making sure everybody was working hard and feeling miserable.

Then every once in a while, a presser would accidently burn a collar or an operator would mess up a hem, and Martino would lose it. He'd be screaming, stomping around the place, cursing in Italian

— three different dialects — and broken English, arms going in five directions.

He'd take the damaged dress and cut it up with scissors or rip it with his hands or pull on it with his teeth, or all of the above.

If it was a particularly expensive dress, he'd be punching walls, slamming doors.

One time he threw a dress and it got stuck up in the factory ceiling, up in a skylight. It hung there for years. It was a frightening reminder to the folks who worked in that factory.

Then, after years of trying, the workers got organized. For $4 a month in dues they could join the International Ladies Garment Workers Union.

All of a sudden they knew about things like holiday pay, overtime, even a little bit of health insurance — maybe an annual cleaning at the dentist or a pair of glasses for the kid.

The atmosphere in the place changed. A lot of the tension was gone. Folks weren't living in fear of losing their jobs, worrying about how they were going to feed the kids.

Back in the shop, Martino never calmed down. Now, with the union in his face, he was even worse. It didn't take a screw-up to set him off. Somebody would simply refuse to work through lunch or come in on a Saturday without getting time and a half.

So Martino was ripping and cursing and slamming even more.

But now these workers weren't afraid of him. For the first time, there was a feeling that they were all in this together and they could deal with whatever he threw their way

Now when things got ugly, they'd even lift their heads, look at each other and smile. Maybe if he was being crazy enough, they'd even have a few laughs.

I thought of all that and, by the time the parade passed, I remembered why the ironworkers have to hang together.

Neighbors step in to help a guy who's hurting

September 13, 2004

Freddy Lange was in bad shape to begin with.

He's 55 and was born with all kinds of health problems — mental and physical. He recently had a heart attack.

He can barely read and write, and he spent the first 16 years of his life in the Woodward State Hospital.

These days he's living on the $556-a-month that he gets from Social Security disability, and most of his food comes from local churches and other charities.

He works about two hours a day cleaning an east-side bar and carrying the empties out back.

That work is good for a few meals, even an occasional treat like lunch at Burger King.

So he was struggling, barely hanging on and then — the way Lange and his friends tell it — he got ripped off.

Ever since his parents died back in the '70s, Lange has had a payee, someone with access to his bank account. That person pays his bills because that's not something he can deal with.

He's saying the woman used his money to gamble.

So he lost his gas and electric and he doesn't have the $1,150 to fix the problem.

The woman he's accusing says it's all a misunderstanding. She says she did pay the bills and doesn't know why the power was cut off.

The two of them go back and forth, but the bottom line is that the guy's hurting.

He's living in the dark and can't even make himself a cup of coffee.

Lange's home is a small one-bedroom house about five blocks north of the State Fairgrounds. He bought it years ago with money from a lawsuit settlement — a long, complicated story involving an assault by another inmate during a night Lange spent in the city lock-up.

Now the house is a wreck. The few pieces of furniture are torn and broken. The floors and walls are filthy, thick with cobwebs and dust. Garbage is piled all over the place. The air is filled with bugs. It's tough to even breathe in there.

Lange is upset and depressed. For the first time since his parents died and left him alone, he's worried about ending up in a home.

But there's some good stuff going on here. This latest disaster with the electricity has gotten the attention of folks who know Lange — from the neighborhood, from the bar, from the church. They're pulling together, making sure he'll get through this.

The other morning there was a stream of folks in and out of his place.

Patty, his next-door neighbor, came over to start cleaning, and she says this will be an ongoing deal so the place never gets this bad again. She's got a few others lined up to help.

Orville Deaton, an old friend, stopped by with a pot of coffee.

Betty Bishop checked in and Roy Davis came over from across the street to make sure the batteries in the lantern he gave Lange were still working.

Roy's wife, Diana, has been Web surfing, trying to figure out how to get Lange on food stamps and see if there's a way to get the state or the county to help handle his money.

Mike Kulisky is rounding up a bunch of guys to do some heavy lifting and fix up the house.

Joe Gosek, the bar owner, set up a little fund to raise money and get the heat and lights back on before the cold weather hits.

Some others are bringing him clothes and there's talk about trying to get some decent furniture in the place, maybe even curtains on the windows.

Lange just sits, listens and doesn't say much more than "thanks."

Everybody who comes by tells him it's not a problem. They tell him to let them know if he needs anything.

Immigrant family is haunted, yet 'blessed'
January 12, 2005

He sits in the living room of a small house he rents on the east side of Des Moines, just blocks from the fairgrounds. He goes by the name Juan.

He talks slowly, in broken English. His oldest kid is 15 and sits by his side, helping out when Juan struggles with the language.

The other kids — 10, 7, 4 — are on the floor behind him playing a video game, laughing, goofing around.

The sound of those kids playing is a good background when Juan says he's got everything he ever dreamed about — the family, the nice house, a decent job, a lot of friends, support from his church and the rest of his community.

But it's strange to hear them giggling as the mood in the room changes, when Juan starts talking about this cloud hanging over his life.

He's in this country illegally and lives with the fear of getting caught, deported and losing it all.

"I've got the children. We have a life here, and I just can't let go. I like Iowa. It's good for the children. They grow up safe, and I have money to feed them. In Mexico, we would eat meat only once a week."

He doesn't make excuses. He understands what's going on, why some folks are angry at him — "the whole terrorist problem, the money it costs Americans. I know that. But I'm not a terrorist. I pay my bills."

He's asked for help, and the guy he works for was willing to sponsor him. But then the guy was told to submit three years of returns to show he was paying his taxes properly and not shortchanging Juan and other workers.

The employer heard that and pulled out.

So it's been grim on that front, but there's a bit of hope right now. The Iowa Supreme Court is looking at the possibility of granting driver's licenses to folks who are in this country illegally. It's causing a major buzz in the Latino community.

Juan prays it'll happen.

"This would help. If I can drive, maybe I can have a bank account and buy a car from a real car dealer. I could get insured and protect the children. This is their home."

It's the only home these kids have had.

Juan, now 42, slipped over the border near Tijuana in the late '80s and worked on a farm picking strawberries and tomatoes from 5 in the morning to 6 at night. He lived two hours from the farm and had to share an apartment with seven other folks.

In those first few years, he got married, had a kid, went back to Mexico for a while, and one night he was approached by a guy who told him about a meatpacking plant in Iowa. They'd pay decent money and not ask a lot of questions.

The family came here, and for 11 years this state has been home.

Juan quit the packing plant after being tipped off about an immigration raid that was coming down. He moved to Des Moines — the Drake area — and lived in a house with his wife, kids and a dozen other people.

He found work on a hog farm and eventually set his family up in their own home.

His day sounds like a nightmare, but he keeps saying, "I'm blessed."

He gets up at 5 in the morning and drives his wife to her job in West Des Moines — she's a hotel maid and dishwasher. Then he goes back home and takes the three younger kids to day care at the church. The oldest goes to East.

When the wife and kids are taken care of, Juan drives about 45 miles to the farm and spends the day working with pigs — everything from feeding to helping them give birth.

He gets back to town in the late afternoon to pick up his wife. Sometimes she has to wait three hours for him to get there.

On weekends, they do a lot of community service — mostly through their church. Juan does house painting and garden work. His wife takes food to folks who are homebound, and she helps them with cleaning and cooking.

Folks who know the family are impressed with the parents' devotion to their kids and to each other. They talk about the couple's willingness to get out and help people. One friend mentions that this town is lucky to have them here.

But ask around, and nobody wants to talk about that dark cloud hanging over this family.

"So I'm talkin' to this guy . . ."

Chapter 2: Politics

By Mario Cuomo
Former Governor of New York

Being out of public office has its advantages: one of them is not having to wake up and see Rob Borsellino having fun with your missteps in the morning paper. His political columns are a lot more enjoyable when someone else is the subject of his smart alecky humor.

Rob was a reporter covering me when I was governor of New York. He was tenacious, and sometimes a pain in the neck.

But he's willing to say things others wouldn't have the guts to, whether it's feeling skeptical over Saddam Hussein's capture or observing Iowa lawmakers helping themselves to freebies

While not letting politicians take ourselves too seriously, he never takes himself too seriously either. That's a skill in short supply among pundits and political observers.

Phelps brings grandchildren
on an Iowa field trip
April 18, 2000

At about 7:30 Monday morning I was on the corner of East Ninth and Grand, standing next to a trio of kids — a 9-year-old boy and two girls, 7 and 12. They were holding signs that said: "Thank God for AIDS," "Fags Doom Iowa," and "AIDS Cures Fags." Next to the kids were folks holding other signs. One had two stick figures of men in an anal-sex position and the words "Fag Sin." Another had figures of women and the words "Dyke Sin."

And there was a woman holding a "God Hates Fags" sign. That woman — Shirley Phelps-Roper — was the kids' mom. I asked why the little ones weren't in school.

"This is a field trip. Kids go on field trips all the time. Children are taken out of school for far less than this. They're getting a better education here than they get in school most days."

Then Phelps-Roper went off on a tangent about the line, "God loves everybody," dismissing it as "the fag battle cry" and wondering, "If God loves fags, why does He send them to hell?" Then, barely catching her breath, she got into a jag about "the sea of fag lies that we swim in. They say all kinds of things about us. They say my dad molested his daughters."

Interesting that she brought it up. Dad, standing a few feet away, is the Rev. Fred Phelps of the Topeka-based Westboro Baptist Church. This is the guy who shows up at the funerals of AIDS victims to mock the families and tell them their dead children are burning in hell. He and his people quote Romans and Corinthians and — when talking about sex, which is pretty much all they talk about — they can throw around the F-word with the best of them. Even the kids can go on about sex, after asking: "Mommy is it OK if I say that stuff?"

Mommy says it's OK and gives the kid a big hug when he's finished.

They do all this in the name of Jesus Christ.

They were in town Monday to burn the Iowa flag and bring attention to the governor's "eagerness to pimp for the fag agenda."

Phelps brought along several of his 10 kids and a handful of his 48 grandkids.

As far as political props go, the grandkids were excellent. They got everybody's attention, even Robin Echer's. She was parking her car and heading to work at the Wallace Building when she saw the crowd. Then she saw the signs. Then the kids. She couldn't help herself. She got in Shirley Phelps-Roper's face.

"What on Earth is going on here? You've got these children out here spreading hate." She threw around a few John 4:11s and the like. Phelps-Roper fired back with a Romans 9:11. Then she laughed off Echer's knowledge of the Bible.

Echer was beyond outrage. And she was late for work. As she hurried off she asked who these folks were. Someone mentioned the Phelps church. Echer gasped. "They're Baptists. Are you serious? I thought it was just some hate group."

Echer took off and the small crowd ambled down to the parking lot for the flag burning. They found a garbage can, lifted the flag and poured nail polish remover on it. Phelps asked around and found a cigarette lighter.

But he couldn't figure out how to use it. Two of his daughters came forward to help. They pushed the old man off into the background and got in front of the cameras. Eventually, with the help of more nail polish remover and a second cigarette lighter, they managed to burn the flag.

One of the kids, 9-year-old Zacharias, was impressed. "That is so awesome. Totally cool."

His sisters agreed and the three of them gave mom a hug. Grandpa was behind them, telling the TV cameras that the governor's turning the state's children into "a bunch of anal-copulating fools."

The kids waited for grandpa to finish his soundbite. Then it was time to head home to Topeka.

They walked off. I was wondering if they'd get up in front of the class today and talk about what they learned on their field trip.

A cloud of sadness, sense of worry follow Cataldo

July 20, 2000

Late Tuesday Michael Cataldo stood outside the Warren County Courthouse and smoked one more Marlboro. His hands were shaking, and he kept shuffling his feet. He was due on the witness stand in about 10 minutes. He said he was looking forward to this.

"I've been waiting for six months. Now's my chance to prove I'm innocent. I'm a target because I'm a politician. Everybody knows that. I'm innocent. I'm not worried."

He kept shuffling and shaking, smoking and moving around. He looked worried.

Cataldo is a state legislator from Des Moines, a south-side Democrat who's up for re-election. In January he was arrested and charged with making obscene phone calls to a woman and her teen-age daughter. It's a misdemeanor that carries 30 days and a $200 fine.

Two other women have come forward saying they also got calls. The cops say he made 604 calls over five months. Cataldo's phone records back them up. Most of the calls were made between 2 and 5 in the morning. Sometimes there'd be 10 or 15 calls a day.

In his defense, Cataldo says he wouldn't be stupid enough to do something like that when people have caller ID and other ways to trace calls. He says somebody obviously had access to his number. He never checked his bills; he just paid them. He lights another cigarette and talks a little about the toll this has taken on his life, his reputation.

The day he was arrested he could only focus on "what the press was going to do to me. That's the only thing going through my mind. It'll destroy my reputation. And my wife is probably going to kill me. Those were my biggest concerns."

He thinks the media is out to get him because it's a sexy story involving a politician. And he says his wife has stood by him "because she knows I didn't do it."

He put out his cigarette, walked into the courthouse lobby and huddled with his wife and his parents. Bill Kutmus, Cataldo's lawyer, came over and tried to get his client pumped.

"You ready to get on that stand and kick butt? This is it. We're going in."

They walked off. Karen Cataldo watched her husband head into the courtroom. She was on the witness stand a day earlier, and it was learned that she didn't find out about the charges until a month after her husband was arrested. And she only found out at that point because the story was going to break in the morning paper.

Asked about that by the prosecutor, she said: "His attorney advised him not to tell anyone because it was no big deal. It would blow over."

Tuesday, Karen wasn't eager to talk about the case and how it's affected her marriage. All she'd say was: "You have to be strong."

It was pretty much the same with Cataldo's parents. George Cataldo shook his head and said: "This is tough on the family. It's tough to see your kid go through something like this."

On the stand Cataldo was aggressive and angry to the point of being cartoonish. He seemed like he was over-coached. Every question — from his name and occupation to things about his guilt or innocence — was answered in a loud, confrontational manner. It got to the point where the judge had to tell him to calm down, saying: "You have to listen to the questions."

Asked about it later, Kutmus said Cataldo's behavior was the fall-out from all he's been through.

"He's an innocent man accused of this. Wouldn't you be the same way?"

The questioning went on for about 40 minutes. Prosecutor Jane Orlanes talked a lot about sexual gratification. She quoted Cataldo going on about orgasms, and she quoted him saying: "Picture me inside you."

A couple of character witnesses took the stand and said Cataldo was honest.

Judge Joe Smith said he'd have a verdict by early next month.

It was over and outside the courthouse Cataldo grabbed a smoke and shared a laugh with his wife and parents, his mother-in-law and his attorney. But even the laughs couldn't mask the sadness around them. It felt like something was wrong, they all knew it, and nobody would talk about it.

Well, citizens, aren't you glad to get rid of the guy?

August 17, 2000

So the guy had sex with an intern, in the White House, lied about it on national TV, lied about it under oath, disgraced his family, humiliated his supporters and gave the right everything they needed to bash the left — and the moderates — for years.

Now the morally challenged Bill Clinton is just about done and I figure the American people couldn't be happier. I hit the streets the morning after Clinton's convention speech to bask in the euphoria, to connect with my fellow Americans. It took a while, but I finally found someone who actually heard the speech.

Ron Dunham is a Republican and he works for Principal. I mentioned Clinton and stood back, giving him plenty of room to vent.

"Well, to tell you the truth, in spite of what's happened, I might vote for him a third time if I could. I'm just not that impressed with what's out there. I don't know how to explain it. I've always been impressed with the guy, with his ability to connect with people."

But Ron, you're a Republican, a businessman in the Midwest. What about Monica? The lies?

"It bothers me, but I'm forgiving. Maybe I shouldn't be, but that's just my nature. Haven't you done things you're ashamed of?"

This is not about me, pal. Thanks for your time.

I moved on. I ran into Billie Martin. She didn't see the Clinton speech because she was at church. Perfect. A woman of God. Talk to me about Bill Clinton. Are you disgusted by his behavior? Glad to see this sorry era coming to a close?

"I'm not the one to judge him. I will say this: He's done a lot for the African-American community, a lot for diversity, and I admire that about him. I would vote for him again."

What about morality, the sleaze factor?

"I'll just say that everybody has something in their closet."

Enough with the closets. One more question: Will you vote for Gore or Bush?

"I really don't know. I'm a Democrat, but J.C. Watts is married to my first cousin and he talks about Bush all the time. I'm still undecided."

I was mulling over Ms. Martin's indecision when I met up with Fred X. Adams, a man who doesn't know from undecided. He's a Gore supporter — "He'll do a hell of a job" — and a Clinton guy. He heard the speech and liked it.

"Weren't you impressed? I thought it was humble. He gave credit to others and he pointed out that we've never been in such good shape. What more do people want?"

How about honesty, morality? The affair bother you?

"I am so damn sick and tired of hearing about that. Who gives a damn? I just wish that when it all came out he'd have stood up there and said: 'Yeah I did it, but it's none of your damn business.' I would have been so proud of the guy."

Adams then said a few other things, but we'll let it go at that.

I'd been at it about an hour or so and still no serious Clinton bashers. I needed a good hard-nosed Republican with a sense of outrage. A no-nonsense type. I found one, but he was a Democrat — a Democrat who didn't vote for Clinton either time. Gary Sly owns a couple of fast-food joints and a coffee shop. He saw the speech and dismissed it as "a bunch of bull. I can't believe anybody takes the guy seriously."

Now we're talking. So what do you look for in a president?

"I look for somebody who understands what it means to be a world power. Someone who's tough. Someone who's willing to say to these other countries: 'Do this or else.' And if they don't do it, that's it. No second chances."

While he was getting all worked up, a woman named Joyce Lewis came by. I asked about Clinton.

"I'm sure he's not the first to conduct himself poorly in that office, but I'm terribly disappointed in his morals." A thoughtful pause. "But otherwise he's done a great job running the country. Can you imagine how much he could have accomplished if he hadn't had to spend so much time defending himself?"

Yeah. But then it wouldn't have been the Bill Clinton we've known for the past eight years. The Bill Clinton who leaves office with a job approval rating of 65 percent — a point or two higher than the beloved Ronald Reagan.

Sharpton impresses local clergy
February 27, 2002

They lined the streets outside Creative Visions, standing in the cold, the snow, waiting for him to get there. They were waiting to escort him into a breakfast meeting for the clergy. Inside, they lined the halls, waiting to greet him, waiting to let him know how pleased they were to have him here.

When he showed up they were all over the guy, calling this "a day Des Moines will never forget . . . an historic day . . . a chance to show people Iowa is more than just cornfields."

They came up to pay homage, to thank him for coming, to ask for his autograph, to bring him a plate of fruit and eggs, a cup of coffee. They came up to just revel in the presence of a national celebrity, a guy who's been profiled in the New Yorker and written up in the New York Times repeatedly in the past few weeks.

For his part, Al Sharpton didn't seem all that impressed. He showed up late, walked in with a phone pasted to his ear, made his way to the dais and then spent the next 15 minutes or so fielding calls, checking the messages on his PDA. He picked at his food and sipped coffee while looking like he'd rather be someplace else.

But then — after listening to the fawning intros — Sharpton got around to doing what he does best. He got around to the reason he was in town. He got up to speak. He's no Jesse Jackson, but he's good. He should be. He's 47 and he's been at it for for almost 40 years. At the 1964 New York World's Fair he preached at a gospel night event. In high school he called for a boycott of the lunchroom because the food was lousy. It hasn't stopped.

So getting up in front of about 30 church types in Des Moines wasn't heavy lifting as he continues to glide from the fringes to the mainstream, trying to decide if he'll run for the White House. He said he's about three months away. And leaning toward a run.

Tuesday morning he moved easily from the cornerstones of his rap — civil rights, police brutality, racial profiling — to his latest interests, things like Enron and corporate bailouts. He talked about Social Security and the Florida vote count with the same ease as he talked about Amadou Diallo.

He threw out a line about Iowa farmers struggling to make the mortgage — cut him some slack; he's from Brooklyn — and he paid tribute to folks like Medgar Evers and Marcus Garvey, Malcolm X and Frederick Douglass.

He's even got some of the applause lines down, calling the current crop of Democratic contenders "Republican elephants in donkey overcoats." And saying: "If you're drowning in 10 feet of water and I pull you up to 6 feet of water and tell you you've made progress, you still have to be saved."

If there were any doubters going in — anyone wondering why this guy's hot on the speaker circuit or why they bothered to show up — an hour into it they were with him.

The Rev. Tom Burkhardt from the Covenant Christian Church said he showed up for a couple of reasons. He was curious about what Sharpton had to say and — Burkhardt said kind of reluctantly — because he doesn't connect much with blacks in this town. When it was over, Burkhardt was impressed.

"I liked a lot of what he had to say and it was an education in how to preach. He's very good."

Father James Kiernan came over from St. Ambrose and he had no trouble finding good things to say about the guy.

"He's thought-provoking. He reminded me that with the destruction of unions in this country, we have no control over business. I'm glad he's speaking out."

And Pastor Clara Glover — a pacifist with the Church of the Brethren — didn't much care for Sharpton talking about "fighting for peace." But she also came away with a positive take, saying Sharpton made her think.

"When he said 'silence is acceptance' and how we should speak out against things we don't like. That was very powerful."

But she's not ready to join the Sharpton for President campaign.

"I don't think that's his calling. It's one thing to be a troublemaker in the ranks. But having a troublemaker at the helm would be a problem."

I hear troublemaker and the words "axis of evil" and "collateral damage" come to mind.

'Flagg Parkway' is a real stunner

March 22, 2002

You're driving along in a new town, passing Main Street and First Avenue, you're cruising, and you look up and see David Duke Drive on your left and George Wallace Way on your right.

You're stunned, outraged. You're wondering why they'd name public streets after people who have exhibited such blatantly racist views.

And that's pretty much how I felt the other night when I was driving down Fleur, looked up, and saw that Valley Drive was renamed George Flagg Parkway.

Flagg is the Des Moines city councilman who retired in December after 20-plus years. He's also the one who admitted that for years he routinely rejected liquor license applications from people with foreign-sounding names.

An investigation last year by the Register's Jeff Eckhoff showed about 90 percent of the licenses Flagg opposed were from Asians, Indians, Hispanics and Bosnians. When Eckhoff asked about that, Flagg said he did it because the city wasn't checking to make sure these folks were here legally: "Nobody seemed to give a damn. So I thought the best I could do under the circumstances was to vote against what I thought were illegal enterprises."

Did he have proof that anything illegal was going on? No, he didn't. Then why do this to these people?

"If you study carefully, you will find that any number of immigrants have been responsible for murders in our country and in our city."

And they're naming a street after this guy?

So I asked around and I heard it wasn't a done deal. They put the sign up to recognize his decades in office, but there are still a few legal hoops to jump through. There's a hearing down at City Hall next month, on the 22nd.

Then I heard folks who own businesses along Valley Drive are upset with the name change and they've got a petition drive going. They're asking the city to reconsider. Now I'm impressed. I figure these people are taking a moral stand. They're ready to go to the wall for their beliefs.

I want to meet these folks. I get in the car, drive along that road, and stop at the Valley Bait shop. Bob Knudson owns the place. He's been there 25 years and he's got a petition on the front counter.

So are Flagg's political views driving this?

"Not at all. I'm happy to honor him. During the flood in 1993 he was the only one who answered my phone calls. I just wish they'd name another street after him. Not this one."

What about that deal with the liquor licenses? "I trust his judgment. He's the councilman. Not me."

I thanked Mr. Knudson for his time and went up the road to Ideal Floors, a place that sells rugs, carpeting.

Shawn Eldredge was in his office — in the shadow of two deer heads and about a half-dozen stuffed birds. He wants no part of this name change, but Flagg's not the problem.

"The problem is that we'd have to change all our stationery, our business cards, everything. It's expensive."

I ask about the licenses and Eldredge is ready to cut Flagg some slack.

"It sounds like discrimination, but politicians are human. They say and do things they'd wished they hadn't done. Haven't you done things you wish you hadn't done?"

I'd rather not go there right now. I change the subject. I ask about the birds — "These are spring snow geese and those are mallards."

Then I hit a few more places along the road and I end up at the Izaak Walton League, the folks behind the petition drive. John Huss is the GM over there and — like the others — he says: "George Flagg isn't the issue. We're not political."

They just think the name Valley Drive is a better fit with the league's role as a conservation group.

I'd heard about enough. It was time for a reality check, time to go to the source. I called George Flagg and asked whether he had any regrets about what he'd done. He's direct, to the point, offering up the kind of thoughtful insight we've come to expect from Mr. Flagg.

"The only thing I regret is having stupid people like you trying to make me look bad."

I hear that and I'm wondering if maybe it's my foreign-sounding name that's got the guy upset.

English bill recalls an '80s scrap

March 27, 2002

A friend of mine came by the house for dinner the other night, and he got into a jag about how naive I've been on this official-English business. He said I should back off. The governor had to sign the bill because he's up in November and most Iowans are with him on this. He mentioned — only three or four times — the Register poll that showed around 80 percent favor it. And he's not the only one making that case.

Folks in Vilsack's inner circle are saying that if he didn't sign, the Republicans would beat him over the head with it for the next seven months. By signing, he's managed to get it off the front page.

The political types on both sides are saying that by summer, people aren't even going to remember this. Besides, the folks he's dissing on this one — the PC bunch, the lefties, immigrants in general, Hispanics in particular — are stuck. They're not going to vote Republican. Vilsack will throw them a bone in the next few months — veto the abortion bill, stay cozy with labor — and they'll come around. Besides, it's a toothless bill. So just chill and give the guy a break

I'm listening to all this, and I'm reminded of another election, another politician. This was in the early '80s. The governor of New York wasn't going to run again, and the lieutenant governor, Mario Cuomo, wanted the job. But he had a problem. Crime was spinning out of control. The usual mix of muggings and murders was being joined by the crack epidemic — with the gangs, the drive-bys, the drug houses.

People were fed up. Some polls were showing that 70 percent of New Yorkers wanted the next governor to support the death penalty. Cuomo's problem was that he was opposed to the death penalty. He said it was immoral and the state must not "become like animals" and kill people. He called it a simplistic response to a complex problem.

And Cuomo had something else to deal with: Ed Koch, another Democrat who wanted the job. Koch was the mayor of New York City, home to half the state's 16 million people. Talk about name recognition. Koch had beaten Cuomo about five years earlier in the primary

"So I'm talkin' to this guy . . ."

for mayor. And he was a big supporter of the death penalty. When someone would say it wasn't a deterrent to crime, it was revenge, Koch would say there's nothing wrong with revenge. The crowds seem to like that. The political wisdom was that Cuomo didn't have a prayer, it was hopeless.

So I watched Cuomo travel the state that spring and, unlike some politicians, he never avoided the tough issues. If people didn't bring up the death penalty, he did. He'd get in their faces, telling them: "If the electric chair is what you want, then vote for somebody else."

His ability to articulate his reasons, to lay things out, muted even the loudest critics. One biographer wrote: "As is the case with Ronald Reagan, Cuomo's apparent integrity and willingness to stick to his beliefs attracts people to him, whether or not they agree with him on all issues."

Come primary day, Cuomo won, 52 to 48. Then he won the general election — the first of three. The death penalty issue never went away and — for 12 years — neither did Cuomo. So how did this guy survive? I called his Manhattan law office the other morning and asked him about that. I asked if he ever signed a bill for political expedience. He laughed.

"Of course. Every politician does that. The question is where do you draw the line?"

So where did he draw the line?

"On what I'd call human dignity issues. Never do something that punishes somebody for being homosexual, never on religious liberty questions. You get the idea."

He was in no position to discuss human dignity in relation to official English — "I'd have to read the bill." But he said he wasn't buying that 80 percent favorable number. "Don't give me that. I've been out there to Iowa. People are smarter than that. Come on."

Talking to him reminded me about what a pain he could be to deal with, his eagerness to argue, to be confrontational.

It also reminded me about what made Mario Cuomo a leader — his willingness to take chances, to take unpopular positions, to stand up to a tough Legislature and, when necessary, to take out his veto pen and use it to tell them to go to hell.

From: Borsellino, Rob

To: Tom Vilsack
Cc: Des Moines Register Readers
Sent: Friday, July 12, 2003 6 a.m.
Subject: Where have you been?

July 11, 2003

Dear Governor,

I know you won't be able to call up this e-mail, but maybe somebody on your staff will be kind enough to print it out or read it to you. And don't worry about e-mailing me back. You might hurt yourself trying to use a computer.

I just wanted to let you know I caught your e-mail riff in the paper yesterday and I was LOL. I haven't laughed that hard since your Winnie the Pooh routine.

You destroyed state records because you're not computer savvy? Talk about mass destruction. You are one clever dude. (:

So tell me, what's really going on here? You've got these high-priced advisers on the payroll, so it couldn't be sheer stupidity. Is this part of some long-range political plan? I know it's a chance to get your name out there — big time. Something this off-the-wall could make you one of those little crawl items on the cable news channels. You'll go national. Even global. They'll be laughing about this one in the cyber cafes from Dubuque to Darjeeling. You can't buy that kind of attention. It was really smart of you to pull something like that. And it sends the right message to your supporters. It appeals to those Roosevelt Democrats, that handful of 80-and 90-somethings who don't have a computer.

But what I want to know is why now? And how are you going to cash in? I'm thinking maybe it's not so long range. Maybe you really are looking at the White House in '04. A line like "I don't read my e-mails" could get you there faster than you can say, "I didn't inhale."

And here's another thing you must have thought about: This'll make you look like "an even newer Democrat." No one will confuse

"So I'm talkin' to this guy . . ."

you with Al Gore, the inventor of the Internet.

Whatever the plan, it's brilliant. Those advisers are really earning their paychecks.

Just look at this. No e-mail means you don't have to spend all your time rifling through the spam. You're not sitting there plowing through hundreds of messages about everything from Viagra knock-offs to news about shifts in the Bolivian economy. And you don't have to put up with that constant whining from those crybabies in Sioux City and Burlington — "Nobody picked up my garbage. . . . I can't afford health care."

And not being tech-wise means you won't be sitting in some trial lawyer's chat room rehashing the Michigan affirmative-action case. Or just Web surfing, trying to hook up with folks you haven't seen since fourth grade.

So that's good. That frees you up to do more important things, like try to decide what kind of image you want to project after Friar Tuck and the Mad Hatter.

Or maybe — if you're really bored — you can use that time to try to figure out how to plug those pesky little holes in the state budget. Important stuff like that takes time, especially if you can't figure out how to use a calculator.

Anyway, GTG. I just wanted to touch base and find out what the hell you were thinking.

Here's your visa to limbo, sir

August 1, 2003

In mid-December Farhad Mian got on a plane in Des Moines, made a few stops along the way, and about 20 hours later was back in Pakistan.

This was going to be a one-month trip. He was there to meet and marry the woman his family had set him up with. The couple would spend about a month together in Lahore, then she'd get back to her college studies and he'd come home to Des Moines. He's a financial analyst at AmerUs and a graduate student at Drake University.

So that was the plan.

Mian had done research, he checked the U.S. State Department Web site, and he knew it would take about a month to get his return visa. He figured he'd be back in mid-January.

Seven months later — a week ago last Tuesday — Mian was finally back at his desk at AmerUs. The company's CEO had to call in a favor from a U.S. senator to get him back. And this is a guy who's in the country legally, no police record, nothing like that. He's kind of soft-spoken, but he gets pretty worked up when he tells his story. He keeps saying, "I still can't believe what I just went though."

Mian came to the United States in '97 to go to Drake. He graduated with a bachelor's degree in business administration. Then he started working on his master's, and he got a job with AmerUs. Roger Brooks — the CEO — describes him as "someone with critical skills."

So Mian settled in here and things were going along fine. Even after 9/11. Mian — a Muslim — says he never experienced hostility.

"Nothing like that. Not at Drake, certainly not at work. People were curious about Islam, but that was it."

Then in December he left the United States for the first time since 9/11.

"I got to Lahore and I went to the U.S. Embassy for my return visa on Dec. 31, and they told me they had to do a background check. I understand that. I figured that would take a few weeks. So I waited. When I didn't hear back, I started calling. They wouldn't tell me what was going on or even discuss it. They make you feel like you're guilty until proven innocent. But they won't even tell you what you did wrong."

What he found out later was that under new security rules, the paperwork goes from the Embassy to the State Department and then to Homeland Security. Then Homeland Security has to bring in the FBI and a number of other agencies to investigate. Then the process goes in reverse. And because it's so complex, it's all backed up.

For the first few months Mian would get up in the morning, call the Embassy, and spend the day on hold, being shuffled from one desk to another, but never finding out what was going on. Sometimes no one would even ask his name or what he wanted. People would just tell him they couldn't help him.

So he waited. He had tests coming up at Drake, so he'd try to study, but he couldn't concentrate. He had all kinds of commitments in Des Moines. He had to stay in touch with his office, pay his rent, take care of his car insurance, his utilities. He ran up hundreds of dollars in long-distance phone bills.

He met other folks in the same situation, workers losing their jobs in the United States, students who couldn't get their degrees.

"I was very depressed not knowing where I'd end up. You feel angry, frustrated. Maybe I was naive, but I didn't get it. I was never in trouble, I worked and paid my taxes and I didn't pose a security risk. Why do this to me?"

At one point he called his supervisor at AmerUs, who spoke to Roger Brooks. Then Brooks ran into Sen. Tom Harkin at the WineFest, told him what was going on, and Harkin got his staff involved. They got the attention of the State Department. Mian got his visa. He figures he'd still be sitting in Lahore if he didn't have these connections.

And it was Harkin's folks, not the Embassy, who let Mian know he'd gotten the OK to come home.

"When I called the Embassy, they still didn't know. But since a senator told me, they figured it must be true."

Now he's back and he's feeling a little wiser, a lot more worldly.

Under jokes at DMACC is sadness
March 14, 2003

I get to the DMACC campus Thursday morning, and the first thing I see is a guy outside the student union building wearing a Woodstock T-shirt. The guy — Brad Beverley — sees the way I'm looking at him and says it's just a coincidence.

I go inside and there's another strange coincidence. Some private investigators are in the school theater attending a seminar on drugs. Larry Rogers, a Des Moines cop, is up there running the show, talking about heroin, crack, meth and — finally — marijuana. But you wouldn't know anything is going on from the way Rogers and the others handle this. I check and am told this seminar has been in the works for months.

I keep walking, and I start hearing the jokes. I hear how people are trying to cope with a situation that could lead to jail time for someone who's been a player in their lives for almost two years.

I run into a friend of mine, a teacher. We talk, and a friend of his comes by and says, "Hi." And my pal wants to know, "Is that 'hi' or 'high'?"

I keep walking, and a student stops me and wants to know if I'm "here to write about President Pothead." The woman he's with makes like she's smoking a joint. They both giggle.

People are joking about "Reefer Madness," rolling papers, bongs. One student is wondering "if he thought he was living in Holland in the '60s or something."

The jokes are cropping up on campus and off, things like this:

* How could you tell something was up at DMACC? The president was calling board members "dude."

* The new botany building was named Mary Jane Hall.

* Brownies have been disappearing from the culinary classes.

* The school's name was changed to Decriminalize Marijuana At Community Colleges.

Some of it is pretty silly, but that's how folks are dealing with the news, less than 24 hours after school President David England was busted on charges of possession with intent to deliver and conspiracy to manufacture marijuana. There's a lot of nervous laughter and a reluctance to have their names attached to this story right now. Not when you're talking about a guy facing felony charges.

But dig a little deeper. Get folks to talk about how they really feel, and just about every one of them mentions shock and sadness. They talk about the grieving process and how tough it was to watch the news and read the paper.

And then those same folks talk about a guy with good ideas and the energy to make things happen. In the wake of the bust, a lot of what they're saying sounds funny. But they are serious when they say he's raised the profile of the school and made the staff feel good about working there. They talk about his willingness to do things in an unorthodox way and his open-minded approach to running the school. They call him ambitious and a guy not afraid to confront the Legislature to get as much as he can for the college.

This is a guy who was running a $120 million operation, with six campuses and about 20,000 students. And another 40,000 in the continuing ed program. This is a guy with a lot to lose.

One woman who worked with England compares him to Bill Clinton.

"He was extremely good at what he does, very likeable and — if what we're hearing is true — very self-destructive. No self-discipline."

She and others say he was very hard to get to close to.

But there is someone who did know him well. I find her at her desk, just outside England's office. Trudy Little was England's secretary from the day he took over as president in October 2001. They were close, they spoke every day, and she can't say enough good things about him. But after a lot of denial, Little's ready to accept what happened.

Late Wednesday afternoon she got a phone call from a board member who heard about it on the news. He told Little, and she didn't believe it. Then there was another call, and a third and fourth.

"After about an hour I couldn't take it anymore," she says. "I'll miss him. He was a good guy."

I don't think it's any coincidence that Little and just about everybody else speaks of England in the past tense.

At least one cynic remains amid those cheering the capture

December 15, 2003

The phone rang about 5:30 Sunday morning. It was my friend Kim calling to let us know they'd caught Saddam Hussein. She sounded pumped, excited. Finally some good news out of Iraq.

I wasn't convinced. I hung up, turned on the TV, and the cynicism kicked in.

Are they toying with us again, lying like they did about the weapons of mass destruction and the Iraq-9/11 connection?

Can we believe them when they say it's Saddam Hussein, or did they dress up one of his look-alikes?

Did they really catch him now or were they holding him until Sunday morning so the Bush team could do the talk-show circuit?

Is this just one big stunt to raise Bush's poll numbers?

It's gotten to that point with me. I've been burned a few times and now I just don't believe these guys. It's not a particularly good feeling, but I know I'm not alone. I've talked to a lot of people who feel the same way.

Back in the summer, a friend admitted that she was actually taking comfort from the terrible news coming out of Iraq and Afghanistan. She'd hear about explosions, ambushes, the killing of U.N. officials, pro-American Iraqis, innocent children, and she was saddened by the deaths. But ultimately she thought it was a good thing. She'd thought that enough bloodshed and disaster would create a movement in this country, a demand to get our people home and save some lives. Maybe enough death would wake folks up to the fact that we have no business running around the globe killing people.

She felt terrible. As an American — someone who genuinely loves this country — she was horrified at her own reaction, embarrassed.

And she's not alone, but it's not the kind of thing people feel comfortable discussing.

So how do you get at the truth on something like this?

There's no problem finding folks who will tell you this is a wonderful thing. Folks like Doug Reichardt, who was having his Sunday-morning coffee at Zanzibar's and going on about how "this is a great day for America. We have caught a brutal dictator who raped and pillaged the men and women of his country."

That reaction is standard. You could find that anywhere.

But we've got something unique around here. A perspective you can't find in other states. Not yet.

I went by the various presidential campaign offices to talk with the workers, the people who have a vested interest in this kind of development. I made the rounds.

The Edwards office was locked and dark. So was the Kucinich office. Kerry's place was open and busy, but nobody wanted to talk. They couldn't. They might say something that would reflect poorly on their guy. Any statements would have to come from the press secretary.

I didn't want the party line. I wanted gut feelings, an honest response about what this means on the political front.

I went down the street to the Dean office and got pretty much the same thing. Nobody wanted to even talk on background, off the record. No schmoozing. Not even a wink and a nod. This is too delicate a subject at a time like this. But they did have a prepared statement from their guy.

I said thanks and headed out to West Des Moines to the Gephardt office.

His press guy, Bill Burton, sounded a lot like Doug Reichardt.

Said Burton: "This is a great thing. It makes the world a safer place and it makes the U.S. stronger."

But this helps the president. Doesn't this hurt your candidate?

"Not at all. The capture of Saddam is not enough to paper over the president's miserable record on the economy."

That's about as cynical as it got Sunday — a day when folks were trying to convince themselves that the capture of Saddam Hussein will be a defining moment.

I'm still not there.

It's a wonderful life
December 19, 2003

After Saddam Hussein was captured Sunday, I wrote a piece for the paper saying that I was skeptical of the Bush administration. I felt we'd been misled too many times to take them at their word. It was depressing stuff.

So I came in Monday ready to write about something joyous — the holiday season. I started to describe the smiling faces of the children as they sat on Santa's lap. I wrote about three words and the little bell on my computer went off, letting me know I had an e-mail. Figures. You criticize a popular president during a war and you hear from people.

I open it:

You owe the State of Iowa, the Military and the US Government an apology.

Interesting. I go back to writing. I want to capture the beauty of the falling snow, the warmth of the fireplace. The e-mail bell goes off. Three new messages:

You are disgusting . . . You are an idiot not a cynic . . . PARASITE!

Try to stay focused. Think about those family traditions, like reading "The Night Before Christmas" to the children on Christmas Eve. Three more e-mails.

Doesn't liberals always support those types of citizens? Low-income, underprivileged, homosexuals, homeless, welfare losers, drug addicts, etc, etc . . . You are mentally ill. . . . Can't you stick to society gossip and leave the lefty angst to your wife and the editorial page?

Then three more:

Every time a Democrat gets in office he screws up the economy so bad but makes it look so good that when a Republican gets in office he has to fix the past four years before it finally starts to look up again. . . . I can see why you write editorials up in Des Moines. You're probably for abortion too aren't you . . . The Republicans work harder and longer and have more heart than any sleazy Democrat could ever attempt to do. Now, go crawl back into your hole.

At that point I realized my column had been posted on some national Web site and the mail was coming from around the country. A bunch from Texas. Go figure. One more:

You are a prime example of why the Lord has seen fit to have some mothers eat their children.

That's the cool part about this job. You learn things. Then four more e-mails:

You're a disgusting pig. . . . Your column reminds me of an overly indulged child who whines at his sister's birthday party because the presents aren't for him. . . . You are a nut. . . . If you were to be blown up, disemboweled and defecated upon, the world would be a much better place.

I've gone global — hate mail is coming from Tokyo, from Canada.

Back to work. I want to describe the joy of going out in the woods, romping in the snow, looking for the perfect Christmas tree. Three more e-mails:

At age 66, I long-ago learned to tell chicken salad from chicken you know what. . . . May I suggest suicide . . . As a member of Porn Emails you will get access to special sites which have loads of videos, pictures, stories, and much much more!

I close those down, two more pop up:

My personal response to you sir, being a New Yorker who saw the 2 planes hit the twin towers no more than 15 blocks away from me on 9/11, is to HELL with you and all zombies of your stripe!!!!!!!!!!!!! . . . What have you ever done to defend this country other than sit behind a typewriter while real men protected you.

Typewriter? Real men? I'm thinking that guy must be a vet from an earlier time. Maybe the Spanish-American war. Three more:

I have no use for you, you're pond scum. . . . Its a shame you weren't in the WTC on 9/11 . . . You' re anti-American scum.

A lot of scum talk. Wondering if maybe Rush is talking about Bill and Hillary again. Another e-mail.

Are you in competition with Rekha for the most obnoxious columnist?

It's good to hear from an Iowan again. And one more:

Fag lover. Let's hope that Mr. Bush continues to back a ban on same-sex marriage.

Finally, someone who's ready to get over it and move on. Someone with enough vision to see the big picture.

Snowstorm can't dampen
Iowa's moment in the sun

January 5, 2004

This is what Iowans wait for, the caucuses. All that national — even international — attention. You run into Tom Brokaw out at Jimmy's, and Tim Russert is doing lunch at Centro. You see Larry King at a back table in 801 and there's a film crew from Tokyo setting up at the Kerry office on Locust.

It's Iowa's moment in the sun.

But it's snowing. Hard. It's cold, the wind is blowing.

So on a Sunday morning — the perfect time to tuck in with a hot cup of coffee and read the paper — I'm driving.

Going about 20 miles an hour on I-80, trying desperately to keep my car on the road. On my left there's a jackknifed truck. Up ahead there's an SUV that did a 180 after hitting the guardrail.

I keep going. I have to. There's work to be done. It's the day of the big debate. Seven Democrats each making the case for why he or she should be the candidate of choice in the caucuses.

So I'm risking my life to hear Dennis Kucinich explain — in great detail — his position on NAFTA.

And hear Carol Moseley Braun wax poetic on the question of why protectionist positions hurt Iowa farmers.

If I live, if I get there in one piece, I'll be able to hear Howard Dean explain what he really meant when he said he'd cut Osama some slack.

And I'll get to hear each one of the seven say: "I'm the only candidate on this stage who" did or didn't do something or other.

And then I'll get to hear each of the other candidates jump in and explain why that's not the case.

There's a pickup on the median with a smashed front behind a little sedan with a smashed rear.

I keep driving, and at one point I skid and hit the curb pretty hard. I think about turning around and heading home, but I can't imagine not being there when Edwards and Kerry go at it over the question of U.S. trade policy.

I'm getting close. I'm off the highway now, and the streets are lined with Edwards and Dean signs. Even closer, there are people waving Kerry and Kucinich signs. With this kind of weather, I was expecting to have the whole place to myself, but there's not even a decent parking spot.

I pull up on a snowbank, lock the car and head for the door.

Security is tight. The guy in line in front of me — Tom Vilsack — is showing his ticket and his driver's license to the guard. The guard checks the mug and lets him in. I'm up next. I go through the same routine, but I get a smile from the guy.

I get inside, look around and the place is packed. Shoulder to shoulder.

Don't these people have lives? I'm wondering what kind of political fanatics come out on a day like this.

I walk through the door and there's Sally Pederson and Leonard Boswell. They're with Tom Miller and Gordon Fischer, Matt McCoy and Pam Bookey. Makes sense. Die-hard Democrats.

But there's more to it. There's a Republican piece to all this. Bob and Billie Ray are there, and so are Steve Roberts and Bud Hockenberg. Joy Corning shows up.

Look around, and there's all kinds of folks who maybe don't have a stake in this. They're here for other reasons, big-picture stuff.

You see all that, and you're reminded that it's not just about party politics. It's about Iowa, about showing the flag, getting out there and letting everybody know this is important. It's about this state's identity and what helps to make this place unique.

Without the caucuses, you're not going to get that Des Moines dateline on the front page of the New York Times. And Brokaw won't do the nightly news live from Iowa.

Probably most important, you won't have folks here and other places talking about how Iowans are plugged into the political process like nobody else. How Iowans do their homework and take pride in being able to discuss — in detail — Kucinich's take on NAFTA.

So once I remember all that, it makes sense that folks would risk their lives to hear Gephardt get in Dean's face about Medicare.

In media Mecca, GOP offers up exclusive
January 20, 2004

It was caucus night and Iowa was hosting close to 1,000 journalists from 27 states and 13 countries. So it was going to be tough to find my own story, something unique, something nobody else had. I thought about spending time with Dennis Kucinich or trying to find out what Al Sharpton was up to.

In the end, I decided to go see what the Republicans had going on. They already have their candidate, so what do these folks do on caucus night?

They were gathering at Valley High School and I figured I'd have the story to myself. That was good, but the downside is that Republicans tend to be a serious bunch, not much on irony.

I walk into the lobby of Valley, the place is packed, shoulder to shoulder, with about 700 people. I wasn't the only journalist. I ran into Gwang Chul Go from the Korean Economic Daily.

I looked around and the walls were covered with Bush-Cheney posters. There on the wall — hanging over all the Republicans — is this huge banner that says, "VIOLENCE IS NEVER THE ANSWER."

A joke?

No. This is a high school and that was a message for the kids. So I found some of the irony I was hoping for.

I worked my way through the crowd and had to listen to about a dozen cracks about latte-drinking, sushi-eating liberals.

Then I ran into John Strong, an activist on veterans' affairs. I've seen him around town at various rallies dressed as Uncle Sam and carrying Saddam Hussein's head on a plate.

This night he was in jeans and a sweater, and he was handing out fliers that said: "Hollywood and Jane Fonda Liberals have taken over the leadership of the Democratic Party."

John means well. He's angry because he feels veterans — particularly guys his age — are getting a raw deal from the system, losing their benefits when they need them the most.

We got to talking politics and we got around to the Iraq war. He's not a big war supporter, but he says it's necessary. He doesn't blame

Bush. Like I said, he's a Republican.

He blames Clinton.

"If it wasn't for him, we'd have caught Saddam during the first Gulf War."

But Clinton was governor of Arkansas at the time.

"Yes, and he was leading the whole liberal movement to get us out of there as quickly as possible."

I wanted to hear more, but it was showtime. The GOP caucus was about to start. I found a seat in the auditorium and got ready to hear the guest speaker — Mary Matalin. The guy next to me was wearing a cowboy hat and kept mumbling "Jesus, Lord Jesus" over and over.

Some speakers got up and did some more liberal-bashing in the guise of welcoming the crowd. Then Matalin took the stage.

It was interesting. She kept calling the Democratic candidates the "benign nine" — even after the crowd stopped laughing. She said "the Democrats don't understand what freedom means" and she called them "sad and shallow."

Then she called them "puny, petty and partisan." That was good.

When she was done, one of her handlers came over and asked if I'd like a little one-on-one time with Matalin. I said sure and — after asking the usual boring nonsense about the upcoming campaign — I asked the question that was on everybody's mind.

What the hell are you doing married to James Carville?

Apparently, she's been asked that question once or twice. "He's passionate about what he believes in and he's hot, hot, hot. Very hot."

Then she left and — since Gwang Chul Go was not around — I'd gotten my exclusive.

Chasing our 'most crucial issue'

March 3, 2004

I'm thumbing through the New York Times, and I come across an ad that talked about the "most crucial issue for our nation." I read that, and a whole bunch of ugly possibilities flash through my head — each more frightening than the next.

The war in Iraq? Terrorism? The deficit? Massive job loss? The health-care crisis? John Ashcroft?

I keep reading, and it turns out that gay marriage is the big threat, the place we better focus our attention, or we'll be looking at the end of life as we know it.

I knew this whole business of marriage was in trouble — a 50 percent divorce rate was a dead giveaway. But I didn't realize that same-sex unions would kill it altogether. Then I saw the ad in the Times. It was a gushy, full-page thank-you note to the president for his commitment to marriage and family. It laid out the dangers of a court system that ignores the Constitution and threatens "our representative form of government."

It was signed by 85 people — 80 men, five women. Not sure what that means, but it was interesting.

It was a rundown of the usual folks who spend their lives — and earn their money — trying to make sure the rest of us believe exactly what they believe.

You know the self-righteous crowd: Jerry "Moral Majority" Falwell, Gary "American Values" Bauer, James "Focus on the Family" Dobson, Bay "American Cause" Buchanan, Franklin "Billy's Boy" Graham.

Mixed in were a sprinkling of Southern Baptists, Midwestern Baptists, and folks from groups called Family Research, Family Council, Family First, Christian Coalition, Traditional Values.

And in the middle of the pack there was Chuck Hurley of the Iowa Family Policy Center.

Perfect. I know Hurley. He's smart, thoughtful and very accessible. I could track him down and find out why I should be scared. I could ask him why I should feel threatened by same-sex marriage. Ask him why he feels threatened.

Hurley is a former state rep who now spends a lot of time up at the

Statehouse lobbying, making sure lawmakers don't stray too far from where the Lord wants them to be. He wants to make sure we have solid — boy-girl — marriages, and don't even think about getting divorced.

He organizes "Marriage Matters" rallies and pushes the state to come up with millions of dollars to promote marriage and two-parent families.

I'm impressed. I can barely find time to get the oil changed in my car, and this guy is going around worrying about everybody else's marriage.

He was at the Capitol when I caught up with him. So here's the first question: If you're so pro-marriage, why not encourage more folks to sign on?

"That's an excellent question."

Thoughtful silence.

"Personally, I have several friends who are homosexual. I love homosexuals as much as I love heterosexuals. God loves us all, and all of us sin."

From there he glided off into the fact that he has 10 kids — some of them adopted. He talked about how, as an attorney, he tends to be very pragmatic and how he's studied the evidence on all this.

"Lengthy analysis has shown that children tend to do best with a loving mother and loving father."

Then, with a little smile, he mentioned anatomy and said: "God designed marriage. It's not an invention of man."

I got that part, but I still didn't get the threat. I kept pressing and Hurley — nice guy that he is — kept assuring me I was asking the right questions. And he kept talking about God and love, Jesus, sin. He talked about growing up on a Kansas farm, his wild days in college and how much he loves his wife and kids.

I gave it one last try. If you're so pro-marriage, why not encourage more folks to link up in loving relationships?

"Every loving, caring relationship is not a marriage. There are brothers and sisters, parents and children."

Again, thoughtful silence followed by a warm smile. He was trying to explain this in a way that even I could understand.

"I love my dog, Skipper, and he loves me. But that isn't enough to call something marriage."

Now I see what I'm dealing with.

World can't get enough of 'Governator'
March 31, 2004

I've never laid out money to see an Arnold Schwarzenegger film, but I've always found the guy interesting — the hulk-like size and shape, the thick accent, the attitude, the Kennedy connection.

I've found it curious the way he's been able to go from the unbridled violence of "Conan the Barbarian" or "Last Action Hero" to warm and fuzzy kid flicks like "Jingle All the Way" and "Kindergarten Cop."

And I've found it curious how he was able to get himself elected governor of California.

Early on I dismissed the candidacy as a joke. I lumped him in with Gary Coleman, Arianna Huffington, and the various porn kings and queens.

It made sense that he announced his political plans on the Leno show — even though MTV would have seemed more appropriate. I wasn't surprised when he refused to debate unless he could see the questions in advance.

But I was surprised when he got elected. I couldn't get my mind around this.

Then last week I spent some time in and around Southern California. I was reminded how star power can overrule common sense. How movies and real life get all mixed together.

It hits you the minute you get there.

Driving in on the Santa Monica Freeway you see billboards — with huge Arnold mugs — announcing "Terminator 3" is now available on DVD. You see the same posters in video stores all over the place.

Walk down Hollywood Boulevard and you see the Arnold star. Go into the Wax Museum and there are four Arnold statues — from his early movies through his latest role as the state's chief executive.

Take the Universal Studios tour and there's a whole exhibit devoted to Arnold. He's up on-screen using a pistol-type shotgun to blow away some robot-like bad guys.

Walk along Venice Beach and you can buy "Governator" T-shirts. In the coffee shops and sushi bars you hear folks doing the "I'll be back" shtick with an Arnold accent. "Hasta La Vista, Baby" is also big.

And it's not just the locals. Or just the Americans. There was a Page One story in the L.A. Times last week about how ambassadors and other diplomats from Hong Kong and Israel, Italy, Pakistan, Ireland and dozens of other countries are making their way to Sacramento for a photo op with the governor. Interview requests are coming in from Dubai and Australia, Peru and Bulgaria.

Now it's getting beyond the celebrity phase. The article talked about how the Iraq invasion has damaged U.S.-European relations and it quoted the pride-filled Austrian consul general saying it helps to have someone in power who knows what Europe is all about.

And it quotes a retired Japanese schoolteacher saying: "Japanese people did not know where Sacramento is. Now it's the center of the United States."

So Arnold is all over the place, and it's not all good. The news was also filled with stuff about a lawsuit involving a woman who says Schwarzenegger groped her. A judge ruled that the governor will have to answer written questions from the woman's attorney.

In Washington, that's the type of thing that could ruin a political career.

But this is Hollywood, it's California, a place Michael and Janet Jackson, Robert Blake, Scott Peterson and O.J. Simpson have all called home.

It's a place where stories about a $15 billion hole in the state budget get a unique spin. They become stories about how the governor is going to get out around the world and sell his state. About how carefully the marketing strategy has to be handled, and about how he has to decide just where he'll go.

As the governor's press secretary explains it: "Think of it in terms of co-branding: Schwarzenegger and California. You're going to dilute the brand by accepting every offer. Then it's not special."

I read that and I began to wonder if this guy could really pull it off. If he could use his celebrity to turn this state around. It's too soon to tell, but as I was leaving the coast and heading east, I decided to keep an eye on this.

I kept thinking, "I'll be back."

'Great Communicator' had at least one good lesson

June 7, 2004

Now's the time to trot out the cliches, use all kinds of fancy language to dance around reality and hide what's really on your mind.

It's time to go on about how: "Even though I didn't agree with Ronald Reagan politically, he was a great American, a man of conviction and commitment. I respected that he was a man of faith and a man with strong vision. He will be missed."

The tough part is being honest.

Personally, I feel he ushered in an era that continues to divide this country and alienate a lot of people.

But, now's not the time to diss the man. And, more important, I owe the guy.

I spent about 15 minutes with him once, and I learned something that's stayed with me for almost 30 years. Something that helped me personally and professionally.

It was in the late 1970s, I'd been in the news business about two years and I was struggling to get a handle on how this works.

You're a reporter, a paid observer who goes to a news event and writes about it in an unbiased manner.

But how do you go to an abortion protest and write an objective piece about the head of Operation Rescue when he's getting in the face of young girls and calling them baby killers?

How do you go cover the trial of some guy who murdered an old woman and threw her body out with the garbage?

And how do you go cover a speech by a politician who is so far to the right that he's come to symbolize everything you don't believe?

I was about to find out.

Reagan was between jobs. He'd just lost a bid for the White House, and he apparently had time on his hands. So he agreed to come to upstate New York and be the guest speaker at the annual dinner of the Ulster County Republican Party.

It was a major coup to get somebody of his stature. The GOP up there usually had to settle for the assistant secretary of state or some guy who carried bags for Dwight Eisenhower. But Reagan was out laying the groundwork for 1980 and agreed to come.

I got there early, wandered around the dinner hall and the hotel, walked through a few doors and found myself face to face with Ronald Reagan. The sheriff and one or two deputies were in the room with him, they knew I was a reporter for the local paper and started to usher me out.

Reagan said it was OK if I stayed.

Perfect. I was young and arrogant enough to think this was a chance to get in the guy's face and help change his mind on everything from the death penalty to school prayer.

But he took control of the interview. He started out by asking where I was from, what did my father do for a living, were my parents still alive?

When I mentioned the Bronx, he talked about the Yankees. He knew Joe DiMaggio. That got my attention. I wanted details about the Yankee Clipper. It was a lot more important than convincing Reagan we ought to lift the embargo on Cuba.

So we just schmoozed, had a few laughs and then it was time for him to go.

I thanked him for his time, and he thanked me for mine.

I don't remember what he spoke about that night.

What I do remember is coming away from there thinking that it was interesting how he was able to neutralize my political feelings. What stayed with me was the idea that I could sit across from someone I disagreed with — totally disagreed with — and find some common ground. And actually have a good time.

It's something I carried with me over the years. It helped me keep my cynicism in check when I was getting ready to sit across the table from folks like George W. Bush and Dan Quayle.

So I owe that to Ronald Reagan.

And while I still think his politics and policies were a disaster, I have no trouble understanding why people who knew him can't say enough good things about the guy.

Looking for new voters is an eye-opening process

September 22, 2004

It sounds easy enough. You grab your clipboard and pen, go out to the dollar store or a trailer park, and you get folks to sign up to vote.

Nothing partisan. You're not pushing a particular candidate or shoving your agenda down somebody's throat. You just want them to register.

But hang out with Derrick Wilson and Sarah Wang, and you get some idea of what's involved. You see why this is not easy.

The two of them were working out in front of the motor vehicle office Tuesday morning in Des Moines.

Wilson is 24, black, and goes to DMACC. Wang is 19, Chinese, and goes back to the University of Chicago next week.

A lot of folks around here see these two and assume they're a couple of liberals. Folks hear Wang or Wilson use the word "vote" and just wave them off, saying "I'm Republican." That was particularly true when they were working the crowds at the State Fair last month.

But waving is the least of it.

They both have stories about how folks can be rude and crude, even racist.

Wang has been given the finger and pushed.

Wilson talks about approaching a woman at a supermarket who yelled the f-word and threatened to call the cops if he didn't back off.

He was telling that story Tuesday morning, and a guy named Jack Rethmeier came by.

Wang asked if he was signed up to vote. Rethmeier, a 52-year-old cash register repairman, got all worked up and started lecturing her on how "this is the beginning of the end for the United States. Soon there will be foreign symbols on American money."

How does he know that? Rethmeier fell to his knees.

"God told me. He whispered to me. There was a voice in my head. He warned me about 9/11 and told me Bush would take us into war."

Wang was polite, listened, waited until he was done. Then she asked again if he was registered.

Rethmeier got back on his feet, assured her he was, and kept walking. He had to get his license renewed.

Wilson shook his head and said: "This job is an excellent learning experience. It really builds your self-confidence and gives you a real sense of purpose."

Wang was less philosophical: "What I can't believe is that there are people who don't even know who the candidates are or what party they belong to."

The two of them are part of a team that's been at this since May. A Des Moines union activist named John Campbell is running this voter registration drive on behalf of the Iowa Citizen Action Network, which is part of a national movement called USAction.

The plan is to sign up 10,000 new voters — Republicans, Democrats, independents — around Des Moines, Waterloo and Davenport. They're now close to 8,000.

Folks like Wang and Wilson are working about 30 hours a week, averaging anywhere between 10 and 20 new voters a day. Because they're looking for people who aren't already registered, they tend to focus on minorities, young folks, low-income types.

So they come up against people who'd love to vote but can't — felons, illegal immigrants.

They also come up against guys like William Lowe, 44, who is voting for the first time in his life. He's a Bush backer.

"The president is a Christian, and he will fight to keep God in schools. Besides, John Kerry threw away his medals. That's a disgrace."

Then there are Bush bashers like Mike Beener, a 43-year-old construction worker who's voted before but can't remember when.

Beener said his sister used to work at the Pentagon, and she knew George W. Bush before he was president.

"She told me that if that guy got elected, he'd start a war. Everybody knew he was looking for a fight."

That's pretty much the same story Rethmeier got, but he had better sources.

And as far as Wilson and Wang are concerned — Bush, Kerry, God — it doesn't matter.

They just want to make sure you sign up and vote.

Legislators are back — and so are the freebies

January 26, 2005

I find January pretty depressing. The holidays are over, the lights and the upbeat music are gone. It's dark, cold, slippery.

But there is some fun stuff. There's the Iowa Legislature.

They've been back in town for two weeks, and I wanted to see what's new up at the Capitol. So I went up there Tuesday, walked through the security gates, and that put me in the cafeteria.

I immediately noticed a change. They have all these new high-energy drinks — like Red Bull and stuff that comes in a variety of flavors, including cactus and Siberian cherry.

So I'm figuring at least this will be a high-energy crowd.

I keep walking, and the first things I see are lobbyists.

There's Ned Chiodo getting his shoes shined and looking half asleep. Then there's Steve Roberts looking half awake. Roberts was on the food line waiting for a server to dish up the entree du jour — a pile of red-and-yellow mush that was billed as spaghetti and meatballs.

Next to Roberts was a guy named Rick Orta, and he was wearing a Marine Corps do-rag and yellow cowboy boots made out of python skin. He's a lobbyist for the downtrodden and couldn't understand how "these Republicans call themselves compassionate conservatives" while children in this state are hurting, starving and being abused.

I started to get into the whole red state-blue state deal — complete with gay marriage and abortion — but I got distracted by another lobbyist.

Mark Maxwell came by, decked out in jeans and a leather vest with an American flag and a bald eagle on the back. He was wearing 11 pins and ribbons, and he had three gold rings on his fingers.

Maxwell is the guy in charge of protecting bikers in this state. They don't want to wear helmets, and they shouldn't have to. Nothing left to be said.

I noticed Maxwell's approach to lobbying was more in-your-face, very different from guys like Chiodo and Roberts. He's not a schmooze-over-a-coffee type.

Besides, he's busy. He has a life. He owns a collision shop on Easton Boulevard.

So he's a lobbyist who resists motorcycle safety rules and also owns a collision shop.

It was time to head upstairs and see the show.

When I got to the next level — the rotunda — the place was packed, and it looked like some sort of high-end farmers market.

This was the fourth-annual Iowa Insurance Day on the Hill. There were 36 companies that wanted to remind the legislators that insurance provides 40,000 decent-paying jobs that don't pollute and rarely cause injuries.

These folks had stands set up, and they were giving out little gifts and goodies to the men and women of the Iowa Legislature.

The lawmakers walked from table to table, snacking on Tootsie Rolls and Butterfingers.

But all politicians don't come cheap.

ING and a few other companies were doling out mint, chocolate and coconut truffles. There was peanut toffee. And they were giving out free lunch.

So how can these public figures accept gifts and lunch from these companies?

It was explained that they can accept it as long as the event is open to the public. Which this — technically — was.

I still wasn't convinced that this was a good idea.

I watched Dolores Mertz, a House Democrat from Ottosen, as she made her way from table to table. She was carrying a shopping bag and filling it with pens, coffee cups, drink holders, notepads.

I stopped her and asked how she could possibly take these things and not be influenced.

"It doesn't affect my decisions. No way, no how."

She was talking and at the same time eyeing the little battery-operated flashlight/key chains on the IMT table.

Mark Davitt, a House Democrat from Indianola, was standing next to her, eating his free lunch. Like Mertz, he insisted this was not a problem.

"Do you think I could be bought for a ham sandwich? Seriously?"

I don't know the guy, but I would guess it would take more than that.

So I let the guy finish his sandwich. Then he could get started on the chips, cookies, apples, soda and ice cream that came with the meal.

I felt bad. I'd forgotten how much pressure is on these politicians.

In a troubled world, his faith is restored

February 16, 2005

So I'm channel surfing the other night, and I come across two guys arguing about what God was thinking when He unleashed the tsunami.

One of them saw it as a wake-up call to the world — time to fall to our knees, beg and get our act together.

The other had some long tortured theory about how it wasn't really God, but some clerk who handles bad things.

Then they got into the genocide in Sudan, the rising death toll in Iraq and the rest of the Middle East, North Korea and about a dozen other disasters.

Listening to that, I got to wondering myself: Not only what is He thinking, but is there a God?

Since I try to stay in touch with Him on a regular basis, I felt uncomfortable going there.

But looking around lately, it's been on my mind.

Then Sunday I was in Borders and saw a book by Essie Mae Washington-Williams, the illegitimate and biracial daughter of the late Strom Thurmond, a guy who ran for president in 1948 as a Dixiecrat, a racist who established the segregationist Southern Manifesto.

I'm thumbing through the book and thinking about the irony and the outrage. I was thinking it's too bad Thurmond wasn't forced to own up while he was alive.

I was also thinking it's great that this guy — dead or alive — was finally outed.

That got me thinking that maybe there is a God.

But I wasn't there yet.

Then Monday night on CNN I saw an interview with Maya Marcel-Keyes, the daughter of Alan Keyes, one of the more conservative political types on the American landscape. He's a former U.S. ambassador who has run for president twice, for the U.S. Senate three times, and he's a relentless gay-basher — calling them sinners every chance he gets.

He caused a buzz last year when he got into this whole deal about homosexuality being "selfish hedonism" and applying that description to Mary Cheney, Dick Cheney's lesbian daughter.

Another line Keyes uses regularly is: "I do not say that homosexual relations are an abomination — the Bible says so."

And Monday night there was Keyes' 19-year-old daughter speaking at a gay rights rally in Annapolis, Md., coming out, talking about the need to support gay and lesbian kids who have been abandoned by their families.

She talked about a friend who got sick after his family threw him out of the house. He died recently.

She said she was speaking out because of her bad relationship with her parents: "Things just came to a head. Liberal queer plus conservative Republican just doesn't mesh well."

Marcel-Keyes said her folks "were not too pleased" when they found out, but she still loves them.

I watched and listened, and I felt guilty because I was glad Keyes would have this shoved in his sanctimonious face.

This was great stuff. It was like Rush Limbaugh getting busted for drugs, Bill O'Reilly having to buy his way out of a phone-sex case, Bill Bennett's gambling problem going public.

So I was dying to hear what Keyes had to say about this.

But Keyes — a guy who usually won't shut up — was unavailable for comment.

He issued a statement saying: "My daughter is an adult, and she is responsible for her own actions. What she chooses to do has nothing to do with my work or political activities."

Such a restrained, thoughtful response from a guy known for his slashing, vitriolic, take-no-prisoners rhetoric.

I was pleased because — once again — there's no doubt in my mind that there is a God.

And he has a great sense of humor.

"So I'm talkin' to this guy . . ."

Chapter 3: People

By Geneva Overholser
Former Editor/*The Des Moines Register*

Some journalists write so the reading is easy. Some people know how to really see others. Very few have both these gifts. Rob Borsellino, bless him, is one of those precious few.

So good is Rob at empathy that he finds as strong a story in a disgruntled philanthropist or a fallen college president as he does in a 63-year-old who is learning to read or a "Jesus bus" driver. So good is he at journalism that he gets a quote like this, from a teenager coming back from drug addiction: "Back then I was always thinking about suicide. I was already dying slowly, so why not?"

Borsellino knows – and cares – an awful lot about people. I'm grateful to him for sharing these gifts with us.

These boys of summer having too much fun to quit

February 24, 1998

Dick Myers can't go from first to third on a single the way he did in his 20s and 30s. And he can't go to his right on a grounder up the middle the way he did in his 40s and 50s.

And he can't hit for average the way he did in his 60s. But he can still play the game. He can still turn the double play, and he can still stroke line drives to all fields.

In fact, last year Myers — second baseman for Des Moines Sanitary Systems — hit well over .500.

"But I was only in my 60s then. I'm 70 now. My average is probably down a few points."

Having said that, Myers walked to the plate with one out, took a strike and lashed a hard single to right. He took the turn at first, thought about it for a moment, and held up. Two outs later he was still there. Back on the bench he was wondering if he should have gone for second.

"I've been playing this game all my life. I go to Mesa in the winter, and I'm in a league down there. Every RV park has a league. These guys are good. Some were pro, semipro. You gotta be 55 to play."

Myers — with two gold medals in the Iowa Senior Games — had a quadruple bypass in 1986 and was told he had to slow down.

"So I sold my cows and quit farming — which means I quit borrowing money — and started going to Arizona."

Every Sunday night Myers makes the 120-mile round trip from his Wayne County home to play in the "50 Plus" men's slow-pitch softball league in West Des Moines. How long does he figure he can play? He's amused by the question.

"I'll play till I drop. What else?"

The Jordan Motors Tigers were down, 17-13, in the top of the seventh — their last at bat. They'd been trailing Mr. B's Clothing since the first inning. The Tigers — in their bright orange T-shirts with black shorts — have an average age of about 63.

Mr. B's — tastefully attired in white T-shirts, blue lettering and shorts in an assortment of muted colors — has the oldest player in the league, Bill Graney, 74. Graney — who played three years in the

Phillies organization in the '40s — is the exception on a team with an average age of 55.

But the Tigers refused to be intimidated by Mr. B's kiddie corps. If they were going to lose, it would be respectable.

Carroll Edwards, 65 and retired from the post office, led off the Tigers' seventh with a single. Dick Cummings, 67, retired from an oil company, walked. Chuck Lathum, 67, retired from Firestone, hit into a force out. A few more singles, two more outs and it was over.

The Tigers — with a roster that includes a former bank president, a teacher, a farmer, a car parts salesman and guys who are retired from DMACC and Maytag — lost by three runs and their record fell to 10 and 4.

When it was over, the two teams exchanged handshakes and good-natured insults. Wives, kids and grandkids cheered. Ken Clark, the Tiger manager, told the players they had a game next Sunday at 6:15. "Show up rested. We gotta win that one." Telling retirees to show up rested may seem redundant. But these guys didn't look like they were sitting around all week playing checkers and shuffleboard, waiting for Sunday to break loose.

Tom Laurenzo, Charley Ill and Chris Siberz have been playing softball together for 36 years. The trio — now in their early 50s — are the cornerstone of the Des Moines Sanitary Supply team. Ill and Siberz own the company that sponsors the team. Laurenzo — a partner in a West Des Moines ad agency — is the manager.

It's this team's first year in the over-50 league. Until now, Laurenzo said, they've been playing in a league with their kids.

"Age forced us into this. I love this game dearly. This is good because it's easygoing, but these guys are competitive. We all play to win."

At the plate, Bud Barron — Laurenzo's 50-year-old catcher — waved at a bad pitch, and Laurenzo let him know what he thought about that.

"Make him throw strikes."

Duly noted. Barron lashed the next pitch to right for a single. The bench erupted in cheers.

If there was a larger message in all this, it got lost in the excitement of some guys having fun on the ball field.

Long road to Hall of Fame
February 26, 1998

In the winter of '56, five kids from New Haven went into a Connecticut church basement and, in a couple of takes, laid down the tracks for one of the most enduring songs in rock history.

Within six months of recording "In the Still of the Night," the Five Satins were playing the Apollo with Little Richard, Chuck Berry and Bo Diddley. They toured the U.S. and Canada, singing their million-seller. By year's end they had one of the top two hits of 1956 — Elvis' "Don't Be Cruel" was fifth.

Two years later the group was pretty much out of business and Jim Freeman — he sang bass — was working construction and doing odd jobs. The glamour of being married to a rock singer wore off and his wife left, taking their three daughters back to Philadelphia.

In 1970 — following his brother, then a Drake law student — Freeman moved to Des Moines. Today he runs a pest control business out of his Norwalk home and tonight he's in New York City getting some long overdue recognition for his role in the evolution of pop music.

Freeman is being inducted into the Rhythm and Blues Hall of Fame, along with Gladys Knight and the Pips, Screamin' Jay Hawkins, the O'Jays and some others. Smokey Robinson will emcee. Bonnie Raitt is on the selection committee.

For guys like Freeman — black artists who laid the groundwork but never hope to get into the Rock 'n' Roll Hall of Fame — tonight's $500-a-ticket deal is top shelf.

"There's gonna be a limo to pick us up at the airport and take us to the hotel," Freeman was saying the other day, sitting in his Norwalk living room amid his memorabilia, a Satins tune playing in the background. "This is gonna be smooth."

The glory days were fast and furious. The group — unlike the polished acts they shared the stage with — was unprepared for the fame that visited them in rock's toddler years.

"We didn't have photos of ourselves, no routines, no uniforms. We were playing six shows a day at the Apollo and people would be in the audience all day watching. The other groups would change clothes and we'd be wearing the same stuff for six shows. And folks would be yelling 'When you gonna change them clothes?'

"They were not shy about letting you know what was up. That whole thing came and went real quick."

Since moving to Iowa, Freeman has been been a substance abuse counselor, heading up Black Hawk County's drug council, and even owned a nightclub — the Five Satins in Ankeny. He opened in May of '85 and closed three months and $15,000 later.

"The first week we opened some woman called and said she was upset that we was running a place called Satan's. I knew right then I wasn't gonna make any money."

It's been an interesting ride. Any regrets?

"No, because I never expected much. We never thought about making money, you know. The girls liked it and that was enough in those days. Everybody had a group back then. Every street corner, in the hallways they'd be singing. Black kids, white kids. But we got lucky. Real lucky."

Then he was quiet a few seconds, thinking.

"You know what I regret? That my mother didn't live long enough to see me get something out of this. She was a single parent, raised five kids in the projects . . . doing maid's work, cleaning people's clothes. She always came up with a few bucks for car fare to get me to the gigs or down to New York. She'd liked this."

Doing the State Fair — the Knapp way
August 18, 1998

At the end of our phone conversation about Court Avenue, Bill Knapp mentioned he'd be spending the week camping out at the State Fair and "if you're out this way, stop by." I had a hard time getting my mind around the image of Knapp and his mate, Susan Terry, hunkered down in their modest campsite, with Susan driving in the stakes to secure their little pup tent and Bill out scrounging around for dry wood to get dinner going.

When I finally got out there, the scene I found was a bit more Knapp-like — more in sync with a guy who has made hundreds of millions in real estate and development. Their 500-square-foot trailer — with a black BMW out front — was off by itself, out behind the cattle barn. Inside I found Bill sitting in one of two recliners, air conditioner going, several cell phones at his side. Susan was in the well-appointed kitchen/dining area, writing on a laptop. I was offered a glass of what looked like a nice French red — I declined. But I did take them up on their offer of sushi. I went with the tekka maki, with a slice of ginger and a dash of wasabi-laced soy sauce. If I'd known this was coming I wouldn't have spent the four and a quarter on that greasy, half-raw turkey leg.

As I drank some designer water, I looked across at Knapp and he said: "Now this is the way to do the fair."

He did have a point.

But this wasn't always the way Knapp did the fair. When he was growing up on a Wayne County farm, the State Fair was a rare treat for his family. Getting away from the farm for even a day was too much of an effort. So he'd only been there a few times as a child.

As an adult, his involvement was significant, but kind of detached — a few years ago he wrote out a check for $1 million to help revamp the Varied Industries Building.

Then he started hanging around with Susan Terry, a West Des Moines native who spent her childhood entering — and sometimes winning — food contests at the fair. She still does. Her potato salad won first prize and her German chocolate cake came in third this year.

So Knapp — to keep peace in the home, so to speak — moves his operation out to the fairgrounds for 11 days in August. He says he's spent more time at the fair in these last two years than he spent in all of his previous 70.

"For all practical purposes, I'm living here. It's a good experience. This is so typical Iowa. I like to go out real early, before folks get up, and see the kids sleeping alongside their animals. This is a time for them to learn how to win and learn how to lose. There's really a lot to be learned here, for everybody."

About a half-mile up the hill — and a world away from the Knapp camp — the Arvidsons of Poweshiek County were getting ready to throw a few burgers on the grill.

Home during the fair is a 9-by-12 tent, pitched next to their Ford pickup. The Arvidsons — like Knapp and Terry — were gracious people. Brent offered me a Bud, Marveen said she'd throw on a burger if I'd like to stay for lunch, and the kids — Ben, 10, and Andrea, 7 — were more than willing to share their potato chips.

I started to tell them about the sushi and the greasy turkey, but they were such nice folks I decided to spare them the details.

Like Knapp, Brent Arvidson said getting away from the farm and going to the fair was a luxury growing up and he came for the first time in the mid-'70s, when he was about 14 "and we camped in the back of Dad's pickup."

He stopped coming in 1986 "because it got away from farming and agriculture. But the wife wanted to come this year so I came and, to tell you the truth, I'm impressed with the farm machinery."

Brent, 38, works in a manufacturing plant, but the family still lives on the 120-acre farm where he grew up. The property is rented out "because you can't make a living off the land anymore, not when you're getting a buck eighty-seven for a bushel of corn and it's costing you a hundred bucks to plant an acre. Or you're getting 38 cents a pound for hogs. I don't even know what's going on with cattle anymore.

"The thing is, this is Iowa. If agriculture doesn't click, nothing clicks."

I thanked Brent for his time and as I left I asked if he planned to come back next year.

"I would, but I'd sure like to see them lower the price. That's six bucks just for me to get in and then three bucks to park. I'm a working man. You're talking about almost 10 bucks for openers."

But if the wife wants to come to the fair, Brent — like another guy I know — said he'll do what it takes to keep peace in the home, so to speak.

David Belin gave everything he had to everything he did

January 21, 1999

The room looked and felt like David Belin was expected back any moment. Newspapers were laid out on the desk. His briefcase — overstuffed, bulging — was on a chair next to the bookcase. And the bookcase was thick with everything from the three books Belin authored to his tattered copy of the Warren Commission report to cookbooks to the Manhattan phone book.

For the past four years it's been Tina Patten's job to make sure Belin's law office is in order, a job she describes as "horribly demanding." And now it's over. Tina's boss died Sunday, and she fears she'll never again find the kind of challenge she's enjoyed working for David Belin.

You work closely with a man like Belin and you become well versed in estate planning and Jewish culture, the Kennedy assassination and classical music, the CIA, education, justice, the media, art and tax law.

Going in, Tina Patten knew little about most of that — she was 3 when Kennedy was shot. Coming out she's a better person for the time she spent with David Belin.

"I wasn't just his secretary. I was his personal assistant, his driver. I handled his personal finances, paid the bills. I'd keep an eye on his house. He was working on his new book and he'd read me something and say, 'Do you agree with this?' He appreciated my opinion. I always felt good that I mattered.

"Now he's gone and I'm stunned. I don't know what you can do after this. Where do you go next?"

She sat in Belin's office at a stone and glass table that's more art than furniture. On the walls around Patten were the markers of Belin's life as an attorney, a musician, a family man, a public servant, a sage.

Along with the pictures of his late and current wives, his late mother and his five kids, was an autographed photo of Arturo Toscanini. Beside that were photos of Belin with Gerald Ford, Nelson Rockefeller and William F. Buckley. There are pictures of Belin on "Meet the Press" and "Face the Nation."

His degrees from Michigan — B.A., law and a master's in business — were next to the citations he got for working with the Warren

Commission in the '60s, the federal panel investigating the CIA in the '70s and Ronald Reagan's commission on arts and humanities in the '80s.

And getting equal weight in that lineup is the award he received for his contributions to education in Iowa.

It's been said he had the resume of 10 people, but the folks around him say his most important accomplishment was the way he raised his children after his wife died in 1980. The kids live in every corner of the country now — and one daughter studies at Oxford — but Belin made it a point to speak to each of the five just about every day.

"One thing he would never quibble about was the phone bill," said Patten, whose thoughts on Belin had her alternately smiling and teary-eyed. "And he had the luxury of being able to put everything he had into everything he did. There are so many lives that he touched in so many ways."

One of those lives belongs to Mike Reck, an Ottumwa native and Harvard law grad who was working in D.C. four years ago when he landed a job with the Belin firm. Reck remembers his first day at work, when Belin took him to lunch and explained the firm's history and culture.

"He's a sophisticated man and the culture around here is such that we work together, like a family. No one would think to raise their voice at a colleague. Not at a partner or a secretary or a clerk. That's David. The irony is that what's lost in all his accomplishments is that he was a better person than he was an attorney, and that's saying something."

Another life Belin touched belongs to Ruth Barkley, who knew him through Temple B'Nai Jeshurun. She would have to call around each fall and get people to do things for the high holy days. Some of the temple's heavy hitters wouldn't return her calls or they'd give her the runaround.

"Mr. Belin always called right back, always participated and always treated me with respect. He made me feel good about myself."

Barkley, 53, worked for years at Norwest. When her eyes went bad, she got a job at a south-side McDonald's where she hauls trash and busses tables. She couldn't get Wednesday off to go to Belin's funeral "but I will pray for him, I will say kaddish for him at home tonight."

I didn't really know David Belin, but I met him a few times. And I got the feeling he'd appreciate Ruth Barkley's simple prayer as much as he'd appreciate all the beautiful words used to describe him Wednesday by grieving relatives and friends.

Latest twist in the Johnny Gosch saga a strange, sad story

November 2, 1999

This latest twist in the Johnny Gosch story has the feel of an Elvis sighting. Given the history of this case, it's hard for me to believe Noreen Gosch saw her son two years ago and didn't tell anyone.

It felt like the case was out of the spotlight for a while and Noreen decided to jerk the chain and get it back in the news.

And that's what happened. I called and asked her to meet me for coffee. When I got to the coffee shop, I reached out to shake her hand and she said: "Are you here to chop me to bits like everybody else is doing?"

I told her I didn't believe her story. She smiled a strange, sad smile and shook her head.

And she let me have it.

"I don't expect you to understand. How could you? You don't know what it feels like to walk past your child's empty room every day and know that somebody took him. You don't stay up at night and wonder if you've done everything you possibly could to find him and help him.

"The only way you can understand is for you to give up your child for 16 years. I'm doing the best I can to cope. It's not enough for some people and that's too bad. My first responsibility is not to the press or to the police or anybody else. It's to my son. He'll know I did all I could to help him."

As she was talking I was wondering what it must feel like to not have closure on something like this. There's no grave, no urn of ashes on the mantel. And — as years go by — less hope that you'll ever hold your child again.

I pressed her for details. I wanted to know exactly what happened that night.

Here's what she said:

It was 2:30 in the morning on March 18, 1997, and she answered a knock at her West Des Moines apartment. Two men were there and she recognized her son, who was 27 at that time. They talked for about 90 minutes.

"He talked about what he had endured all those years. He didn't discuss every detail of the sex abuse. He would have been embarrassed and he didn't want to hurt me. Sons take the role of protector when it comes to their mothers."

She offered to call the police, but he wouldn't let her. He said his abductors are out there and he's in danger. He left at about 4 in the morning.

I still didn't buy it. If that was my kid — under those circumstances — I'd sell everything I own, borrow, steal, do what I had to to get some money and run with him to Europe or Asia or South America.

She shook her head.

"I don't have anything to sell. Everything I had went into trying to find my son. I was working three jobs at one point. I don't expect you to understand. You can't understand."

She's right. I can't. But Patty Wetterling can. And she's not buying Noreen's story.

In October 1989, Patty's 11-year-old son and two other boys were going to the video store in the Minnesota town of St. Joseph when a guy with a gun approached the kids. Jacob was thrown into a van and hasn't been heard from since.

Patty — like Noreen Gosch — spends her waking hours trying to piece together every scrap of information she can find. She's fought to get legislation passed — locally, nationally. Today, 10 years later, Jacob's photo and bumper stickers saying "Jacob's Hope" are still plastered around their hometown, about 75 miles west of Minneapolis.

Patty's in touch with Noreen. They spoke just two months ago, but Noreen didn't mention that she saw Johnny.

"I can't believe she'd have information and not share," Wetterling said the other night. "I've never heard of something like this when a parent wouldn't share information and try to help. I have a vested interest in Johnny's case. She knows that. She told me she's working on something big. Very big."

Noreen told me the same thing. She said for the past year she's been working with a major TV operation — "bigger than 'Inside Edition' " — and at some point all the details of her son's kidnapping will come out. And, I assume, that will give rise to another round of publicity.

"I'm at peace because Johnny knows I've tried. If I don't keep going, I'd think I failed as a mother."

I still don't believe her, but — having sat across from the woman and looked at the hurt in her eyes — I don't feel so smug about it.

War photographer is left numb by the Balkans' total despair

July 27, 1999

A bullet caught his leg in the Gaza Strip and he lost some of his hearing to a mortar blast in a Kuwaiti oil field. He watched the Germans bang away at — and finally bring down — the Berlin Wall. He had his wrist fractured by a rocket in Croatia and he was in Agra the day Hillary and Chelsea visited the Taj Mahal. Through the lens of his camera, he's witnessed bloodshed and misery — and sometimes joy and celebration — in Panama, Haiti, Nepal and Sri Lanka, India and Pakistan, in Nicaragua and Bosnia, in Somalia and Bangladesh.

He's covered the last six Olympics and the last 10 Super Bowls. When Mark McGwire was chasing Roger Maris, McGwire did it under the watchful eye of John Gaps. And when LA exploded in the wake of the Rodney King verdict, Gaps gave the world some of the most enduring images of the violence.

But now, back in Des Moines after six weeks in the Balkans, Gaps is hurting in ways he's never hurt before. This one got to him.

"I've never seen such a mass concentration of human suffering — in the camps, settlements, processing areas. Children begging through the bars for food and candy. An entire society uprooted. The absolute despair on the faces of people who've given up, tens of thousands of them. It was too much, just too much, too much."

The problem, said Gaps, "is that I'm just not right. There's a heaviness, a sadness. As best I can explain it, I feel numb." It hit him when he was walking the greens at the Senior Open and it hits him as he prowls the state with Clinton and Bush and Gore and Dole.

He'll be OK for a while and then something will set him off — usually something innocuous. Walking through Sam's Club with his wife, he saw people pushing pallets loaded down with food. He had an anxiety attack. He couldn't catch his breath.

"All I could think was that the Kosovars would have killed for that food. I just looked around me and saw all this pure, naked consumption. I just stood there and put my head down and stared at the floor hoping the moment would pass."

In the past, he'd get home and hit Cooney's or some other neighborhood bar, hang with his pals for a while, and he'd unwind. Or he'd find comfort working on Stand Alone, the monthly literary magazine he publishes with the help of his wife and his son John Henry — the oldest of their four kids.

It's not helping. He's even talked with combat veterans — and one in particular, an ex-Marine who served in Korea. The guy actually approached Gaps, sensing something was wrong.

"He said people who haven't been in combat just don't know. They haven't seen it. This isn't post-traumatic stress syndrome. I've been through that, and this isn't it. I'm just feeling totally overwhelmed."

This could be a problem — like a pilot who develops a fear of flying or a surgeon who faints at the sight of blood.

This kind of work has been Gaps' life since he joined The Associated Press in 1985. In some ways it's gotten pretty routine. There's trouble, he hears about it, he packs two bags and waits for the call. A few hours later he's leaving Des Moines and heading for a hot spot somewhere on the planet.

It's an odd role for this Iowa photographer — a Dowling grad — who is supposed to cover only this state, Nebraska and the Dakotas. But he made his mark early on and now — according to the head of the AP in New York — Gaps is: "Our global fireman."

And he loves that role. He wants to be the first one off the copter when they get to the line of fire. He's done it so often that when he hits the ground he knows where to look and what angles to play.

He's been on call for the better part of two decades and doesn't mind traveling 200 to 250 days a year.

But something's eating at him.

"I just wish there was a moment of closure in all this. It's like I'm hoping there's some larger message, some lesson to be learned."

And then there's the question of what happens when the next call comes in. When mass graves are uncovered, when starvation grips half of a continent, when misguided missiles hit a nursery school or old-age home a world away from here.

Given John Gaps' history, he won't have to wait long to find out.

Thanks can be a tough word to write, even think

November 25, 1999

It's been a long time since Lori Jipp had a good day. Some days are better than others. Most days are lousy. Thanksgiving week is the worst. Two years ago this week Lori and Chuck Jipp found out why he was having that nagging problem with his left foot.

Chuck worried that it was some sort of nerve problem that would require back surgery. And that would interfere with his passion — long-distance running.

What they learned, Lori says, "was worse than anything we would have considered. Far worse than anything we could have imagined."

Chuck, now 48, was in the early stages of Lou Gehrig's disease — amyotrophic lateral sclerosis. With ALS, you gradually lose control of your motor functions. Your arms and legs are useless. After a while you can't even breathe.

At best, he had four years before it would kill him. And they had two days before the family was gathering at their home for Thanksgiving. They called Chuck's mother in Boone and his sister in Atlanta. They called his two sons — living in northeast Iowa with his ex-wife.

Dinner that Thursday was a solemn event. Folks arrived, some with a few tears in their eyes. There were hugs and kisses, but nothing was said. Over dinner it was all small talk, the usual family fare.

After dinner they gathered in the living room for a long talk and a good cry.

There have been a lot of tears since then. The decline has been swift and painful — emotionally, physically. They thought they'd have more time together.

Just a year ago Chuck was getting around with a cane, helping raise money for his church, speaking before hundreds of people. This year he can't move and he can't speak. He can barely swallow. Solid food no longer is an option.

Months ago he gave up his accounting practice. Lori works for the state, and she's set up to work at home part of the day.

He spends his days in a recliner, sleeping, watching TV. He has to use his right hand to get his left hand to move. If he works at it, he can manipulate the remote and change channels. His neck is in a brace. An electric IV machine pumps fluid into his system, and a catheter pumps it out.

In the morning, Lori uses a lift with chains and hooks to get him out of bed and into his wheelchair. The couple is buying a machine that'll help him communicate. If he can type words into it — and that gets tougher by the day — the machine will then speak those words.

With a lot of effort he can answer a question by writing a note. Or he can just let you know what he's thinking, like when he heard his wife talking about how quickly he's slipping away.

Chuck wrote: "Toughest thing is you can feel your body weakening every day. Biggest fear is death by suffocation."

His wife sits at his feet and massages his legs. And when asked whether there's anything to be thankful for this holiday, she manages a half-smile.

"There are things you don't know until something like this happens. You don't know how much you're loved. Chuck's running group called last spring and told us to meet them at AK O'Connors in Beaverdale. They had taken up a collection to send us on a trip. We figured we'd get a room in Omaha, just get a way for a night. They collected enough to send us to Hawaii.

"Last weekend my friends came over with their husbands and they cleaned my house. They cleaned my windows. That helps."

Their health insurance doesn't cover the equipment Chuck needs, high-end stuff like the van with a lift on it. They had to remodel the house so he could get around. That took money. All kinds of friends — business friends, high school pals from Boone — raised all kinds of cash.

Two weeks ago Lori's friends put together a package that she describes as "girl stuff" — scented body lotion, gift certificates for a massage and pedicure, small luxuries beyond her reach.

"So yeah," Lori Jipp said the other day, "we've got something to be thankful for."

Chuck smiled. Lori smiled back. She was still massaging his legs.

Storm brewing on horizon between locals, Lost Souls Café

January 12, 1999

Sitting around and having coffee on a Sunday afternoon, Randy Sieberling and Jeanette Gavigan seem like reasonable people. Gavigan works two restaurant jobs and is raising her 3-year-old grandson. Sieberling has two kids and works in the tech department at an insurance company. Both of them live near 35th and Cottage Grove, across from the Lost Souls Cafe.

And both want the place muzzled or moved.

Dan Inzeo and Jules Westegaard — the couple who own the Lost Souls Cafe — also come across as reasonable. They've brought something to town that was missing: a hip space where young people can feel comfortable. Inzeo and Westegaard understand how to make a room like that work.

What they don't seem to understand is why the city and some neighbors are trying to close them down.

"This is what the city's lacking," said Inzeo. "Look at (the cities) where young people are flocking. This is what's lacking in this community. We need more places like this."

At midnight Saturday, the Lost Souls Cafe was pretty mellow. A few teens and twentysomethings stood out front on the 13-degree night, smoking and getting dusted by a light snowfall. Inside, the handful of cafe tables were taken — about 20 or so guys and gals sitting around drinking coffee and soda, talking. A few were on the computers. Two were playing cards.

In the next room — a space that looks and feels like somebody's family room — about a dozen teens were hanging out on the couches and chairs, talking and laughing. One guy was reading a magazine. Another was thumbing through a book.

It was a scene you wouldn't mind seeing your 16-year-old involved in. Or the kind of place that would be nice to walk to for a coffee.

That's what Randy Sieberling was figuring two years ago when he heard a bookstore/coffeehouse was opening a few doors down the block. He was thinking about long winter evenings sipping coffee,

"So I'm talkin' to this guy . . ."

and scanning best-sellers and cutting-edge magazines.

And he wouldn't have to tramp out to the 'burbs to do it.

When the Lost Souls Cafe finally opened — less a bookstore than a cafe and teen hangout — Sieberling gave the owners piles of wood so they could build a fence on the property.

And Sieberling's kids sometimes go into the cafe to hang with their friends. But now Sieberling's thrown in his lot with the city and the folks who say the place is in violation of the zoning ordinance.

"It's not what it claims to be. They've got kids hanging out in front of the place, making noise. You can't park around here. There's music in the summer and you can't keep your windows open. It's not a bookstore. Why should we have to put up with this? These are not bad kids or anything like that. It's just that this business is in the wrong place."

Jeanette Gavigan agrees. Her two jobs sometimes keep her out of the house from 7 in the morning until 10 or 11 at night. She also complains about the parking, the noise and the occasional beer bottle thrown in her yard.

"There's nothing wrong with these kids. They're fine kids. I just want to be able to sleep."

Inzeo says the noise complaints are overblown and he's dealing with the problem.

"I patrol the front of this place like a cop. We have zero tolerance. Kids mess up and they're banned for 30 days. The regulars know that and they police this place themselves. The kids know the only way this can work is if we respect the neighborhood."

Mayor Preston Daniels has offered to find a different spot for the cafe and get somebody to help them move. Westegaard and Inzeo say they're ready to duke it out with the city in court.

"They can take away my license to do business, but I'm not closing these doors. We're morally and legally right and we're not going to back down."

It was after midnight and the snow had picked up, but the crowd thinned out. One lone kid stood on the cafe's steps, hands deep in his pockets, snow gathering on his hair, eyes straight ahead — looking like he didn't see the storm gathering around him.

Thomas critic stands on principle
February 6, 2002

Sally Frank spent Monday night working on her signs, practicing her chants, getting the routine down.

Tuesday noon, it was showtime.

Frank and about a dozen other lefties took their act out to the front of the Drake Law School. They started waving those signs — "Justice Thomas is a Contradiction in Terms" and "I Believe Anita Hill."

And they were chanting: "Hey, hey, ho, ho, the right-wing court has got to go" . . . "We cast our votes, but they won't count 'em, Thomas will select without 'em."

Those were some of the more cutting-edge lines and signs.

So that raises this question: Why is a grown woman — a tenured law professor, president of the Drake chapter of the American Association of University Professors — standing outside in subfreezing weather, waving these signs and chanting tired slogans?

Ask Frank about that, and she sort of laughs. She mentions how much she's mellowed — she hasn't been arrested for disorderly conduct since 1982. And then she affectionately blames this life of activism on her parents.

"They took me to my first protest when I was 11, in fifth grade. It was 1970 at Foley Square in Manhattan, and it was about the treatment of Soviet Jews. Then when I was 15, they let me take a day off from school to go and protest against Arafat. They weren't real liberal. They just believed that if something is wrong, you should bring attention to it and try to deal with it."

What Frank was trying to deal with yesterday was Clarence Thomas' weeklong gig at Drake. He's in town teaching a class on constitutional law, and he's holding informal sessions with students and teachers. Folks around the school were saying it's an honor to have a Supreme Court justice on campus — even if you don't agree with the guy's politics.

Tim Coonan, a third-year law student, said having Thomas in town "is a rare and important event. Politics aside, how could this not be worthwhile?"

But Frank wasn't buying into that. Not even close. She can't put politics aside. She's got a long, thick list of complaints about Thomas, starting with Anita Hill and going right up through the court's decision on the 2000 election, an event Frank casually and consistently refers to as "the Coup."

She's relentless in her complaints about Thomas' stand on abortion — he's against it — and the death penalty — he's for it.

She can't mention the guy by name without referring to his "right-wing radical activist agenda."

While Frank and her gang were going on about Thomas, a bunch of students were gathering on a balcony at the law school. They started mocking Frank and the rest of them. They'd yell out whenever a TV or radio mike was stuck in Frank's face.

Scott Kaspar, a second-year law student, stood on the edge of the small crowd of protesters, shaking his head, staring at them with a look that was somewhere between anger and disbelief. Kaspar describes himself as a political moderate and says he's not exactly in sync with Thomas, but that's not the issue.

"We've got a member of the United States Supreme Court who is willing to come here and meet with us. And look at how these people behave. We should be happy he's here, regardless of his views. If Ginsburg or one of those others came to teach or speak, would there be a bunch of wild conservatives out here carrying on? I think they'd be a lot more respectful."

Frank insists she and the others are being respectful. But they're not going to ignore Thomas and his record.

Then — about an hour into the protest — Frank's people start drifting away, saying they have to get on to other things.

She says that's not a problem.

"You look for the small victories. You don't expect to achieve peace on Earth."

But before they call it quits, she gets them chanting again.

"One, two, three, four, it's justice we are fighting for."

Not exactly Dr. King's "Dream" speech, but they got their point across.

Drummer's death leaves sad silence

March 8, 2002

Kathy Hill woke up, looked across the room and saw the guy she was about to marry was dead on the floor. There'd been a fistfight the night before between her fiance and his son. Some ribs were broken, his spleen was ruptured and Kathy Hill spent her wedding day making funeral arrangements. She quietly buried a man who was anything but quiet. He was 48 — already a great-grandfather — and spent 40 years drumming, making a lot of noise in this town. He was banging away until the day he died.

That was at the end of January. Kathy Hill's spent her time since then sorting through a long, complex relationship, going back to that afternoon in the early '70s when she was hanging with her friends over in MacRae Park and Ron Hill blew in on a motorcycle.

"He was the most gorgeous thing I'd ever seen. Blue eyes, the hair. I can still remember how I felt when I looked at him that day. It's almost embarrassing to talk about it."

That wasn't the first time she saw Ron Hill. They grew up together on the south side of Des Moines and went to the same schools from elementary through high — Watrous, Kurtz, Lincoln. But she was always a few years ahead of him, and that day at the park was the first time she saw him as something other than a kid from the neighborhood. He was 18 and had been drumming and playing in bands for about 10 years. He was already making a name for himself around the city.

She was 22, divorced with a 4-year-old daughter.

Over the next 30 years they were close friends, got married in '87, got divorced in '98, stayed close friends and were about to get married a second time when Ron Hill died. This happened while they were visiting Ron's father at his Texas getaway near the Mexican border. Ron and his son — a twentysomething from a previous marriage — had a fight. Punches were thrown, and the kid is facing involuntary manslaughter charges.

Now Kathy Hill is living alone in the south-side house they shared. It's painful for her to walk from room to room because it's all Ron. On the fridge she's got pictures of him — from his childhood through the days before he died. There's a drum in just about every shot.

"So I'm talkin' to this guy . . ."

The dining room has hundreds of CDs and stacks of albums — Canned Heat and Quicksilver, Deep Purple, Stevie Ray and Cream. His posters of Janis and Jimi are in the living room. His drums are still set up in the basement, with half a pack of Marlboros on the snare and two empty Heineken bottles on the floor next to the bass.

Kathy talks about him and doesn't try to gloss over the rough edges. She doesn't kid herself or try to convince you that Ron was some homebody who enjoyed sitting in front of the tube with a bowl of chips and a Pepsi. Ask around — talk to club owners, other musicians — and you hear about the women and the drinking and every other thing you'd expect from a guy who spent his life playing bars.

But no matter how much you hear on that front, there's always another piece to it. They always come back around to stories about Hill behind the drums, playing with Roze, RH Blues Factor, Pelican Peace.

Randy Van Hosen plays bass with Roze and shared a stage with Hill hundreds of times over the years. And he can't say enough about him — good and bad. He had to throw Hill out of the band more than once. But he always took him back.

"Huge ego and a terrible pain in the ass to deal with, a living hell. But it was worth it because once he got on that stage he gave 100 percent and he was the best. What a showman — stick twirling, jumping in the air, mooning the audience, phenomenal solos. Playing drums, performing was his life."

Talk to Kathy Hill about that — tell her what folks are saying about Ron as a musician — and she takes you back downstairs to where the drums are set up. She says she can't believe how quiet the house is. She can't believe Ron Hill won't spend at least part of this weekend in some club, sitting behind these drums.

She's talking and she's slowly running her hand along the top of a conga, stroking it.

Violent racist turns life around

December 13, 2002

I'm listening to him talk about his collection of butterfly wings. He's got thousands in glass cases. He's going on about the beauty of the Madagascar urania and the uniqueness of the Atlas moths.

I'm nodding along, trying to act like I know what he's talking about. I'm buying time. I want to get past the butterflies and get him to tell me about that tattoo on his hand.

But for now we're doing insects.

His name is George Van Meter, and he seems like a nice enough guy.

He's kind of low-key, soft spoken. He's sitting there in a torn sweat shirt and jeans, a gold cross hanging from his neck, a couple of days' growth on his face. We're in a back room at Urban Dreams. Van Meter's one of the few white folks who is employed at that inner-city social services operation. He does everything from construction and roofing to window cleaning and taking out the garbage. The folks at Urban Dreams — Wayne Ford, Harry Flipping — can't say enough good things about the guy.

Van Meter spends some of his down time helping out at his church or giving teddy bears to hospitalized kids or doling out food to hungry people.

So this guy's a real sweetheart, one of those folks who makes this a better world, somebody who says things like: "I will spend the rest of my life serving people and serving God."

But it wasn't the do-gooder stuff that got my attention when I first met Van Meter. What caught my eye was the swastika tattooed on his left hand. This is not some little blot that gets pasted on for a few days. This is a real tattoo. He's 37, and he's had it since he was 17.

When I get around to asking about that, Van Meter takes it a step further. He pulls off the sweat shirt and shows me he's got all kinds of Jesus stuff and Bible quotes tattooed on his arms and chest. Then he turns around, and he's got the words "White Pride" tattooed on the back of his arms — elaborate letters each about 3 inches high.

Van Meter says he's been born again for about six months, and he's been a hard-core racist for most of his life.

I ask about it, and he takes me back to his Missouri childhood and the father he's never met. He talks about the mother who abandoned him and ran off and had kids with a black guy. But mostly he talks about the grandmother who raised him. This is the abusive woman with a drug and alcohol problem, the one who had a string of men in and out of her bedroom every night.

Because of his mother's deal with the black guy, this grandmother took to calling Van Meter all kinds of racial slurs. And it was no problem for her to get others in the family and in the neighborhood to do the same. The kid — starting from when he was about 9 — took his anger out on black people. By 13 he was in juvenile hall on a variety of assault and theft charges. By 15 he was into drugs and drinking. A year later he quit school, and a year after that he ran away to St. Louis.

At one point he ended up in jail for five years. He had two marriages that lasted less than six months each — "I beat both of them repeatedly. That's just who I was." He had friends in Des Moines, and he moved here in the early '90s. He discovered meth, he continued to drink and steal and get into fights. He kept getting fired from his construction jobs, and he kept getting busted — forgery, burglary, grand larceny.

A few years ago he met Shannon Dudley, got her hooked on meth, beat her. But he loved her, and when she left him and got into treatment this past summer, Van Meter started going to meetings with other addicts. Then — with Shannon — he started going to church.

He's come to terms with his racism.

"I just didn't know black people. I came here to work at Urban Dreams, and they didn't judge me by who I was in the past. Now I've got black friends, and I've never been happier."

And as of this morning he's been clean for 109 days — a lifetime for this guy.

Cynic offers a break to Cyclones' Eustachy
May 1, 2003

I was on the phone the other morning with a friend and we got around to the Larry Eustachy story. This guy was going on about how Eustachy said he used "poor judgment" when he got drunk and was caught kissing young women at a party.

My friend wasn't impressed. This was his take on it: "When an adult says 'I used poor judgment,' it means he had a good time and the newspaper found out about it."

That line was in my head Wednesday afternoon when I was waiting for the Eustachy press conference to start. Even before he said a word I could hear it all.

He'd be talking about the tremendous embarrassment he's caused his family and his players, the school and the state. He'd talk about how words alone could not express his remorse and he'd never be able to apologize enough. He'd say he was getting help, in treatment and — if he's really savvy — he'd refer to his drinking problem as an illness.

He'd ask for forgiveness, say he was disappointed in his behavior, but proud of himself for dealing with it.

How could the university — and the entire community — be so coldhearted that they'd fire someone with such a crippling health problem.

The press conference lasted about a half hour and Eustachy didn't let me down. He used every phrase I expected to hear, even "illness." And he went a step further, saying his grandparents died of alcoholism, a nod to the theory that heredity plays a role in all this.

But some of my cynicism was tempered. I was sitting there looking at him and his wife, hearing him talk about his kids, and thinking maybe this guy gets it. Maybe he's serious and ready to put the glass down and get on with his life. A tough move for a guy who's been drinking as long as he has — at least 25 years. So maybe he knows he bottomed out. No easy thing, but it's a moment every recovering alcoholic faces.

For some folks it doesn't hit you until you have no choice. You can't drink because you're behind bars or being held in some detention center or some court-ordered treatment program. For some, that moment comes at 2 in the morning on the side of the road when you're handcuffed, charged with drunken driving, and being read your Miranda rights. Maybe you're standing in the doorway watching your spouse leave. Or having your kids look at you in disgust after you've embarrassed them one more time.

Some reach that moment in less dramatic ways — reading a book or an article about alcoholism and what it does to you, deciding to become a health freak. Seeing a friend losing it, making a fool of himself at a party and knowing how easily that could have been you. Maybe getting religion.

One guy I spoke with sobered up the night he left a half-glass of bourbon on his desk, the boss found it, and told him to get into rehab or he'd be out of work.

"The toughest part was going home and telling my wife."

Another guy talked about the night he tried to choke a friend, hurt him badly, "and the next morning I didn't even remember what happened. It was time to stop drinking."

Those stories brought me back around to what Eustachy did to himself.

Here's a guy whose drinking problem is the lead story everywhere from his hometown paper to the national sports shows — TV and radio. Pictures of him drinking beer and kissing young women were flying around the country on the Internet.

So when I wondered if he realized he'd bottomed out, I was willing to believe him.

Besides, most of us aren't in a position to wag a finger at the guy.

Valley student is truly special

May 9, 2003

Take a look at Paul Krupko — sitting in his wheelchair, struggling to lift his head and speak — and it's hard to believe what you're hearing about this guy. He's 18, graduating from Valley High School, and he's going to Drake in the fall.

He's got a 3.6 grade-point average — higher than most students — and he's taking advanced placement classes. He's the only person in this state to ever win the "Yes I Can" foundation community service award, something he got this year for his work with the Variety Club Telethon.

He does volunteer work, he was a Boy Scout, he likes books — epic fantasies like "Lord of the Rings" — and he likes to play computer games.

That's one piece of Paul's story. The other piece is what makes him unique.

He's got cerebral palsy, he's legally blind, he can't write, and he reads at the second-grade level. But he's gone through 12 years of school and was never marked on a curve. He did the work the other kids did and earned his diploma.

Jim Garbison is a special-ed teacher at Valley and he's been doing this kind of work for 35 years, handling about 20 students each semester. He's been working with Paul.

"He's got an incredible memory, he's a good thinker, he participates in class discussions, he's very focused, and he can deal with extremely abstract concepts. He can visualize algebra equations."

Garbison thinks a moment.

"There was a time when the education system would have looked at Paul and thought he was incapable of succeeding. Now he motivates people — staffers, students. Everybody's amazed. You can't spend time with him and not come away impressed."

Paul was born in Chicago in 1984. He was 10 weeks premature, spent five weeks in the intensive care unit, and underwent three major surgeries — on his hips, his ankles and his knees. On a scale of one to four — four being the worst — his cerebral palsy is at level 3.

From the beginning, his parents read to him. By the time he was

5, the family had moved to Des Moines and he was ready for school.

He worked hard to keep up. He still does.

"It can be very difficult, but I work at it. Every night I spend hours doing my homework. I use one half of my brain more than the other so I get real tired. My mother reads to me and I have to do physical therapy. My dad helps with that. It's tough, but I've had a lot of help from my mom and dad, and in school from my classmates and teachers, everybody. I've got a full-time associate at school that just works with me."

And there's help on another front. Paul calls it "assistive technology."

At a basic level, it's books on tape, something Paul's been using for years.

Then there's a program called "Dragon Naturally Speaking." It's software that lets him talk into a mike and get it back in print. The software adapts itself to each person's speech pattern, and that's how Paul does his reports, his term papers, anything that has to be written out.

And there's a process called "Kurzweil" that scans the text and reads it back to him. That works great in school, but at home — because of Paul's interest in fantasy tales — it's a bit flawed.

"With all these fictitious names it doesn't work that well. They don't always get it right. So mostly my mom reads to me. But it's a big help with stuff like English and history."

Paul would like to take it easy this summer and get ready for college in the fall. Looking ahead, he has no real sense of what he wants to study, what he wants to do with his life, but he's giving some thought to law, maybe education.

"Math is difficult because the problem has to be blown up big so I can see it. One thing I can't be is a chemist. It's just too much to do all those complex equations."

You hear that and you go back an hour to when you first met this guy and you were thinking he can barely function. Now you're thinking that if Paul Krupko put his mind to it, he could be a chemist.

His good deeds don't go unpunished
May 14, 2003

David Kruidenier is the closest thing this city has to a leader. He's the one who makes things happen.

That cuts two ways. On the downside — like most movers and power brokers — he can be a pain to deal with. He can be demanding and insist on getting his way.

On the upside, Kruidenier has put his time and his money and his energy into everything that works around here. Think of what this place would look like without him.

He's poured millions into the Art Center and raised and invested $9 million in the Civic Center. He built the Forest Avenue Library and put up $5 million for the new downtown library. He's heavily invested in Nollen Plaza, the Simon Estes Amphitheater and Salisbury House. And he's got "a significant investment" in the Temple for Performing Arts.

Then there's Gray's Lake. He put up $1.5 million to make that happen. And it wasn't easy. After he offered to donate the money, the city didn't return his phone calls. He finally got through, and then they lost the $100,000 check he gave them as a deposit. He had to stop payment and write out another one.

Then when things were getting started, they wanted to build a four-story building next to the lake. Kruidenier told them what they could do with their building. So they backed off and decided to build a lighthouse in the lake.

Again he said no. "What is this, Maine?"

Then they had this plan to put up a railroad bridge with steel girders and six metal sailboats around the lake. Kruidenier was ready to pull out.

"They kept saying, 'We need a focal point.' And I kept telling them, 'The lake is the focal point.' "

Eventually he got through to the city, the path around the lake was built, they put in a state-of-the-art bridge, and the place is hot. Hundreds of people are there every day, thousands use it on weekends, and it's one of the few places around here where you find a mix of colors and ages and backgrounds — economic and ethnic. They're showing movies down there, having concerts. The pavilion is available for parties and weddings. It's working.

So Kruidenier — at 81 — ought to be sitting back and soaking up the good feelings that are flowing his way. Instead, he's sitting in his downtown office and stewing about the grief he's getting. It's the kind of grief you expect when you have to push people out of the way to get past the talk and the meetings and make something happen.

Local activists and loudmouths are going after him on the Net, e-mails are flying around about his heavy-handed approach in getting the AIB building leveled. Others are ragging on him for saying the city should limit the use of Gray's Lake. For the most part, Kruidenier can deal with it. He was in the newspaper business most of his life and knows how the game is played.

"I'm a big boy and can take the hits. I know it's fun to take potshots at people. But what bothers me is people are writing and saying things about me, and not one of them even calls to get my side."

This is Kruidenier's side: "All I'm saying is that the lake is designed for recreation and it's not a venue for special events. We should limit the noise and try to maintain a natural setting. No movie screens and Jet Skis. Maintain some balance. That's all I'm saying."

But there's one more thing he's saying. Kruidenier says he's pretty much had it with Des Moines. He doesn't see the city as a good long-term investment. He says it's losing ground, nobody's in charge, and people are too comfortable with the status quo.

He spent 10 years in Minneapolis and points to that city as an example.

"Go look at the energy level up there, the positive attitude, the self-confidence. Do you see that here? In the city or the state? We have a Legislature still fighting between rural and urban, and we're going no place."

It's tough hearing that from Kruidenier. Beyond the cash, this guy has invested 90 percent of his life in this city and state and now he's dissing the place. And what he's saying makes sense.

Long shot is long on ideas
May 28, 2003

So you're a Democrat and you can't seem to get jazzed about the nine presidential options. You can't decide who has the best shot of taking down the Bush administration. Sharpton? Kucinich? Moseley Braun? It hasn't been this tough since the Republicans had to pick between Keyes and Bauer.

But not to worry. I've got one for you: Fern Penna.

This guy is just what you're looking for. He's never held office, so he doesn't come with a lot of political baggage. He's not some know-it-all. He couldn't even tell me who the mayor of Kingston, N.Y., is — and Penna lives there. He couldn't figure out how to use his cell phone when it rang, and he's the guy who pronounced Dubuque "Duh Buh Key."

He's 39 and a millionaire, so he's not beholden to special interests. But he can't quite explain how he made all that money. Or how he was able to retire 10 years ago. He's been on his own from the age of 13, and he started a floor-sanding business at the age of 15. He's been a "consultant on government policy" for a number of senators and congressmen.

Which ones?

"Moynihan, for one. I can't tell you the others because they're still alive."

He says he's an architect, and he says he's been to law school. Where?

"It was a home-study deal."

And he recognizes insightful probing when he hears it. Like when I ask him: "Why are you running for president of the United States of America?"

I catch him off guard with that one. He thinks for a second and then says: "That is a very good question."

He goes back to his childhood.

"I decided to run when I was a teenager. I was an angry kid. It's just something I've always wanted to do, and now the time is right."

Penna is from Brooklyn. He lived out in Anaheim for a while, and now he lives up in the Catskill Mountains. He's campaigning in

Iowa this week. He drove here in his Saturn with his wife and 2-year-old daughter. Along the way he locked up party support in Pennsylvania and Ohio. He's also a favorite in Germany and France. "But it's still 50-50 in England." No problem. The election isn't for another 18 months.

He's still cobbling together his platform, but some things are already in place.

Ask about farm policy, and he's on it.

"We have to study the weather and use the lakes to prevent drought. We have to put underground silos on every farm, that'll provide jobs. We have to clean up the oceans and stop wasting money. We're spending $57 million to study ketchup, and we're paying Florida for crops that don't exist. There's $3 trillion missing from the budget. Did you know that? DID YOU?"

He's raising his voice. He's obviously passionate about farming. I manage to get him to calm down, to focus.

"The day I take office I'll declare a state of emergency in every state. I want to rebuild the entire country."

Let's talk about something less volatile. The environment?

"The oceans are dying, the killer whales are dying, and nobody is doing a thing about it. The Green Party is with me."

How about foreign policy?

"It's a beautiful world. It all comes down to money."

So talk to me about the economy — the one thing people really care about.

"I don't believe in welfare or food stamps. I say we close the cookie jar. China makes $135 billion on us. We need an import tax to feed Social Security."

He goes on to talk about the 250 terrorist cells in Canada and the need to explore Mars — "That'll open a whole new field. We'll hire 3 million people to start that project. We have to. We're losing this planet."

It's time to wrap it up. In my mind I start to dismiss Penna as just another publicity freak who's running without a shot of winning. Then I think about some of the head cases and lightweights who've run for president — and won.

England looks beyond downfall
June 20, 2003

The first time I saw David England was at a DMACC dinner. He was working the room, going table to table, glad-handing, slapping folks on the back, charming people with his Texas accent and his smile. The guy was a star and he knew it. He had the job he wanted, the $400,000 house, the six-figure income, the marriage, the kids. The folks who worked with him and for him had nothing but good things to say about England.

That was about a year ago.

The last time I saw him was Thursday morning in court. He'd just been sentenced on a felony drug conviction. The smile's gone, the job's gone, he's almost broke and he's tens of thousands of dollars in debt. His wife and kids were also convicted on drug charges — related and unrelated. Groups looking to legalize pot want him as a poster boy. He's been written up in High Times magazine and newspapers around the country. He's getting all kinds of national attention.

He's sad, embarrassed, looking for some way to salvage his life and career.

It's been a quick fall.

England was hired two years ago as president of Des Moines Area Community College, a school of almost 20,000 students. They paid him $175,000 to lure him out of Texas and it was looking like a good move all around. With his energy and insight and 24 years experience, he managed to shake up a sleepy school. He got folks jazzed about working there and going there. He was up at the Legislature making his case for funding, talking to all kinds of community groups, raising DMACC's profile in the right ways, with the right people.

Then on March 12, drug agents — acting on a tip — raided his Johnston home and found a few pounds of marijuana and about 70 plants. He was smoking dope when the cops got there. He eventually pleaded guilty to two felony counts and was sentenced Thursday to two years' probation and 100 hours of community service.

And anybody who hears England's story comes back around to the same question:

What the hell was this guy thinking?

The other morning I asked him about that and he tried to explain it.

"I saw it as a very private thing. I only smoked when the kids weren't home or late at night in my room with the window open, the door locked. I never took it outside, in the car or anything like that. It never interfered with my life or career. I grew it because I didn't want to go out and buy it. But I'm not trying to justify what I did. It was wrong; it was illegal. It was a big mistake. A terrible mistake."

And why get the kids involved?

"I didn't. They didn't know a thing about it. What they were doing, they were doing on their own. I wasn't pleased when I found out."

England is 51 and started smoking dope in college. He kept it up, smoking three or four times a week. He kept his plants in a small basement room behind several locked doors. He kept his stash in a freezer, also behind locked doors. He lives in a three-story, 4,000-square-foot house and he makes the case that he was able to keep it all away from the kids — his 23-year-old daughter and 16-year-old son.

"I wouldn't do anything to harm them. I made one mistake and I just hope I'm not totally destroyed."

If he behaves, he'll get away with no jail time. But that's about all he'll get away with.

Since the bust he's been out of work, his wife gave up her job at the Art Center and the debt's piling up. He's been in therapy, drug counseling. He's been trying to write a book about what happened and he's been applying for jobs at community colleges around the country. He's well-known in the field and says he's gotten some good response. Now that he's been sentenced he wants to get on with his life. He talks about how much he misses the work and people. He says he spends a lot of time thinking about how much he's lost.

And — he mentions several times — he hasn't smoked dope since the bust.

South-side family grieves, asks, 'Why?'
September 25, 2003

Frank Ounlokham was fishing at Easter Lake. It was getting dark so he packed up and headed home. When he pulled out of the park he came up against a mass of traffic and flashing red lights — cops, firetrucks, an ambulance.

It was a car wreck. A bad one.

He stopped, got out and saw some kids he recognized, some friends of his 15-year-old brother, Nick. They were on the roadside crying and when Frank walked up to them and asked what was going on, they turned away and cried harder.

Then Frank looked at the crash, with the broken glass, the pieces of metal and plastic, engine parts. In the middle of that mess he saw his brother lying dead in the street.

"I just felt angry. So angry and sad. I stood there and looked at him and kept looking and I couldn't even cry, I was so stunned."

He finally got it together and then there was a round of phone calls — his mother at home, his father at work, his sister at the U of I, uncles and cousins and friends. He didn't offer details. He just asked them to meet him at the hospital. He got in the car and started driving, and still no tears. He just couldn't cry.

But Frank Ounlokham had no problem crying Wednesday morning while he sat in the basement of his family's south-side home and talked about his brother. They were eight years apart but they were close. They played basketball together, wrestled, hung out at the mall, listened to music. Frank had a son three years ago and Nick was just devoted to his baby nephew. Nick would stay up past midnight and rock little Christian to sleep.

"That's what I'll remember. He loved being Uncle Nick."

Frank talked and friends and relatives came by to give him a hug and a kiss, to cry with him.

The men gathered in the family room to comfort Sai Ounlokham, Nick's father. They listened to Sai talk about a tough-acting teenager who never forgot to kiss Mom and Dad good night, or to greet them with a morning smile and hug.

Over in the living room, about two dozen women — from their

teens to their 80s — sat around Nick's mother and tried to comfort her. They tried to spoon-feed her some soup and they tried to just hold her and let her know she wasn't alone in this tragedy.

But there was no way to comfort Bounmy Ounlokham. She lay there on the floor of a room that was dotted with family photos — Nick as a baby, through his graduation from Weeks Middle School. And she cried out her son's name — over and over.

All morning long the friends and family kept coming. They brought all kinds of food and drinks. Some gathered in the kitchen to cook. Some were on the deck and some were on the front lawn.

They all cried.

Bettina Ounlokham sat alone on the bed in her brother Nick's bedroom and talked about the kid who could make her laugh and smile just by saying hello.

"I'd come home and he'd do this little routine, saying, 'Hey sister,' in a funny way. It was something between us and we'd just laugh. He was very sweet and kind and very funny."

Nick's bedroom was an interesting mix, a life in transition — stuffed animals and techno CDs. Pictures of Nick's baby nephew were on the wall with a Barnstormers sticker and a Michael Jordan poster.

Bettina talked about how her brother loved to shop for clothes and sneakers. She opened the closet and there were stacks of shoe boxes.

And then 19-year-old Bettina talked about that moment when she heard her brother was dead.

"I just screamed, 'WHY?' as loud as I could."

That was the question that hung in the tear-soaked air at the Ounlokham home. It was the question in a lot of places on the city's south side.

At 63, she's learning to read

October 10, 2003

Norma and Katie are both learning how to read, both having a hard time. So they help each other out.

At night they sit and go through these kids' books, back and forth, each reading a page. Then they test each other — throwing out words to be spelled and defined.

Katie is 11, and it's the kind of struggle a lot of kids her age go through. But she's having a good time with it.

So is Norma. Not only does she get to spend time with Katie — her granddaughter — but for the first time in her 63 years she's not embarrassed because she can't read.

"I basically gave up a long time ago," she says. "I just thought I was too stupid and that wasn't going to change."

Norma Kenoyer grew up on the east side of Des Moines and went to Brooks elementary. In third grade, when it became obvious she had a learning problem, she was shuffled to the side and put into what was then considered a special ed class. It was basically a baby-sitting operation. The kids sat and drew pictures, played with coloring books, did some basic math, and spent a lot of time in the cafeteria. And nobody taught them to read.

Kenoyer drifted from grade to grade.

"When I got to ninth grade, they called me in and told me I should just quit because it would be too embarrassing to go on. I just cried because I wanted to go to high school so bad."

But she quit school at 16 and got a job busing tables at a buffet place. She got married at 17, had two kids, and never learned to read.

"My mother taught me the alphabet, and I could recognize some words, like 'cat,' 'the' and 'this' and 'that.' I figured out how to sign my name, and I managed to memorize enough stuff to get a driver's license. But that was all. Then my husband left me and took the kids. He got tired of having me leaning on him all the time, and the court said I couldn't raise them because I couldn't read."

She fought and got her kids back. She remarried and worked as a housekeeper for about 25 years. For the most part she was able to hide her problem. Then about 10 years ago she was working for this woman, cleaning her house, and the woman left her a note asking her to clean the refrigerator. Kenoyer could figure out the word "clean," but that was it. She cleaned everything in sight. Everything but the fridge. That blew her cover, and the woman realized Kenoyer couldn't read. That was one of those curses that turned into a blessing. The woman helped her get into a program at Drake. It's at the Adult Literacy Center.

Now Kenoyer cleans houses for about 50 hours a week, and she spends just about every evening reading — alone, with Katie or with one of her three other grandchildren. She spends a few afternoons at the center.

At her age, learning to read is tough and tedious. It's taking years. She's got to deal with the most basic issues — "My brain just isn't used to this. It's all trial and error. Mostly error."

But Kenoyer is driven, and Anne Murr, her teacher, is with her on this. They start every session with the alphabet and then get into these word games with names like "multisyllabic sound tapping" and "consonant blending."

Murr lays down the words — base-ball, camp-fire, class-mate, in-sult — and Kenoyer figures them out. She's pretty smooth but with a few stumbles. She has trouble with "critic." She keeps seeing "cricket." But Murr walks her through it a letter at a time, and Kenoyer gets it.

By the end of the hour they are both feeling good about themselves.

And Kenoyer is even looking ahead, talking about where she wants to go next.

"I've got this dream that someday I'll be able to use a computer. That would really be something to be able to do that."

After seeing what this woman has accomplished, you've got to figure it won't be long before she's checking her e-mail.

Eager for change in the inner city
November 19, 2003

The senior center at Martin Luther King and Forest is usually a pretty quiet place. You've mostly got older folks sitting around sipping coffee and playing cards and dominoes, reading the paper, making small talk.

It's comfortable and easy, a chance to get away without going too far.

But that wasn't the deal the other night. It was high energy in that place. No small talk. It was time to deal with serious problems. It was a chance to brainstorm, kick around ideas, get folks to sign up for the caucuses, register to vote. It was a time to argue, disagree, get in each other's face and then come together to make things happen. It was a good time to get organized and make sure some issues stay on the table — at the Statehouse, the county, the city and even the school board.

It wasn't so much a meeting as a semi-organized free-for-all.

The whole thing was pulled together by a group called Sisters on Target and they had help from the African-American Coalition, Blacks in Business and some others. They put out the word, saying it was time to sit down and give folks a chance to vent, talk about what's wrong — and even right — with being black in Des Moines.

It wasn't just about seniors. It was a mix.

Jesse Taylor has been an activist in this town for just about every one of his almost 80 years, and he was there. So was Joshua Brown, a 19-year-old from California who's been here two months and wants to connect.

Some politicians realized it was a good place to be, a chance to hear what people are thinking, a chance to get their name and face out.

Wayne Ford and Jack Hatch showed up. So did folks from Tom Harkin's and Leonard Boswell's offices. New school board member Ako Abdul-Samad — the guy some folks credit with energizing the black community — stopped in on his way to another meeting. Ruth Ann Gaines stopped in to plug for her City Council run. Ted Sporer heads up the Polk County Republican Party and he was there with Leon Mosley from Black Hawk County, interim head of the state GOP.

About 75 people broke off into about 12 groups, each at their own table. Every group made a list and at the top of everybody's list was health care and the fact that folks can't afford it.

Just about every list had stuff about racial profiling, and how tough it is for ex-cons to readjust and re-enter the community. There was talk about drugs and jobs, about how the inner city is shabby and needs a face-lift. There was a lot of talk about education, after-school care, the need to support local businesses.

It's the same stuff you can hear folks talking about when they buy clothes at Hip Hop Heaven, get their hair cut at Harlan's or sit at the tables in the Forest Avenue Library.

But this was different because there was a feeling that they could band together and get some things fixed.

Yolanda Shavers is 27 and she's been in town for about six months. She's got some issues with the other blacks around here and she doesn't hold back. During the session she talked about rude store clerks and how blacks don't treat each other with respect.

By the end of the evening she saw another side, a chance to maybe even change things.

"It's very impressive to see people come out like this, disagree, respect each other's opinions and hang together. It was vibrant and emotional but never hostile. I came because I live here now and don't want to be on the outside. But I wasn't expecting a lot. I just wish more people were here."

Other folks said pretty much the same thing. They showed up thinking it was a good idea, but figuring it would be another one of those meetings — sitting there listening to somebody drone on, keeping one eye on the clock.

When this was over, folks were in no hurry to leave. They stood around the room, the halls, the parking lot and they kept talking. They exchanged phone numbers and business cards. Ask around and just about all of them said they'd make the December meeting. A lot of them said they'll bring a friend or two.

Jesus bus gets trashed, but owner's faith unflappable

October 13, 2004

Willard Van Sant called the other morning to let me know the Jesus bus has been vandalized, and pretty much destroyed.

So I go out to meet him and he shows me the damage.

Every window and light shattered, tires slashed, paint thrown all over it, the inside set on fire.

Van Sant — the guy who owns the bus — wanted to talk about it, get the word out and let people know what he's been through. He mentioned several times that it would be nice if folks came up with some money to help him out.

But he won't call the cops.

"They've got other things to do. The Lord will make things better. Vengeance is mine, sayeth the Lord. I will recompense."

The bus is a traveling mission with about nine beds. It's completely covered with stuff about Jesus, prayer and sin.

Van Sant has been driving this around Des Moines for the past few years offering desperate people a place to sleep, a meal and a safety zone.

This is how he spends his life. I know this guy, and on some level he's one of the sweetest, most selfless human beings you will ever meet.

And on some level he comes across like a complete nut case.

We're talking and I'm looking at his denim overalls with the word Jesus spray-painted on the left leg and Christ on the right. The front of his vest says: RU SAVED?"

The back says: "RU REALLY SAVED?"

There are about 20 other Jesus-related comments on the vest, his pants, his shirt and his T-shirt.

I keep trying to get him to focus on the fact that a crime has been committed. He wants to talk about the big picture. He's quoting the Bible — Corinthians, Matthew, Luke and a bunch of folks I'd never heard of.

In all of these quotes he hears the Lord telling him to get that bus back on the road.

"I made myself poor for righteousness. Jesus says: 'Feed my

sheep, feed my lambs.' I've got to do the greater work that he did."

It's tough to figure out, but you get the point.

This past spring he bought a mobile home — "God got me a good deal. Only $1,000, but I had to fix the roof."

So he hasn't been driving the bus. He's been keeping it on a 12-acre flood plain off Beaver on the north end of the city. He set up a little camping area with a grill, some chairs, a prayer space and a large water tank for baptisms.

But the vandals have been coming through there all summer, chipping away at the bus, splashing paint on it, breaking the headlights.

This past weekend they set it on fire and finished it off.

Van Sant thinks he knows who did it. When he got back to his place last week there were six or seven teenagers there. They were just hanging around, but Van Sant got a bad vibe from them.

"The Lord let me feel fear, like they wanted to kill me or something. I think these boys were running on Satan's thoughts. They were devilish, demonic, ornery and mean."

So why would the Lord allow this to happen? What was he thinking when he created these kids?

"Man has free will. You can serve the Lord or serve the devil."

I nod, he pauses, looks at what's left of his bus and then looks toward the sky.

"I will not be defeated. I will serve the Lord no matter what happens."

Then he mentions once more that it would be nice if folks came up with a few bucks to help him out.

I threw the guy a 5 and told him I still think he should call the cops.

Racism fueled a life of growth

March 10, 2004

You don't meet many folks with the style, energy and self-confidence of Veola Perry. She's a dancer and a teacher, a parent, a political activist, a mentor. She does yoga and tai chi.

And she's the same woman whether she's talking to group of several hundred or if she's in your face one-on-one.

You see her around Des Moines and she's all smiles, upbeat, a back-slapper. Catch her with the Gateway Dance Theater and she's a star. She'll tell you she's "happy and proud. I love who I am."

But right below the surface there are the remnants of another Veola Perry. There's a self-hating child — who hated her black skin, her hair.

Talk with Perry about how that girl became this woman and she takes you back about 40 years to a cotton field in Collierville, a Tennessee town outside of Memphis. She takes you back to that day when she was in fifth grade. She was a quiet kid who loved to read, and that day she was doing what she did every day after school — she was picking cotton. She remembers it was sunny and she remembers feeling good about things.

She was bent over, working, her eyes down, making sure there were no snakes or bugs.

Then a pickup truck came by with four or five teenagers in it, white boys, and they were yelling at her and the others in the field — her parents, her four sisters, some neighbors.

"Don't put this in the newspaper, but you know what they were saying. They just kept screaming and yelling that word over and over, calling us all kinds of names. I heard that and I just couldn't stand up again. I was stuck there on the ground. I couldn't move. I kept going over it in my mind, saying to myself, 'So this is what people think of me.' I felt like I was nothing. Nothing."

That wasn't the first time Perry heard those words. Growing up black in the south during the 1950s and '60s, racism was a part of the mix. She knew her place, she knew she had to move aside and keep her head down when she passed white folks on the street. She heard the mumbling and the laughter when she passed. Even at 10 years old, she was hardened.

But this was different, and she couldn't get over it. The pain was deep and it stayed. It got worse over time.

For years after that incident — all through her teens — Perry could not look at herself in the mirror.

"I just saw this black face — this face that had been spit at and laughed at — and I felt all this anger and shame, and I had to turn away. I just stopped looking at myself."

The years passed, she went through middle school and high school, and each year she went deeper inside herself, got more angry.

She didn't see it at the time, but there was a positive piece to all this. Her interest in reading became a passion. Then late in high school she branched out from the novels and history books, and started reading magazines that were aimed at a black audience. She read Jet and Ebony, and she saw beautiful black models, black people with nice homes and nice clothes. She started to see the possibilities. Slowly, she started to feel better about herself.

By the time she got to college in the late '60s — LeMoyne-Owen College in Memphis — it was a different world, and Veola Perry was a different person.

She had role models — from Martin Luther King Jr. and Malcolm X to H. Rap Brown and, her favorite, Angela Davis.

"Angela was a woman who wasn't afraid to say what needed to be said. She didn't hide her blackness. I loved her hair. Then I started loving my hair, my skin."

Perry got a bachelor's degree in 1970 and came to Drake for a master's. She kept growing. She graduated and taught around Des Moines for 33 years.

These days she's that woman with all the style, energy and self-confidence. She's spending her time dancing, mentoring young girls.

She's getting involved in local politics — Ako Abdul Samad's run for the school board, Ruth Ann Gaines' bid for the City Council.

But spend an hour with her and, at least once, a sadness drifts in. Perry will have to catch herself, breathe deep and take a moment to deal with that little girl.

Queen of innuendo relishes
her role on stage
March 15, 2004

It's 10:30 at night, the bar's crowded, noisy, smoky. The band's taking a break and Pinkie's on stage doing standup. She's got the place laughing loud and hard.

The jokes — she calls them stories — are funny, and hearing them come from an 87-year-old woman gives them more of an edge.

But here's the hook: She was up there for about a half-hour, told a dozen jokes and it was almost impossible to find even one that I could put in the paper.

Pinkie makes no apologies.

"I tell dirty stories. I used to tell clean stories, but nobody laughed."

She never once used an obscenity. She didn't have to. She's the queen of innuendo.

I'll paraphrase:

These two immigrant women arrive in the U.S. for the first time and they're walking the streets in Manhattan and they see a hot dog stand. One of them says: "I didn't know they ate dogs in America."

The other one says: "I didn't either, but let's just eat what Americans eat."

So they order two hot dogs and the guy wraps them up and hands them to the women. They go sit on a bench to eat and one of them unwraps it, looks at what she's holding and says to the other: "What body part did you get?"

Not her best joke, but you get the idea.

I've been hearing about Pinkie for years. People have been telling me I should go catch her act — "You won't believe it."

I kept putting it off. Then the other night I was sitting in front of the stage at Blues on Grand, listening to her and thinking: "How did this woman end up here?"

Pinkie is Margaret Bernice Pinck from Eagle Grove. She had serious heart problems as a kid, spent one year of her childhood in bed, and wasn't expected to make it past 16.

"I survived. My 16th birthday was the happiest day of my life."

Back in 1940 when she was still living in Wright County, she was voted "Clarion's Most Courteous Working Girl." A year later she moved to Des Moines and in 1946 she was waiting tables at The Des Moines Building Restaurant and was voted "The Second Most Charming Waitress in the City of Des Moines." Then for about 30 years she worked in the budget office for the federal ag department. She's been married a few times — divorced once, widowed once. About 10 years ago she met a guy at her church and they moved in together.

"We have kept it strictly as friends and so it has worked out well for both of us. As far as I'm concerned, he's more like a son. Some people early on thought we were lovers, but I quickly set them straight."

Her comedy act is part of a package. The show opens with the band Fat Tuesday, a quintet of 50-somethings. They play blues-rock, but throw in tunes like "16 Tons" on the outside chance that anybody besides Pinkie remembers Tennessee Ernie Ford.

Then late in the first set they bring on Jimmy "Midnight Cowboy" Pryor, also in his 80s. But you wouldn't know it. He's still got the moves.

Pryor — a member of the Iowa Blues Hall of Fame — rocks out with stuff like "Route 66" and "C.C. Rider."

When Pryor is done, it's time for Pinkie.

This started only about four years ago. She's friends with one of the guys in Fat Tuesday and was always telling him her jokes. One night the band was playing at Buzzard Billy's, she was there and they invited her up on stage to do her shtick. The crowd loved it. They tried it a few more times at different gigs and it worked.

Now she's a regular with the band and she's branching out, working with Lavender Lace and Melanie Wright. There's talk about getting her on the program for the zoo's annual fund-raiser at Hoyt Sherman this spring.

She can't believe what's happening at this point in her life.

"I can be down in the dumps, but I get up on that stage, see people laughing and having a good time and I am quickly out of my dumps."

Seriously. She wasn't trying to be funny.

Shop is closing; owner laments D.M.'s provincial nature

May 31, 2004

Rhonda Fingerman chooses her words carefully. This is her town, and she doesn't want people to get the wrong idea when she calls Des Moines "provincial."

She put it this way: "It's provincial, but still quite charming."

The charming part is what she loves about living here. The provincial part is what makes her crazy.

The provincial part is also what got her to open a quirky gift shop in the Shops at Roosevelt. And now — three years later — it's what helped put the huge "Going out of business" sign in the front window.

Maybe this town just wasn't ready for what she was selling.

Maybe this town just couldn't deal with Fingerman's edgy approach. She's not the type who fawns all over folks when they walk in the store. But she says it's nothing personal.

"I don't like it when I walk in a store and people are all over me. Why would I behave that way here? I'm polite, but I don't overdo it."

She said she's burned out from dealing with the public and has decided to close the shop and try something else. She'll find another way to earn a living. She'll keep looking for ways to make this city more user-friendly.

"You don't want to lose the things that make Des Moines unique and manageable. But we also have to make it more welcoming and more comfortable to transplants. People from other places get frustrated living here. If there's a problem and they can't find what they want, they leave."

Fingerman is 41 and comes at this from both angles. She's a native — born and raised here, Roosevelt class of 1980, Drake graduate, small-business owner.

She's also something of a transplant. She spent all of the 1990s in New York — living in the West Village and Gramercy Park, working for Liz Claiborne in Times Square.

She got used to what she calls "the urban flavor." She loved the action and diversity. She took advantage of what the city had to offer — cooking classes at the U.N., midnight tours of Central Park, the 92nd Street Y.

But she missed her hometown, her family and the manageable lifestyle she grew up with.

"After 11 years, I was exhausted. You can't sleep out there with all the noise. And it's expensive. I was living paycheck to paycheck."

So in the fall of 2000 she sold her 575-square-foot Manhattan apartment and bought a 2,850-square-foot south Des Moines house for one-third the price.

Then she had this idea: open a quirky gift shop, a place that caters to the folks looking for something different, unique. It would be a place with an urban feel.

Fingerman's Drake business degree and her 20 years in retail and marketing gave her some insight and helped get things started.

She put together a business plan and strategy, and then found 96 vendors for the stuff she needed. She got financing, picked a location, and in April 2001, she opened the doors of "Whatever."

It's unique. From the body-shaped corkscrews to the zodiac therapy candles — a different scent for each sign.

Walk the aisles, and you see the curved, mellow-colored drinking glasses next to dinner plates with an attitude.

As one writer described it: "Transparent glass bowls flecked with neon-bright hues sit next to tall, striped stoneware vases. Collections of smooth, stainless kitchen tools by Stelton contrast with a black plastic spice rack that looks like a set of oversized hatpins."

Then there's the bath and beauty area — called "lotions and potions" in the business. It's the first thing you see when you walk into the shop, last thing on the way out.

You have everything from Dirty Girl skin cream to Total Bitch body wash — with a rack of MoFo soap in the middle.

Virgin bubble bath shares shelf space with a whole line of Slut products. And there are a few other things.

It's fun stuff. It caught on with Fingerman's customers.

"This is the fastest-moving category of products. Women in Des Moines like to be self-indulgent."

Having said that, she's closing the shop but staying in town. It'll be interesting to see what's next for Rhonda Fingerman, a woman who can be quite charming, and not particularly provincial.

No shortage of stories about Reichardt's passion

June 2, 2004

It was time to say goodbye and about two dozen people were jammed into the hospital room. They stood around Bill Reichardt's deathbed holding hands, crying and waiting.

They were all there — his wife and three kids, the grandkids. His two sisters had flown in from the East Coast. His pals — guys like Wayne Graham, Bill Krause, Randy Duncan — were there for the family and for each other. There were a few guys who've known Reichardt since grade school in Iowa City. Some played football with him at Iowa. Some knew him from business, politics and the other phases of his 73 years.

Some friends couldn't be there, but they called, folks like Jim Zabel, Barb Henry and Johnny Majors.

At one point a nurse came by to tell them how she used to see the Reichardt TV ads and at the end she'd always chime in and say: "I'm Bill Reichardt and I own the store."

This crowd got it. Smiles all around. They thanked her for sharing.

A priest came in and recited the Lord's Prayer. Bill Reichardt lay there silently, breathing heavily. Two of his granddaughters reached out to touch his arms. They told him how much they loved him.

When the prayers ended, they all drifted out into the hall, holding onto each other.

In the middle of the pack was Sue Reichardt, the woman who married Bill 52 years ago next month. She still remembers the first time she laid eyes on the guy. It was 1951 on the Iowa campus. She was in her car and she saw him in her side mirror.

"He was wearing his ROTC uniform I looked at him and said, 'That's for me.' We started dating, got married and ever since then my life has been an adventure. This wonderful adventure," she said. "He was a very unique person."

Around the hall they were telling their Reichardt stories, sharing memories. More than one person mentioned that he was the Big Ten MVP in a year when the school didn't win a single game.

There was the well-known Reichardt quote about how it costs

more to send a kid to Eldora than it does to Harvard.

His daughter, Barb — in from Denver — told about the time he took her out west to look at colleges and the only thing he wanted to see was the football stadium.

And everybody had a story about Reichardt helping kids. That was his passion and nobody could quite figure out where that came from.

But Sue had a few thoughts.

She mentioned that when he was growing up his parents owned the fabled Reich's Cafe in Iowa City and it was pretty much a seven-day-a-week operation.

"He was a middle-class kid and never went hungry or anything like that. But he was alone a lot of the time and I think that may have opened his eyes to what some kids go through."

She stopped to deal with the tears.

"When he was coaching, there were kids who had to walk miles to get to the field. The families didn't have cars, the kids didn't have bikes. And they'd have to walk in their uniforms. Bill made sure every one of them got a ride. In some ways it was a small thing but it meant so much to those kids and their families."

I heard that story and it reminded me of a I guy I met a few years ago at a Roosevelt sports dinner. He was a big guy, African-American, and he talked about playing football as a kid. He talked about how sports really saved him. And he talked about "that Bill Reichardt. The clothing guy? He made it happen for me. He saved a lot of kids in this town. Ask around."

Last night, I didn't have to ask around. I just had to stand there and listen. The Bill Reichardt stories were in the air.

For desperate mom, piece of advice trumps $100

August 9, 2004

Her kid was sick, and Cathy Westercamp was broke and desperate. But she had an idea, a plan to make things better.

She went out looking for money, knocking on doors, hitting up businesses around Des Moines. She needed $65 and had raised about $22.

Then she walked into this shop, and saw a guy she recognized. He used to own the place. She told him her story.

"I told him I needed money to get my daughter into a swimming program. This was four years ago. She was 5 at that time. Swimming helped with her asthma. It was incredible how much better she was when she was swimming."

Then Westercamp pauses and gets real serious. She chooses each word carefully.

"He looked at me, right in the eye, and he said, 'I'll give you a choice. I can write you a check for $100, or you can take my advice.' I looked around, and this man was obviously very smart and successful. I wanted the money, but I didn't want to be rude, so I told him I'd take the advice."

The guy told Westercamp to go downtown to the YMCA and tell them her story.

"He said: 'You tell them what you just told me, and if they don't help you, you come back here and see me.' He was talking and tapping his finger on the counter. I'll never forget that moment."

Westercamp went down to the Y and told them her story. They took some information about her finances, crunched the numbers, and then gave her family a swimming scholarship.

Westercamp, her husband and three kids all got into swimming. They learned together.

For the first two years they got Y scholarships. Now they've got a few bucks and pay on a sliding scale.

And Elle — the child who was sick — got better. No more attacks where she couldn't breathe. No more being hooked up to a face mask at night.

The doctors were stunned at her recovery. Everybody else is

stunned to see all the other things that happened with her over the past four years.

Elle Westercamp is now a national star.

She's one of the country's top swimmers in her age group, one of the fastest. She's won all kinds of awards in swim meets around the United States.

Folks who know Elle say in time she'll be on the U.S. Olympic swim team. She's already won gold and silver medals in the Olympic-sanctioned State Games of America.

Last month she was in D.C. at a Senate Appropriations Committee hearing where the YMCA announced plans to help communities get healthy. On that trip she met and spoke with federal Health and Human Services Secretary Tommy Thompson.

Her mother talks about this stuff, shakes her head, gets teary-eyed, and swears none of it would have happened if she hadn't been sent down to the Y that day.

"I never would have gone, and I suspect my daughter would still be struggling. I honestly think he knew what he was doing for my family."

Not long after their encounter, she called the guy and thanked him.

"But at the time, I didn't realize how much I owed him. It was too soon."

Over the years she'd see him around town, but didn't approach him. Sometimes she'd see him on TV.

"I'd see him and get this warm feeling, like I was seeing an old friend. I'd stop what I was doing and listen to whatever he had to say."

But she never told anybody what happened, what she owed the guy. Then a few months ago he died, and Westercamp felt guilty. She felt like she just never thanked him enough.

So when she saw one of the guy's sons at the YMCA recently, she went up and told him her story.

"I felt good after I told him. I wanted him to know how his father reached out and changed our lives. And I just know that I'm not the only person he's done this for."

For some folks, Westercamp's encounter with a Des Moines businessman is a life-defining tale of fate, compassion and human kindness.

For others, it's just one more Bill Reichardt story.

Megan's Nazi tattoos fading with the bad old days

October 6, 2004

This started about a year ago, back when Megan was 17. Her life was already a mess. Then it fell apart.

Her best friend was in the hospital after stabbing himself, and Megan was crashing after a six-day drug binge — meth, coke.

She can't tell you where she was living in those days, but she remembers seeing herself in the mirror. She looked at the swastika on her left cheek and the other Nazi symbol on her right, the gang tattoos she got a few months earlier when she joined the Aryan Nation.

She stared at what she'd done to her face.

She pulled her hair forward and tried to cover the sides of her head. That didn't help. She cried.

She thought about how screwed up her life was. She had one of those bad childhoods, complete with abuse. She was a runaway and quit school after spending three years in ninth grade.

She kept going over all that, and she kept crying. That didn't help, so she figured the best thing would be to just kill herself and get it over with.

"Back then I was always thinking about suicide. I was already dying slowly, so why not? Then for some reason I called my parents and asked them to help me get into rehab."

Her folks got her into a program, and over the next 12 months Megan put the drugs and gangs behind her, got her GED and even got a driver's license.

It was the first time she was feeling something that resembled self-confidence. She wasn't quite there, but she didn't hate herself as much as she usually did.

She started to dream about having a life, a family, a job.

But she still had those anti-Semitic tattoos. And she's still not sure why. It wasn't political. She just wanted to fit in.

Out in her hometown — in the eastern Iowa city of Clinton — there was a small gang of kids who claimed to be members of the Aryan Nation. These were the kids she grew up with, went to school with. She wanted to be part of the clique.

"I didn't really think about it. That's all I knew. There were other kids doing it, getting tattoos, getting small ones. But I wanted to show off, so I got big ones on my face. I was high when I did it, and the minute I came down I wanted them gone."

But they weren't leaving, and she figured that would be it for the rest of her life.

Last week Megan was lying on an examining table in Peter Boesen's West Des Moines clinic. She was having her face worked on with a laser. The heat fractures the ink and clears things up — "like butter in a frying pan," according to the folks doing the work.

And there's a real demand for this stuff.

Hang around the clinic and you hear about the woman in her 50s who was on vacation in Hawaii, had a few drinks and decided to have a flower tattooed on her ankle. She got home and now she's having second thoughts.

There are all these twenty-somethings with the names of old girlfriends or boyfriends tattooed on various body parts.

Then there are the ex-gang members, folks trying to do a radical lifestyle change. Folks like Megan.

She's now had the second of about a half-dozen treatments, and the tattoos are getting lighter.

It was painful and there would be blisters, but it wasn't costing her anything because the Boesen crew is offering a free ride to former gang members. It's a growing market.

Jim Boesen is the doctor's brother, and he speaks for the clinic. He said normally this would go for about $1,000.

"But instead of charging them, we'd like to see them go out and do some community service."

Megan said she hasn't locked into any service plan because she just found a job — her first. She'll be on the cleaning staff at a utility company near Clinton.

And as the tattoos fade, she's hoping to move up. Her dream is to get a union job. She wants to be a welder.

"For me, that's aiming high."

"So I'm talkin' to this guy . . ."

Chapter 4: On the Beat

By Dennis Ryerson
Editor/*The Indianapolis Star*

You don't have to be among the high rollers and the literati to have a story, and nobody knows that better than Rob Borsellino.

He's been "on the beat" with ordinary people since his days growing up in the Bronx projects during the 50s and 60s: Shopping for his mother at the fishmongers on Arthur Avenue. Catching the subway for the ride to Manhattan. Hanging out with a special gang of kids who grew up to be business owners and Ph.D scientists but who never forgot their roots.

Here are the stories of the women bowlers at Val Lanes, the priest who tends to the flock at Cooney's bar in Beaverdale, the owner of the pie shop in Bondurant, the singer in a karaoke bar, and many more.

These are ordinary people who, thanks to Rob's gift of storytelling, share their extraordinary lives.

Des Moines apartments benefit from a little tough love

September 24, 1998

Ray Yowell carries the scars from five gunshot wounds, three stabbings and three failed marriages. Over the years he's been a construction worker, a trucker, a horse trainer, a farmer, a welder, a bouncer, a bodyguard and the assistant director at the Ogallala Home for the Handicapped in Nebraska.

He likes motorcycles and he likes action.

But by last summer, Ray, 50, and Annie, 52 — his fourth wife — were touching bottom. He was suffering from something called organic brain syndrome — it causes seizures and blackouts — and they were homeless, camping out at Jester Park. They were out of work, out of money and just about out of options.

Then some guy they knew wired a deal where Ray could take over as manager of a 10-apartment building on 19th Street in the Sherman Hill area of Des Moines. Ray and Annie got one of the apartments for themselves and they moved in last November.

They were told it was a nice, quiet place to live.

Rent runs about $325 to $450 and in those nine apartments Ray says he found two hookers, two crack dealers, a meth dealer and — in one two-bedroom apartment — six people who were raising pit bulls.

Ray Yowell, the son of an Oregon lumberjack, doesn't think he'll ever forget what those first few days were like.

"You come in the building and the first thing you smell is crack and marijuana. They'd be screaming, yelling and fighting at all hours. It don't matter the time. I went up to the third floor just to see what was what and some guy pulled a knife on me.

"The mailboxes was ripped out. We had nobody here that was a real legitimate married type of family. One girl was running a whorehouse on the third floor and she had a 2-year-old and a 6-year-old and one other kid that would come and go. It angers me what these kids learn in these situations. Every night there'd be fights in this parking lot out here. It was anything goes.

"In one 24-hour period I counted 125 people that went in and out of the building. We couldn't even figure out how many people lived here. I been sober now for 11 years, but let me tell you, this place could drive you to drink."

Ray didn't drink. He cleaned up the place. He did the little things. He posted "No Smoking" and "No Noise" signs in the lobby. He put a sign over the mailboxes telling people mail tampering is a federal offense.

He cleaned out the abandoned basement, put in a washer-dryer set and made storage areas to give tenants a place to put their stuff. He removed the car parts and the burned-out mattress that littered the alley behind the building. He cleaned the piles of broken glass in the back yard and set up a little picnic table and barbecue grill. They cleared brush and Annie planted a vegetable garden.

And he did the big things.

He put the numbers of the vice and narcotics squad on the wall by his phone and he called every time somebody got out of line. City police records show they were out to the building 43 times between March and August for everything from narcotics and weapons to cruelty to animals.

He handed out seven-day notices, telling the troublemakers they had a week to get their act together or they'd be thrown out. Some were evicted, some left on their own.

All of them are gone now.

They've been replaced by guys like Hale Wilson, a cook at Zimm's who goes by the name J.R.

He moved there in January, when the madness was still in full swing.

"I don't know what Ray's been saying but I can tell you there was no rules. There was total chaos. The tenants ran the place. You couldn't go in the hall without somebody trying to sell you a rock. When I rented they told me they had some problems but all that was going to change. Now it's really a good place."

And Ray and Annie Yowell — not long ago homeless, down and out — are feeling pretty good about things. Annie's taking a computer course and Ray says he's enjoying some of the peace and quiet he was expecting.

"But it's never really quiet around here," he said. "Some woman that used to live here came by this morning and threatened to kill Annie. Otherwise, things have been good."

Class on Judaism is a good primer for Jews, non-Jews alike

December 15, 1998

You'd figure a 46-year-old guy named Abe Goldstien — from an Orthodox family — would know whatever he needed to know about being a Jew. But there was Goldstien sitting quietly in the temple basement the other night, a student in Rabbi Steven Fink's "Introduction to Judaism."

Goldstien and his 30 or so classmates were an interesting mix of laborers and lawyers, high-powered business-types and folks who are unemployed. There were new arrivals to Des Moines and a few from families that helped build this town. The common thread was an interest in learning more about what it means to be Jewish. And at this time of year — the full-employment season for the Christmas Industrial Complex — there was a lot of talk about Hanukkah.

Goldstien was there with Jackie Garnett, his girlfriend. Garnett's a Baptist and wants to get a better handle on what her man believes and why he believes it. So he was there for her.

That was pretty much the same deal with Steve Nadel, a Des Moines lawyer who's been dating JoEllen Sanders for almost five years. They haven't gotten around to setting a date, but marriage is a possibility.

"I'm cautious about this," said Nadel. "You don't want to force religion on someone. It'll come back to haunt you. But JoEllen wants to know and I don't feel like I know enough. So we're here."

Sanders works at Principal and was raised Catholic. "Very Catholic. I'm one of seven kids. I want to be able to celebrate holidays with Steve's family. I just find it all fascinating. It's a different world and I enjoy learning about it."

And if the two get married, there's the question of children and how they'd be raised.

Nadel says both families "are very supportive of us (as a couple). But the kid issue is unspoken on both sides."

Across the room, Ron Herzog had different reasons for taking the 24-week course. Herzog grew up in a Jewish enclave in New York City in the '50s and, early on, developed a bad feeling about religion.

Like a lot of kids, he got through his bar mitzvah by memorizing the lines and giving little thought to what any of it meant.

"I grew up in a house where they spoke Yiddish only because they didn't want us kids to know what was going on. I believed that everything that went bad, or anything that happened, was God getting even with me. Over the years I tried different churches. I tried Buddhism. But in my heart I was a Jew."

He says the course and the people in it have taught him "this is a religion totally different from what I was led to believe. It's much more interesting."

Fink — who teaches the course with Rabbis Neil Sandler and Martin Applebaum — was glad Herzog said that. He saw it as a step toward the course's goal: giving folks the grounding they need so that Jews who marry outside the faith might raise their kids as Jews. Or, ideally, that the non-Jew will convert.

On this night the talk is not about marriage, but about Hanukkah. It's a rather minor event on the Jewish calendar but, for obvious reasons, Hanukkah and Passover have become the most celebrated holidays among American Jews.

Fink showed an Israeli-made animated film about the holiday. Then Goldstien hauled out his accordion — "I wanted a bike. My parents bought me this" — and they sang some Hanukkah songs.

There was talk about what it's like to be a Jew at this time of year. About how it feels to have the only house on the block without Christmas lights. Or the only house with a menorah in the window. Fink says he and his sister were the only Jews in their elementary school "and it was awful to have to be the one to sing the obligatory Hanukkah song at the holiday assembly."

That hit home with Daniel Klein, who grew up in heavily Catholic Argentina. He talked about "not wanting to stand out, but at this time of year we were always reminded of our identity." Herzog weighed in, saying that for years he was "totally intimidated in a Christian world. But I'm learning not to feel that way."

Then something interesting began to emerge. They started kicking around the idea of Hanukkah as a sanctuary, a time to bond with the family and not get caught in the path of the Christmas machine.

As a time to celebrate and a time to reach back and feel a lot of pride in who you are and where you came from.

Work that takes the patience of a saint, plus a strong back

December 22, 1998

The pay's terrible, the hours are lousy, the work involves a lot of heavy lifting, and when folks hear what Carol Garver does for a living they usually tell her it sounds depressing.

But Garver has a different take on her job.

"It's a joy. I love this, and every time I think about doing something else, something with maybe better pay, I just know I'll never feel about the work the way I feel about this."

Garver's an aide in a Windsor Heights group home for severely retarded children. The place is unique because it's also a foster home, so Garver and the other folks who work there are, in some cases, the only family these six kids have.

The kids — four girls and two boys — are between the ages of 9 and 18. For the most part, they can't speak. Some can't walk. Only one can feed himself. They get up at about 4:30 in the morning. Diapers have to be changed, the kids have to be bathed, fed and dressed.

A simple task — getting a child a glass of water — can become a production. The water is often spilled and the table and floor have to be wiped up and clothes might have to be changed. This kind of work takes the patience of a saint, a good heart and a strong back.

Garver, 36, seems suited for the job

On this morning, she's sitting on a couch cradling a 14-year-old named Katy. In front of them, on the floor, another 14-year-old — Kara — is sitting quietly and staring straight ahead. Across the room, Bryan, 9, lets out an occasional scream. Nikki, 18, is sitting on a chair and has managed to curl her entire body up onto the cushion. Jamie, 13, is in front of the TV.

And Dustin, an 11-year-old who can barely walk and talk, but is considered the highest functioning child in the home, is in the kitchen sitting in his wheelchair and helping to make lunch. His job is to crush the crackers that will be used in the meatloaf.

Garver strokes Katy's hair.

"There's a misconception that working here is very depressing. But the kids are actually happy most of the time. There are things about it that are sad. Katy has a degenerative disease. She might not make it. We know that. So every day we make sure to put a smile on her face, on every one of their faces. It's great to be a part of that."

Garver grew up in Des Moines, graduated from North, was an English major at Iowa for a few years and came back to Des Moines in '86, out of work and looking for something to do.

An ad in the paper caught her eye: "Do You Love Kids?" She interviewed at the Convalescent Home for Children in Johnston and got the job. When that agency opened the group home in Windsor Heights in '89, Garver went to work there.

Before joining the agency, she'd never spent much time around kids and had no dealings with anyone — child or adult — who used a wheelchair.

Looking back, she's surprised she got through those first few years. She was naive, got too emotionally involved and, in her mind, failed the kids. That first year, in particular, was the toughest. One little girl — a child Garver got very close to — died.

"I guess I was just overwhelmed. I felt like I wasn't doing enough for the kids, like I just couldn't measure up. The only way to do this work properly is to approach it as if these are your own kids. And then one of them dies or one of them moves away and it's very, very tough. But this is about the children's needs."

And right now, the children need to have a nice holiday. So the house has been decorated for Christmas, the tree is up, six stockings are hung on the fireplace. Wednesday night, everybody will pile into a van and they'll go to Waterworks Park and see the lights.

Some volunteers and the staffers — whose pay starts at $7.50 an hour — put together money to buy gifts for the kids.

If there's any doubt as to why folks like Garver do what they do, on the wall near the front door there's one of those hokey posters with inspirational sayings on them. This one — called Priorities — was hanging right next to a row of wheelchairs. "A hundred years from now it will not matter what my bank account was, the sort of house I lived in or the kind of car I drove," it says. "But the world may be different because I was important in the life of a child."

Back in the living room, Garver was still sitting on the couch, stroking Katy's hair.

The locals let loose as singing stars on the karaoke circuit

January 19, 1999

Five days a week Joannie McGregor works the counter at an eastside Subway shop, and when she gets the sandwiches right nobody applauds. But come Saturday night — karaoke night at Gene's Place near the fairgrounds — Joannie McGregor is a star.

She takes the stage in her tight jeans and black leather jacket, her long blond hair going side-to-side. Even the guys watching the Chuck Norris show on the wide-screen TV look up. The folks along the bar, the ones on the video games and people at the tables around the club stop what they're doing to catch McGregor's act. When she breaks into one of her signature tunes — "Harper Valley PTA" — the place is with her.

And when it's over, they let her know she nailed it. McGregor bows with the style of a diva on opening night at the Met and takes a seat over near the pool table.

She'll be back later to give them a dose of "Hit Me With Your Best Shot."

But now it's Shirley Slocum's turn. Shirley, an amateur ventriloquist who's done her act out at the Funny Bone, is celebrating her birthday and the crowd knows it. She sings "Hello" — an old Lionel Richie tune. Her friends slow dance in front of the stage, and Shirley — like Joannie before her and everybody that follows — is a star.

If you go to karaoke bars looking to hear folks who sound like Pavarotti, you might just pass. It's mostly off-key singing with a few high spots. This is where the guy who works two jobs can go and have a few beers and let loose with a Hank Williams tune. It's karaoke on Saturday, bowling on Sunday, and come Monday he's back on the line making $10 an hour.

Maybe on Tuesday he'll hit Anthony's Lounge in Altoona — just to see who else is on the karaoke circuit.

At Gene's, Mike King runs the show — keeping track of the play list, making sure the music flows and filling the dead spots. On a busy night King might only get to sing four or five songs. On a slow night he'll do 15. King grew up on the east side, went to East High and he's been singing karaoke for about five years — "I heard the applause one night and I got hooked."

And he runs the show at a bunch of bars: Gene's, Hull Avenue Tap on East Ninth, Waters Edge in Polk City and John's down in Norwalk.

"I love it. I love to put on a show. Look at this crowd. What could be better?"

Friday morning at 8:30 he's hosting a three-hour show at Gene's for a bunch of overnight postal workers and some dispatchers from the sheriff's department.

"It's a good crowd. They come in and sing and they can put away as much as anybody. It's a good way to unwind after work."

Mike's talking and Joannie McGregor comes over and asks him to team up with her on "Stop Dragging My Heart Around." It's a deal. They take the stage, each grabs a mike and the crowd makes them feel special.

A half-hour later and a few miles west, the folks at the Firehouse Lounge are getting misty listening to a guy in a Vikings sweat shirt sing "How Can You Mend a Broken Heart?"

It looks like 3 a.m. in a Brooklyn saloon when Sinatra comes on the jukebox. You could almost see the wiseguys at the bar nodding their heads and getting teary-eyed as Frank goes on about some woman who done him wrong.

But here, just as things start to get mellow, Jim Hamilton steps up and belts out as good a rendition of "Green River" as you're going hear on this side of the '60s.

Hamilton handles the karaoke machine for the Firehouse. He's a student of the genre. He knows it started in Japan and hit the coasts by '79. Hamilton's been at it for about 10 years. Before that he played guitar and piano and was a sideman for a string of touring country singers — from Ernest Tubb and Faron Young to Tex Ritter and Mickey Gilley.

"I got burned out on the band scene and got into this. It's a big draw in these bars. Sometimes you get some real talent."

Hamilton's talking, but it's hard to make out what he's saying. A guy from Nebraska is at the mike and he's rocking the crowd with "Sweet Home Alabama." Hamilton says the best thing is to just shut up and listen. Or, better yet, get up there and sing.

Veteran's photos document horror of concentration camp

June 1, 1999

Bennett Gordon is an elegant man. Soft-spoken, cultured and well-traveled, more prone to understatement than exaggeration. He looks right at home among the white-linen tablecloths, crystal and the other high-end surroundings of the Des Moines Club.

But the story Gordon is telling this day is not about the finer things in life. He's talking about that morning 54 years ago when he stumbled on something that would haunt his waking hours to this day.

It was late in the war — May of '45 — and 32-year-old Maj. Bennett Gordon of Des Moines was with the 11th Armored Division rolling across Austria. They'd fought their way through Belgium — the Battle of the Bulge — and now they were looking to hook up with the Russians. There'd been rumors that something was coming — something big — but there were always rumors in the service.

Then they saw the camp.

"We just came on it. I had no idea when I got up that morning what I'd see that day. There were at least 500 bodies dumped on wheelbarrows to be carted over to an open grave, which was partially full of bodies. The mind doesn't comprehend what the hell's going on. How could one man do this to another? Every cliche you could think of comes to mind."

Gordon and the others walked around the camp for hours, not realizing until later that the coat of ash on the ground was the aftermath of some 45,000 bodies being burned in the Mauthausen crematorium.

Thousands more were gassed, hung, shot, poisoned and beaten to death. The bodies in the wheelbarrows were men — Russians, Poles, Yugoslavs — who died of starvation. There were about a half-dozen men still alive and Gordon said he could count each of their ribs from 50 yards away. Even these combat veterans were silenced by what they saw.

"And there was the stench. God awful. I have no idea how long it stayed with me. I went back to camp and tried to clean up, wash up. I finally threw my clothes away. Everybody in the world should have to smell that, just once. It would remind us of what went on there in ways that I could never express."

Gordon grabbed a camera and took pictures of everything around him — the piles of bodies, the survivors, the open graves, the gallows, the ovens in the crematorium, the other soldiers, the camp factory where the inmates were slave laborers.

The rest of Gordon's time in the Army is a hazy memory. He finished out his four-year military career on the staff of Gen. George Patton, was discharged in '46 and came back to Iowa. Over the past half-century he's told few people his story.

Even fewer have seen the photos.

"When I came home and talked to people, I never went into a lot of detail. Everybody came home with stories. I just never thought people would understand and I never could explain what it was like. Even now I find it difficult to express what my feelings were."

Last year there was a chance dinner meeting between Gordon's son Jim — a Chicago venture capitalist — and Steven Spielberg. In the aftermath of "Schindler's List," Spielberg set up the Shoah Foundation to document the experiences of the camp survivors and their liberators. He mentioned the foundation to Jim Gordon and Gordon mentioned that his dad was in the service, helped liberate Mauthausen and had photos of the camp.

It went from there.

Someone from the foundation came to Des Moines some weeks ago, interviewed Bennett Gordon and made copies of the photos.

Now Gordon's story is part of the record.

And tucked in among the photos in Gordon's collection is a letter from Spielberg, thanking him for taking part in the project.

The letter ends with the lines:

"Far into the future people will be able to see a face, hear a voice and observe a life so that they may listen and learn and always remember."

Bennett Gordon reads that sentence, folds the letter and puts it down on the table. He's silent for a moment and then says he thought about those words recently.

"It was when I heard about that shooting in Colorado, those kids honoring Hitler."

Ride has its wild side,
but it's more than that

July 29, 1999

Back when I first arrived in Iowa — I'd been here about 15 minutes — several people told me: "You have to do RAGBRAI. That's the only way you'll understand the spirit of this state."

Rag Bry? It sounded like a cross between a folk dance and the house special at a kosher deli.

And when it was explained to me, I was cold to the idea. My bike was stolen when I was 10, and the healing process has been slow and painful. In fact, I still can't look at Chuck Offenburger without breaking down in tears.

Then there was the business of pedaling 75 miles in 90-degree heat for the pleasure of pitching a tent at the Kossuth County Fairgrounds, hopping into a sleeping bag and calling it a night.

But I was intrigued by the rolling party — 7 days, 500 miles, 10,000 people. Then I've been hearing that the media turn a blind eye to all the sex and drunkenness — the seedy underbelly of what looks like a family affair.

I've been trying to fashion a way to get a feel for the event without working up a sweat. I wanted to hit some of these towns you only hear about when a 50-year-old guy takes Mom hostage and holds the local cops at bay with a shotgun.

So the other morning I packed up the car, drove to Algona, got a $37 room at what looked like a hot-sheet motel and went out looking for the spirit of RAGBRAI — and maybe a pork sandwich.

It was midafternoon, and bikers were just starting to hit town in big numbers. One woman rode by with a cell phone pasted to her ear. Goofy T-shirts were the preferred mode of attire. I haven't seen that much spandex since the days of Donna Summer and Studio 54.

Downtown Algona was beginning to stir — vendors were firing up the grills and putting $2 bottles of water on ice, musicians were tuning up. The 10-person police force was on duty. I walked around, talked with the locals.

Somebody pointed out a man who looked pleasant enough to be a 1950s TV dad.

Lynn Kueck teaches calculus at the high school and serves as mayor in his down time. Talk about upbeat and cheerful. This was a chance to showcase his town of 6,000. "It's a way for us to get people's attention, let them know we're here and what a great community we have. Otherwise, the closest they come is stopping at Casey's for a few minutes."

I started to ask the mayor about the dark side of this event, but I decided to let it pass. That would be like asking Mr. Rogers about sex.

Now the street was getting crowded. And in the crowd I found Tony Colosimo, owner of Artistic Waste Services — a Des Moines garbage company with the motto "We Talk Trash." This is his fourth RAGBRAI, "and it's pretty tame. The bad old days are over. But it's like anything else — you go looking for something, and you can find it."

Tony said a lot of the action takes place on the road — in the small towns between the host cities. "There's just a certain chemistry some of these towns have. I can't explain it. They all have beer, music, people, but sometimes it just works, and sometimes nothing happens. That's the strange thing about this bike ride."

Algona partied late into the night — on the main streets, at the fairgrounds, at the high school. But it didn't get ugly. This was not Woodstock '99.

The next morning, I got on the road early and went looking for one of those little towns Colosimo talked about. I found Ventura, population 700. As the bikers rolled in, folks lined the streets. Some applauded. Little girls in cheerleader outfits waved pompoms while their parents and grandparents offered up free water and lemonade. Not exactly party central.

Don Friesleben, 62, sat on his front lawn, leaning on his walker and watching the show. A stroke drove him into retirement two years ago and — he laughs — "this is about as exciting as it gets for me. If I weren't doing this, I'd be sitting inside doing nothing."

I asked what all this meant for his town. He said some folks were still talking about the last time the ride came through — 10 or 15 years ago. "I guess by coming here, they make us feel special."

So maybe this whole RAGBRAI deal is no deeper than that. And if some folks want to have a few beers along the way — and get naked — I'm not about to pass judgment.

For Big Earl's little boy, this Goldmine is just a business

September 21, 1999

I spend a lot of my time waiting to interview business types. Usually I'm left alone with a cup of weak coffee and an old copy of Insurance Agent Monthly.

On this afternoon I'm waiting to talk to Melvin Bryson, the guy who runs Big Earl's Goldmine. I want to check in with this young entrepreneur to see how he's handling the family dynasty in the wake of his father's murder and a devastating fire.

I've been shown to a seat in the back of the club. On stage is a dark-haired woman who is about 97 percent naked. Parts of her upper body look like they've been digitally enhanced. She's playing around with a small flashlight, shining it on herself, out at the crowd.

Bryson will be with me shortly. So I wait. The music is loud. "La Vida Loca" is coming at me from all sides. There are maybe 40 men in the place, some sitting around the dimly lit stage, most at tables farther back in the room.

There are large-screen TVs on either side of the stage. On the left, ESPN is doing a special on Joe DiMaggio. On the right, CNN is flipping from carnage somewhere on the planet to the aftermath of one hurricane and the arrival of another.

While I'm trying to concentrate on the major events of the day, a blonde walks past me wearing a black thong and a bra that doesn't come close to doing its job. She smiles. I smile.

Just another day at the office.

Two more women walk by. Thongs, tiny little tops, clear plastic spiked heels. Another round of smiles. By now the blonde is lap dancing with a guy who could be her grandfather. He's sticking bills in her G-string. Two other women are escorting customers into rooms behind dark glass for private dance lessons or some such thing.

The woman on the stage has abandoned the flashlight in favor of stuffed animals. She's hugging them, throwing them around.

A moment later I'm ushered into Bryson's modest, backroom office. My eyes give it the once over. With a few exceptions — a blood red loveseat shaped like a pair of lips, a nude poster of Marilyn

Monroe — it's utterly commonplace: hardwood desk, a few leather chairs, pictures of the kids, a pen-and-pencil set with a matching clock, jars of candy, a large bottle of Tylenol.

For Bryson, this is the family business. If his name were Hubbell or Ruan or Cowles, he'd have gone into insurance or transportation or the media. But this is Big Earl Hamilton's kid. Daddy ran a strip club.

"The toughest part is the misconception. It's just a business. People think it's some big orgy, 24 hours a day. It's the opposite. I'm a gentleman with these ladies. My wife works here. She can walk in any time, day or night. There's nothing going on. It's innocent."

I'm wondering if he's given any thought to taking down Marilyn and putting up a photo of Mother Teresa.

Bryson went to Des Moines Tech and then AIB. His parents split up when he was a baby. Over the years his father owned a bunch of businesses around town. Big Earl finally opened the strip club in the early '90s. Three years ago he was gunned down and the murder remains unsolved.

Bryson took over and things went along fine until an arsonist torched the place in March. He reopened a few weeks ago.

For six months the dancers were hustling to find other work. Victoria — her stage name — was working in a fast-food restaurant and a grocery store. She still had a hard time making the $700 rent and supporting her two kids. At 25, she knows this kind of work has a limited shelf life. She came off stage and I asked her to talk to me about her job.

"I'm here four days a week and making a nice comfortable life for my family and putting a few dollars away. I know society still thinks we're the bottom of the barrel for doing this. They think I'm brainless, easy, but they don't know me. Away from here I'm a mom. I don't dress like this. Another year and I'm going back to college."

She's talking and I can hear that whiny Dr. Laura voice saying: "You work as a stripper to support your babies! This is what motherhood has become?"

But she's working to support her babies and there's a lot to be said for that.

Doughnut shop's competitors just keep rolling along

November 4, 1999

I tried to tune out the hype and the hysteria. I did what I could to avoid any discussion of doughnuts — or even muffins, croissants, eclairs.

But I broke down the day an Urbandale woman wrote into the 2 Cents' Worth column and said, "If sex was as good as Krispy Kreme doughnuts, we'd want it all the time." Maybe I was missing something.

Then I started paying some attention to the numbers: About 3.5 million Krispy Kreme doughnuts are sold in the United States every day. That's about 1.3 billion each year — enough to circle the Earth twice. The new store in Clive can produce about 3,000 doughnuts an hour.

When the store's doughnut-making machine broke down last month and no glazed doughnuts came out for about six hours, the story made the front page of the Register business section. A fire at the State Capitol on Monday only rated a mention inside the metro section. It's obvious we know what Register readers care about.

But I didn't really appreciate the extent of the Krispy Kreme hysteria until I found myself on foot, child in tow, braving four lanes of Saturday morning traffic on what may be the busiest street in the state to buy a box of doughnuts. We got into the building alive and waited in a line that snaked around the store and out the front door. The doughnuts were OK, but I'm not a doughnut person. I needed some perspective. I needed a doughnut authority.

I called a cop — Sgt. Dave Murillo of the Des Moines Police Department.

"Rob, why are you stereotyping people? I'm surprised that a mainstream newspaper that's politically correct would do that." After he got that out of his system, he said one of the guys brought in a box the other night and he tried one.

"They're not bad, but I think the hype is greater than the product. The best doughnuts in Des Moines used to be at Smitty's on 19th and Keo. The Donut King is good now, and they've got the best brewed coffee."

The Donut King is actually in West Des Moines, on Grand

"So I'm talkin' to this guy . . ."

Avenue just past 63rd Street. Lou King owns the place. He's worked there since 1964, when he was in high school. His day starts at midnight and ends about noon. He's in there seven days a week. He bakes and sells about 200 dozen a day. Self-promotion is not his strong suit.

"All I can say is that I wouldn't put out anything that isn't good quality — nothing too small, nothing greasy. I start fresh every day." At first, the Krispy Kreme craze hurt his business. But things are back to normal. Has he tried one?

"I haven't, but my customers tell me it's just a doughnut."

Not far from King's place is Dotty's Donuts, where Dolly Wise rules. She's in there baking at 3 in the morning, and she goes through as many as 50 dozen some days. Just ask about her doughnuts, and stand back.

"Our mixture is the best there is. No question about it. We make it the old-fashioned, grandma way. The best way. Ours are cake doughnuts, not filled. This is home baking. We're the best."

And she went on like that for a while. I won't share her comments about the competition, but she did say there was a slight dip in business for a few weeks. "But folks are smart. They're back now."

It was pretty much the same deal at Donutland on Douglas Avenue east of Merle Hay Road. Owner Bob Patel said he's weathered that initial loss of business. "Sure, everybody's got to try it, but nobody has the variety we have."

He offered me a Nibble — sort of a chocolate-covered doughnut hole. I respectfully declined. I don't do holes. Besides, I had to get up to Krispy Kreme for the morning rush.

Tom England, an Urbandale engineer, was paying for his first dozen. He said he had a staff meeting and thought the doughnuts might help. And besides, he was curious.

"It's interesting, because everybody's so health-conscious. Then a doughnut shop opens and we go crazy for it."

I nodded along — couldn't agree more. Right. Health-conscious. Staff meeting.

But I was edging my way toward the car, eager to eat the doughnut before it got cold.

Vilsack's order kicks anti-gay hysteria into overdrive

November 30, 1999

Stealing, cursing, fighting: none of that was a big deal when I was growing up. Everybody did it. Same thing for drinking and wife beating. Guys would get loaded and smack the old lady around a little and nobody got too crazy about it. No reason to call the cops. That was between you and the wife.

Gambling, running numbers, fencing stolen stuff: that was like our stock market. It was all part of the culture, just like racism, anti-semitism and a whole bunch of other isms that make me cringe just to think about.

The Irish beat on the Italians, the Italians beat on the Puerto Ricans, the Puerto Ricans beat on the blacks and everybody beat on the Jews.

There were only two things beyond forgiveness. First, there were girls who slept around. We had an entire vocabulary for those girls — Italian words, Yiddish words, English and a combination of all three.

But the worst thing was being gay. You wanted to hurt somebody, you called him a homo. And then the fists would fly.

I didn't really know any openly gay people. But I was ready to gay-bash with a vengeance if the occasion called for it.

Then somewhere along the line I got out of my comfort zone and started hanging around with folks who had more than an eighth-grade education. I met musicians and actors and guys and gals who were poets and dancers. Some of them were gay. And among those gays there were folks who were scam artists, junkies, the typical mix.

In that respect, gays were like any other group — socialists, Republicans, Christians, atheists. Any group you can imagine will have its share of losers. But most of the gay and lesbian people I came across were normal folks trying to get through the day, go home at night and be with their loved ones.

That was the end of my gay-hating phase. For 25 years or so I never gave gays and lesbians much thought. I had my own problems.

Then I moved to Iowa and I was reminded that homosexuality is a problem. A big problem — in the schools, in the churches, in the workplace.

We've got gays running for the school board who must be weeded out. We've got gay ministers who must be banished. Gay marriages? Not a problem here, but let's pass laws that make it illegal.

Then there's the problem of gays in the workplace, particularly these so-called transgendered types — which is a fancy name for folks who think they were born in the wrong body.

Gay-bashing is one of the few growth industries in this state. People are moving here and making a living off this. Gay and lesbian people who were born and raised here are being driven out, moving to the coasts and taking their talents with them. It's not a healthy situation on either end.

And any effort to deal with this in a sane, rational way is met with more anti-gay hysteria.

A couple of months ago the governor signed an order saying folks wouldn't face job discrimination if they're gay. He included the transgendered. It's limited to the executive branch of state government. It's a small step, mostly symbolic. The reaction?

Tonight there's a rally to whip up opposition to the governor's order. It's being put together by the usual suspects — Bill Horn and Reggie White, guys with a lot of time on their hands. They're bringing in Gary Bauer, a presidential candidate who had to call a press conference recently to say he's not cheating on his wife.

So they'll gather and they'll make their speeches and they'll talk about Jesus and the Bible and they'll push all the right buttons. But when it's over, I don't think any one of them will have been as eloquent as the woman who spoke at the Des Moines City Council meeting last year when they debated a gay rights ordinance.

Linda Christensen, the mother of a gay man, told the council: "I didn't know how to have a relationship with God, where you hate the sin but love the sinner, because having lived with my son for 18 years and knowing him, there is no part of my child that I could hate."

We could have used a Linda Christensen in the old neighborhood.

We're not just 'dealing wit some shmegeggi here'

December 2, 1999

Some religious leaders are quiet and circumspect, on the low-key side with a strong dose of humility and a taste for the simple life.

And some are like Martin Applebaum. Applebaum doesn't know from quiet and simple.

He tools around town in a black Lincoln Continental with "RABBI A" on the license plate. The walls of his office are loaded with autographed photos of him with everyone from Shimon Peres and the pope to Hillary Clinton and a B-list country and western singer he met somewhere along the way.

He can be brash in a city where some folks won't say the word "Jew" too loudly. He can be disarmingly candid — "How did I end up in Iowa? I got an agent. He negotiates. I got the job. He gets a commission. It's not like years back."

He can speak with the eloquence of an English professor or he can lapse into the street dialect of his native Brooklyn. Thursday becomes "Toisday" and this thing is "dis ting."

It's not a problem.

"Jackie Mason made millions of bucks tawking like this. I should apologize?"

He can be laser clear or he can refer to "the letter I got from the whatever, the Asian thing, the lady. . . . They think they're dealing wit some shmegeggi here."

He's controversial. He was sued — successfully — this past spring by a woman who said he didn't pay her for work she did. He's even had his rabbinical credentials questioned. He waves it off.

"It's just Jewish politics."

Applebaum spent 20 years in the Army. He got out in January of '98 and was hired 14 months ago as rabbi at the city's orthodox synagogue, Beth El Jacob.

He wasted no time letting folks know he was here. He's now the official chaplain of the Des Moines Police Department and all kosher affairs are held at the Marriott or the Sheraton, both under his supervision.

He's an interesting mix of the traditional and the trendy — he certified Krispy Kreme as kosher.

And he quickly figured out how to negotiate the alleys of the bureaucracy, at every level.

He wanted to carry a concealed weapon — "I get threats. It's a dangerous world" — and needed a permit. But the test was on Saturdays, the Sabbath. First the county told him he was out of luck. That wasn't good enough. This should not be a problem. He got it taken care of.

The state requires a burial or embalming within 48 hours of death. Orthodox Jews do not allow embalming. What if somebody in the congregation dies on a three-day weekend and can't be buried for 72 hours? A long shot, but why take chances? He called around, found out which legislator he needed to educate, and the law was changed.

There have been a half-dozen of those deals.

"A rabbi has to be able to pick up the phone and get things done for his people. If you can't do that, you're missing your calling."

Now he's ready to take his act to a new level.

Later this month — on Tuesday the 21st at 2 p.m. — he starts a weekly half-hour talk show on the local public access TV channel. He's already lined up his first three guests: the mayor, some folks from the police department and the city school superintendent — "What is it, Weatherspoon? Right?"

He's hoping for some quality time alone with Bush, Gore and Bradley.

The show, called "Des Moines Alive," will be heavy on issues. But not necessarily Applebaum's issues.

"I don't want this portrayed as being Jewish. It's for everybody. I want to create something people will look forward to seeing every week. It'll cover all the issues. I don't have to agree. I'll just ask the questions."

Hard to imagine someone that opinionated and expressive asking a question, then just sitting back and letting things flow. But as hyper and as driven as he seems, Iowa is getting to him. He's learning to relax a bit.

"I like it here. People are knowledgeable. It's close-knit. You feel like you're part of the human race."

But let's not get carried away with this quiet reflection.

"So you gonna help me with the show? You gonna put this in the paper?"

Do I got a choice? Can I say no to this guy?

A comrade remembers Griffin's fight for equality

February 10, 2000

Word came down Tuesday that Edna Griffin was dead, and that got John Bibbs thinking. His mind wandered back to the summer of '48. He was 22, four years out of Tech High School and just back from the Navy, an experience he remembers as highly racist. "I was called nigger and everything else. I got five days in the brig for speaking up about that."

Back in Des Moines, Bibbs was going to college and feeling like he'd been pushed around enough. In those days, Bibbs says, the only difference between Iowa and Alabama was that this state didn't have "Whites Only" signs posted in the shops and restaurants. They didn't need them. Folks got the message. If Bibbs went to the movies, he had to sit in the balcony. Blacks couldn't get a decent hotel room or even a meal.

"I know that's hard for you to imagine, but if we wanted lunch downtown, we had to stand at the end of the counter and they'd sack it up and we'd take it and eat on the curb or in the alley. Between that and the way I was treated in the Navy, I just didn't have much faith in the system."

So Bibbs was looking around. He needed an outlet for his anger. He fell in with the Progressive Party, Henry Wallace's deal, and at a meeting he met a woman named Edna Griffin.

"She was a doctor's wife, and that meant she could do things others couldn't. She could step out and say things. She was a leader, so articulate, so intelligent. I had so much respect for that woman. She motivated me to do what I did."

Then, on a July day 52 years ago, Griffin was refused service at the lunch counter of Katz Drug Store. Bibbs was right beside her. The two of them — along with the late Leonard Hudson — had what they needed to shove this city's racism into everybody's face.

It was perfect. Katz's was high-profile, on Seventh and Locust, right in the center of the city.

What followed were pickets and sit-ins, civil lawsuits and a criminal case that nailed the store's general manager for violating the state's civil-rights law.

This was seven years before Rosa Parks refused to get in the back of a Montgomery bus and 15 years before King's "I Have a Dream" speech.

Bibbs remembers it as a lonely battle fought mostly by African-American women. Black men had to support their families and were worried about being blacklisted. Few whites signed on, and this city's black establishment was no help, Bibbs says. For the most part, they kept their mouths shut.

"They didn't like our tactics, and they didn't want us fooling around with tradition. They thought we were troublemakers. But Mrs. Griffin didn't care. She wanted people to understand what the coloreds were saddled with."

When the protests died down and it was time for Bibbs to again focus on his life — raise a family, earn a living — he realized there was no going back. Folks in this town knew who he was and what he did.

To many people, that wasn't a good thing.

Even with his education, he couldn't find a decent job. For a while he couldn't find any job. Sometimes the family had to eat whatever they could pull from the garden. If all they had were dandelions, that's what they ate.

Then he got work as an orderly at the VA hospital. From there he went to a packing plant — sweeping up, shaking hides, working on the kill floor, doing jobs he calls menial.

Eventually he signed on with Iowa Power and Light and by the time he retired in the late '80s he was a supervisor.

In recent years there's been a lot of attention paid to that 1948 protest. A plaque honors Griffin at the site of the drugstore where she was denied service, and she received an honorary doctorate, medals and all kinds of awards. Two years ago — on the 50th anniversary of the lunch-counter incident — Griffin, Bibbs and Hudson were recognized by the state.

Now, with Edna Griffin's passing, the story's back on the front page and Bibbs says that's a good thing, an important thing.

"We all knew we had a problem, but it was Mrs. Griffin who did something about it. We owe her. Let's not forget that."

Colorful Girls roll on
Tuesday nights at Val Lanes
February 22, 2000

At 77, Mary Risolvato is not the bowler she was in the 1950s when she started playing this game. It's been a while since she broke 200. But she still averages about 132, and not long ago she rolled a 174. Watch her for three frames and she throws a strike and two spares. Then she sits down, takes a pull on her bottle of Coors, laughs and says: "I bet if I got this cataract removed, I'd hit 240."

On Tuesday nights you'll find Risolvato and about 100 other women at the Val Lanes, bowling in the Val Gals league. Risolvato is one of the Rockettes. On the next lane are the Skittles and a few lanes over are the Alley Cats, the Pinheads and the Bogus Bowlers. Some of the team names are a bit less frivolous — West Construction, Retail Data System.

On Lane 4 are six women known as Girls With Balls. It says so on their bowling shirts — the coral-colored shirts with the black trim. This is the same team that has tailgating parties and theme nights — like parents night or homecoming night, when they wore corsages and elected a queen.

One night they hired a male stripper to jazz things up. They've been known to come running into the bowling alley with the Bulls theme song — "Are You Ready To Rumble" — blaring in the background. They've got a little fan club — friends who show up at the alley to cheer them on. Their penchant for cheering has gotten them reprimanded for disorderly conduct.

The team slogan is: "Just because we're bad bowlers doesn't mean we're bad people." Their bowling balls are lime green, pink, purple, red. And they name their balls Bubbles, Suicide, Flubber and a few other things.

Their body language — several of them jumping up and gyrating, trying to keep the ball from going in the gutter — looks like mambo night at the Roseland Ballroom.

Stylewise, watching them bowl next to Mary Risolvato is like seeing Barbara Bush hanging with Courtney Love.

By day the Girls work in marketing and the media. One of them teaches third grade and another is a credit analyst. One is a supervisor for a trucking company and one is a writer. They're all between 32 and 42, all single, no kids.

During the summer they play golf together. And on Tuesday nights — from August to April — they bowl. It's a 33-week season and, as one of them — Diane Cannon — said: "I've never been this committed to anything."

They pay $30 for league dues, $10 a night to bowl. Each lays out $50 or $60 to go to the state tournament every year "and on top of that," said Cannon, "there's the thousands we pay for beer."

This started as a joke. The women were looking for something to do during the winter when they couldn't play golf. While they were kicking around different ideas, one of them saw an ad in the paper that said "Women Needed — Bowling."

"It was a sign from God," says Barb Preuss, marketing director at the Civic Center. "Bowling? We figured it would be fun for four or five weeks."

That was four years ago.

Early on, it was a bit uneasy. The other women didn't know what to make of the Girls With Balls. Preuss says if the league weren't so desperate it probably wouldn't have let them in.

Mary Risolvato doesn't argue with that. "They were strange at first, but now we've warmed up to them. We like them. They're good kids."

The Girls have become an integral part of the Tuesday night gathering. They get invited to weddings, graduations and such. When one of the other bowlers is in the hospital, they go. Last year Preuss was elected league president and her teammate, Jan Kinney, vice president.

Next week they head out to the state tournament in Dubuque. And their game is getting better. A year ago they came in last — 12th out of 12 teams. This year they're in 11th place.

That's got the Girls feeling pretty good about things. But, as Preuss says, it's not just about bowling.

"This is such a departure from who I am the rest of the time. And it's brought us into a whole new community of friends, people we wouldn't have met any other way."

It's her turn. She picks up her pink ball and tries her damnedest to raise that 148 average — not something she ever thought she'd be worrying about.

Southerner's 'good life' has lasted 110 fruitful years

July 18, 2000

One of my first assignments in the newspaper business was to interview the 90-year-old former mayor of Kingston, the upstate New York city where I was working. I got out to the house and immediately realized he was hard of hearing. So I spoke up. Really loudly.

The guy, thinking I was yelling at him, started crying. As it turned out, it didn't matter if he could hear me or not. He didn't remember that he'd ever been mayor.

I was thinking about all this the other afternoon when a woman named Paulette Pace called and asked if I'd like to come out and interview her husband's grandfather.

Why would I want to?

"Because Paw Paw is 110 years old. He's really special."

With visions of the crying mayor dancing in my head, I was tempted to beg off. But I figured if nothing else, I'd get to meet a guy who's 110. I'd ask a few thoughtful, probing questions, things he'd never heard before — "So what's your secret for living so long?" — and see if anything came of it.

But first the cynic in me demanded that I check some records and verify the guy's age. With that done, I headed over to the house and spent several hours with Walter Hickman over several days.

And Paulette Pace got it right. There's sort of an aura about the guy. He gets around with no more than a cane and speaks in a mostly clear voice. He wears glasses but no hearing aid. He's never been in the hospital.

His favorite expression seems to be: "Damned if I know."

Hickman lives with one of his daughters in Tennessee but spends summers visiting family in Iowa — Des Moines, Davenport. There's a lot of family to go around: six kids, 42 grandkids, 133 great-grandkids and 63 great-great.

His mind is extremely sharp, but a few details are sketchy. He couldn't remember if he'd been married two or three times. It turns out he was married three times, but twice to the same woman.

Most things are clear. He remembers he was born on a

Mississippi cotton plantation — "We was so poor we didn't even own a cow" — and for the next 80 years he never moved more than a few miles from there.

He remembers that his grandparents were slaves, and he knows he's the sole survivor of his parents' 16 kids — eight boys, eight girls. He remembers picking cotton and farming for 65 cents a day, $3.50 a week. Out of that he managed to save $1,000 to buy himself 40 acres. How?

"Damned if I know. That's something I wonder about myself. Hard work, I guess."

He knows he never learned to read and write: "It's not too bad. People help you out." He's never been on a plane, and he's never been in jail.

"I never even been pushed around by the police."

No small feat for a black man who spent the last century in Mississippi. But the whole racial thing is something he won't talk about. He's like those combat veterans who come home and try to leave their war stories on the battlefield.

He'd much rather tell you about Sunday mornings when he'd load the family into the mule-drawn wagon — "the mules was named Matt and Ross" — and head down the road to the Methodist church. Or he'll tell you about evenings on the farm, after dinner, when he'd have a little down time.

"I'd just walk and look around at all we had. The blessings. The cotton and hogs and cows. We had watermelon and beans. I told you about the mules. There was fruit on the trees. It's a good life. I'm blessed."

He talked and sort of drifted away. He seemed to be getting tired, and I didn't want to push it. But I had to ask: "So what's your secret for living so long?"

He had his lines down.

"Damned if I know."

Pause for a laugh line.

Then he said, "Three things: Pray, get along with people, and mind your own business."

'I guess I must have known you a long time ago'

November 14, 2000

Her son sat her down and said the words Eva Wamsley waited 65 years to hear: "They found Colleen."

Eva's mind raced back to January 1935. She was 20, a single parent with a 3-year-old son and a 2-year-old daughter, two kids she couldn't afford to feed. She remembered the desperation she felt the day she put her kids in the orphanage in Longmont, Colo., just north of Denver.

She remembered that dark day two months later when she went back to get them and her daughter was gone. Colleen was adopted and there was no way to find out where she was. The records were confidential. Eva had no money for a lawyer, nowhere to turn. That part of the case was closed.

Friends and family were pretty rough on her. Some never spoke with Eva again. The worst part was living with herself, trying to come to terms with what she'd done. Until then she'd been a pretty wild kid — having babies at 16 and 17, no husband. Losing Colleen sobered her up, but she was paralyzed by sadness.

In time Eva realized she had to raise her son, get on with her life. She met a guy and got married, had three more kids — two sons and a daughter who died a few months after birth. The family moved from Colorado to Idaho, and on to Washington and Montana, then back to Colorado. Her husband farmed — wheat, fruit and dairy. He worked in the silver mines and made $4.75 a day for three days' work. When the $6 rent on the mining shack went up to $7, they moved. And they kept moving.

"We moved 47 times in those years, the Depression. Those times lasted longer for folks like us than they did for a lot of other people. It was tough times, so tough. It would get to where we had nothing to eat. But for all those years there wasn't a night when there wasn't a prayer for Colleen. Praying she was safe. Praying I'd see her again."

Now, at 85 — early in March of the year 2000 — Eva was sitting in her Denver kitchen and her son was telling her, "They found Colleen."

She bowed her head. She wasn't sure how to deal with what she was hearing. She wasn't sure if she could.

"I just kept thinking 'My goodness.' I was confused, shocked. All that. I didn't know if I could handle it."

Within days, Eva was able to compose herself. She let it be known she was ready to talk with her daughter. On Monday, March 6, at about 10 in the morning the phone rang. It was Colleen — now Sally Lowry, a 68-year-old retired elementary-school teacher living in Des Moines. They caught up as best they could, but both were nervous beyond words. The call was pretty formal. Sally opened up with something like: "Eva, I guess I must have known you a long time ago."

After that they spoke every few days, with Eva trying to work up the strength to see her daughter. About two weeks into it she was ready. They arranged for Sally to fly out to Denver in early April. Waiting for that day to come, Eva was a wreck.

"I'd sit for hours and crochet and wonder what she'd look like and what she thought of me because I gave her away. It was very strange because I was so scared, but I was thankful I had lived to see this."

Sally got to Denver on April 1 and drove to the hotel where she met her mother, her brothers, nieces, nephews, some cousins — the only blood relatives she'd ever known. Eva laid eyes on her daughter for the first time in 65 years.

"When I saw her . . . words can't describe it. You understand that. But I knew the minute I saw her that she was mine."

There were hugs and tears all around. When she was able to pull herself together, Eva took her daughter aside, held her and told her: "There hasn't been a night in 65 years before I went to sleep that I didn't wonder where you were."

Eva had waited a lifetime to say that.

Sally had been waiting to hear it.

It's the same ol' place: Perfect enough

January 30, 2002

Leave town for a year and you come back ready to deal with the changes. You're looking around, trying to get a feel for what's different, what's gotten ahold of the place over 12 months.

And this gets going even before you hit the city limits. Coming in on I-80, you turn on the radio and start channel surfing, scrolling past the May cattle and the June hogs. You get to some guy on the Mickelson show going on about that fine line between immigrants and terrorists and how we'd better close the borders before they kill the rest of us. Not much new there.

You get to town, grab the paper, and there's a piece about some honcho up at the Statehouse who's insisting we make English "the official language." That's failed just about every year, but it's a lot sexier than talking about budget problems, hungry kids and old people who need help with their medical bills.

You keep looking for something new, something you haven't heard around here before.

You ask what the city government types are up to, and you hear they're still wringing their hands over the Events Center and plans for that mall out in West Des Moines. You hear there are still all kinds of questions about what to do with Court Avenue, the library and the Science Center. And don't even bother to ask about Prairie Meadows.

Just keep looking, keep moving. Hit the south side, and you're hearing that folks there — make that the Mauro brothers — feel as if they're getting picked on because they're Italian. Over on the east side, folks feel as though they're getting shortchanged. That's a mindset that dates to early in the Hoover administration.

Downtown, you hear that Nan Stillians and her gang are all worked up because the business types are still tearing down buildings. And some of those business types, guys like Hansell, Brannan, Weitz — the Ed, Red and Fred Club — are all worked up because those buildings aren't being torn down fast enough.

So you're running all this past a friend the other night, and he wants to know why — if things are so bad, so stagnant — you bothered to come back. You start to explain that you're not complaining, just observing. You start to tell him it was the same thing when you lived in New York, Florida and a few other places. But before you can go there, he cuts you off and says, "You knew this place wasn't perfect."

And that sends you back about three years. Now you're thinking about the go-round you had with your old pal R.J. He's the lawyer in San Francisco, the one with that beautiful house on the Marin side of the bay. He had a wife, no kids and enough money to have some fun — high-end restaurants a few times a week, Venice in June, Negril in January.

Then in the late '90s, his marriage broke up and everything else fell apart. You called one night to see how he was doing, and he went on about how he was lonely, depressed. He might have to sell the house to settle up with his ex.

Then about 20 minutes into it, he asked how you were doing in Iowa. You told him you liked your job, the family's in good shape and it was nice to live in a place where you didn't have to keep looking over your shoulder.

Then you said, "But I'm still living out in the middle of nowhere."

There was a pause, and then R.J. said, "So what you're telling me is that your life out there is perfect, but it's just not perfect enough."

That's the line you kept coming back to over the past year, the year you were down south. And when you thought about this place and what you missed, it wasn't about buildings and politicians. It wasn't about some guy ranting on the radio, and it had nothing to do with whether to put a French cafe or a pole barn on Court Avenue.

It was about people. You missed folks like the ones you saw last week over at the hospice, the ones who volunteer their time and give up their nights to make sure nobody around here dies alone. You missed the guy who shoveled the old lady's driveway because that's what good neighbors do. You even missed the woman down at the coffee shop, the one who remembers you take milk and how much.

A year later, and they're still around. And that's one more thing about this town that hasn't changed.

Who bakes the pies? Surprise!
March 29, 2002

You're on the main drag through the heart of Bondurant. You pass a church, a library, a bunch of pre-fab warehouse-type buildings. And then you see Pie Delight Pies. In your mind you can already picture the owners — a couple of old ladies in aprons and hairnets, reading glasses. And you can already smell those fresh-baked pies.

So you go up to the front door and there's a handwritten note on it that says: "No one under 16 years of age can enter the pie shop unless accompanied by an adult." Strange. But you keep going.

Open the door and the first thing you hear is Rush Limbaugh on the radio, The first thing you see is the glass case with the pistol cleaning rod and the gun locks. And you can smell the pies. You keep going, keep looking for the old ladies who run the joint.

The glass case continues on and hooks off to the right. It's got knives and rare coins and old cigarette lighters, photos of the Pope and a 1946 Iowa driver's manual. On the wall behind the case there's a rifle and a trombone and a framed quote from the Bible, John 14:2 "In my father's house are many mansions . . . "There are photos of Dick Cheney and Ronald Reagan and the Bush clan. Autographed mugs of Newt and Ollie and Charlton share wall space with a sign that says: "I love my country but fear my government." There's a poster of W.C. Fields hawking Old Gold cigarettes next to a Henri Matisse print. And behind the counter there's a burly, tough-looking guy in a T-shirt and baseball hat. He's standing in front of a sign that says: "Shoplifters will be cheerfully beaten, regardless of race, color, creed or national origin. Have a nice day."

You approach the counter and the tough stuff melts away. A smile creases his face.

"Hi. Can I help you?"

This would be Ray Biddle, the owner. This is what you get instead of the old ladies with the hairnets. Biddle's been in the kitchen making pies, filling them with fresh fruit, making the crusts, "hand-fluting the edges of each and every one that I sell."

He cranks out about 20 or 25 on a weekday, up to 50 on Saturdays. You want to know how this happened, how he ended up baking pies in a shop that also sells hand-cranked adding machines and coffee pots that look like they were around the last time the Cubs won the Series.

Biddle takes you back to the south side of Des Moines — Lincoln class of '68. He talks about working after school at places like Johnny and Kay's. Then he did a stint at Poppin' Fresh, where he met his mentor, Paul Tillinghast, the guy who taught him to bake. Biddle moved to Minneapolis and worked in the Pillsbury test kitchens in the mid-'70s. Then he drove a truck for 16 years, had a bad accident — he was crushed against a wall, seven back operations — and opened this place in '92.

The pies are his passion. The rest of it is just spill-over from his hobbies. He's a collector — coins and antiques, political stuff, old books and posters.

He'd love to talk, but it's break time over at the county road department and about a dozen guys come through the door and grab seats at the five tables along the wall. They're calling out their orders: Three coconut cream, two cherry, two banana, one chocolate, a few others. They want coffee and Pepsi. One guy wants a pair of binoculars.

Ask around and they've got nothing but good things to say about Biddle and his pies. Bob Schoonover said he comes in "because I just find this place so damn interesting. And this guy can bake like nobody else." When they finish up and drift out, Roy Stoll comes in with a pearl-handled knife that belonged to his father. He says Biddle is "somebody who can appreciate it." More folks come in and the phone keeps ringing. People are putting in their Easter orders.

There's a break in the action and you ask about the sign on the door — no one under 16. Biddle says the kids in town would come in after school to hang out and he couldn't handle the crowds. He works alone. Then he takes another call.

So you walk off and wait. You check out the table where the Rosh Hashanah and Christmas cards seem right at home next to the used tractor battery and the books, like "Let Go and Let God" and "The Knife Throwing Techniques of the Ninja."

So this priest walks into a bar

March 12, 2003

Typical night at Cooney's bar in Beaverdale. The place is packed, the music's blaring, folks are tossing back beer and wine, watching the hockey game on TV, laughing and talking it up. Three guys in the back are playing darts.

Then this priest gets up on a chair near the front of the bar. He's right under the Harp Beer sign, between the fireplace and the popcorn machine. He checks his mike and introduces himself — Monsignor Frank Bognanno, pastor of Christ the King Church.

With all that these priests are going through right now, you would think they'd low-key it.

Not Bognanno. He wants the crowd's attention.

He throws out a few laugh lines like: "I'm a priest, but other than that I'm a nice guy." Then he tells people what he wants to talk about: "Why Bother Being a Catholic?" By now the place is silent — the music's off, nobody's talking, the guys put down the darts. People are still drinking and smoking, the TV's still on without the sound, but Bognanno — not the Islanders-Bruins game — has their attention. He starts talking about morality, saying, "Sex isn't bad, God invented it. . . . Beer and rib-eye steaks aren't bad. It's when we abuse these things. . . . Wine isn't bad. We serve it at Mass. I'm in the business. Jesus created 120 gallons at a wedding feast."

He talks some more about Jesus, the pope, the Greeks and Romans. He says the Ten Commandments "don't tell you what to do. They are warning you what not to do." He talks about marriage, about sex before marriage — not a good thing — and he slips in some reference to Moses.

Then he sort of laughs and asks, "Am I getting too heavy, too deep?"

Look around at the tables, up and down the bar, and some folks are shaking their heads left to right, letting Bognanno know he's doing good, saying the right things. Some are shaking their heads up and down, letting him know they agree. Some are shaking their heads because they can't believe what they're hearing and seeing in Cooney's.

And some — the folks drinking shots with the beer — are just shaking.

About that point, Mike Canine stops in for a drink, something he does about once a week. This is Canine's neighborhood bar, and he knows the place. But on this night — the silence, the priest — he doesn't recognize it.

"This first thing I thought was that we'd gone to war or something and he was some kind of guest speaker. A priest on a chair? That's the last thing I thought I'd see in a place like this."

But he orders himself a Miller Lite and settles in.

What Canine and the others are seeing and hearing is Des Moines' first "Theology on Tap," something that's been going on in Chicago and Milwaukee, D.C., Boston and Atlanta. It's aimed at folks in their 20s and 30s. The idea — according to the archdiocese — is to bring the church to the people. So they'll be hitting the bars, trying to connect with people, talking about religion in a "nonthreatening, comfortable environment. Pope John Paul II urges people to preach the gospel in the streets. To go where the people are."

On this night, the people are at Cooney's. And — priest and all — they're happy to be there. Belle Alger is pumped.

"It's really, really wonderful to hear about Jesus in a different setting. It's nice to be with people with the same interests, the same moral background."

Ryan Beck is surprised, but impressed.

"I had no idea. I wouldn't have believed it if somebody told me about this. But it was interesting."

And at the end of the night, Bognanno is glowing, happy with the way things went.

"It worked. It was great. Sure some folks think it's extreme to be doing this in a bar, but I don't think that at all. The Catholic Church doesn't think bars are evil."

So where's the next one? Bognanno says that hasn't been decided.

It'll be interesting to catch this show when it plays Hooters.

Potter mania seizes quiet night

June 25, 2003

Friday night after a rough week, the deadlines are over, it's time to turn off the computer and chill, indulge myself. The wife's in New York for the weekend at a high school reunion. I got the kids and I got the night all mapped out.

We'll go to the Y and work out for an hour, go home and clean up, go have dinner at Tumea's, hang with Tony B. and Mario T. and the Chiodos. Get the ravioli — boiled, never fried, don't even ask. Get home in time for the news at 10, catch Leno's monologue, read a little and have the lights out by 11.

That was my idea of a good time and it worked beautifully through dinner. Then at 9:30 my 13-year-old took over. He had his own plan. We were going to a bookstore to wait until the Harry Potter book was released at midnight.

I'd been hearing the Harry Potter stories all week — about the hijacking of a truck loaded with about 8,000 copies of the book. About the New York Daily News being sued for $100 million for printing excerpts before the release date. Then there was the shop in Brooklyn where they accidently put copies on the shelves a few days too soon.

Stores around here were having pajama parties, costume contests and all kinds of readings and giveaways. Barnes & Noble was offering a trip to London.

I tried to explain to my son that teenagers aren't supposed to spend Friday nights hanging out at the bookstore waiting for novels to be released. He should rent a video — maybe one of those poignant, moving Jim Carrey films. Or maybe just channel surf and find some "South Park" reruns. Or he could get online and download some Eminem CDs.

But books at midnight? Reading 900-page novels during the summer?

I keep forgetting this is a new century.

So we went to Barnes & Noble and a block away we saw the lights from the TV trucks, Channels 8 and 13 going live at 10. The parking lot was packed. Kids — from toddlers to teens — were pouring out of the cars wearing capes and pointy hats and those round glasses. The parents were tagging along, trying to keep up, some of them looking like they hadn't factored this in when they decided to have kids. Some were obviously into this — Mom in the cape, Dad in the hat.

Inside the store there were more than 1,000 people — probably a lot more, but the fire code limits what can be said. Folks had been lining up since 5 p.m. and the line went around the building and down to the street. Most of these people had already reserved the book, but they weren't taking any chances.

Some folks were there without kids. I asked what that was about and one guy — maybe in his mid-30s — told me he is really into Harry Potter and so is his wife. They already had one copy ordered from Amazon, but they were going on vacation up to Minnesota and the marriage wouldn't survive with just one book between the two of them. He was serious.

Another guy said his three kids were home and his wife wouldn't let them stay out that late. So she sent him to get the book. Non-negotiable.

The later it got, the more crowded the room was. By 11:30 it was obvious they wouldn't have enough books to go around. We left there and cruised by Borders and saw the crowds spilling out. We ended up at Waldenbooks in the mall. There were only a few hundred people lined up, so it looked empty. By then it was midnight. They rolled out the carts with the books and started selling.

People waited quietly for their turn — with the discount the $30 book was going for about $23. We got our copy at about 12:30 and I was home in bed by 1. I barely remembered where I'd eaten dinner.

I woke up to the news that they expected — and finally sold — 5 million copies the first day, 1 million online, a record-breaker all around. In Britain they sold 1.8 million copies, one out of every 28 people. My wife called from New York and — the big news? — they were selling the book on the street for $17. I found out Preston and Patty Daniels are Harry Potter junkies. It went on like that. It still does.

And I haven't seen much of my kid since early Saturday morning. He's been sitting in his room reading. He's up to page 350.

I'm sitting in the other room watching "South Park."

Does small-town life ring a bell?

July 18, 2003

Beaconsfield, Ia. — I hear "small town in Iowa" and I think of a place with maybe a thousand people. If you want to get ridiculous about it, maybe a few hundred. No schools, no cops, not even a traffic light. Hard to imagine.

And then I heard about Beaconsfield — the smallest of the small towns, population 11. I just had to see this place and meet these people. So I made the 75-mile drive from Des Moines, turned onto the gravel road, made a quick right, and up ahead on the left was the mayor's place, the brown trailer she shares with Spottie the cat.

I wasn't expecting Richard Daley, but I wasn't ready for Lois Davis. Talk about feisty. She's 76, and she's got the energy of a 10-year-old. We got through the greetings and pleasantries, and first of all she lets me know there are more than just 11 people living here. Three folks moved in after the 2000 census was taken and there are a few others "who didn't fill out the papers. They say it's nobody's business where they live."

I ask about her job and what the mayor of Beaconsfield has to do.

"Everything that needs to be done. I go to landfill meetings in Leon and I have to write letters to people who have property but don't live here and don't take care of their weeds. There was a dog showing his teeth to people when they're going to church and that was my problem. Sometimes I have to cut the grass in the park or over at Wilma's because she's 91 and can't do it. And I've got to remember to take her cat to get spayed this afternoon."

She mentions about 10 other things. I ask about her salary.

"It's $15 a month and the three council members get $5 each, but we don't take the money. We put it in the city account, to buy gravel and stuff like that."

There's a dozen other things I want to ask, but enough with the talk. Lois wants to hit the streets of Beaconsfield — both of them. She takes me to the church and shows me where she sits on Sunday mornings. They're having an ice cream social this week. They've got a traveling preacher who does Beaconsfield services at 9, then Grand River at 10 and Kellerton at 11.

We go over to City Hall — a one-time grocery store owned by a couple of guys named Hyde and Vredenburg. This was their first business together. Later they shortened the names to Hy and Vee, put them together and opened some more stores. From there we go across to the old jail, a little shack — "They used to put the hobos in there."

Then we look at the Beaconsfield welcome sign. It says astronaut Peggy Whitson is from here.

"Mount Ayr tried to claim her because she went to high school there. That's because we don't have a high school. But I called the radio stations and newspapers and let them know she's ours. You can't pull those shenanigans with us."

We walk over to the town pump — surrounded by stones and flowers — and that was the end of the tour. Then we went to meet some of the the people — all retired, some weren't home.

Raymond and Dorine have lived there longer than anybody. Raymond can remember the '30s when there were about 150 people living in Beaconsfield. There was a gas station and garage, a barber shop, a lumberyard, even a movie theater.

Eugene and Esther live up the road and they've got 20 acres, seven cows and "God knows how many chickens." Eugene plows the roads when it snows. Esther's the town clerk and keeps an eye on the $5,600 budget.

Clem drives by and waves. Lemar is taking care of his great-grandson, tooling around in a golf cart. We go and visit Wilma.

"She'll be real hurt if we don't stop by. Her hearing isn't good so if you ask a question and get a crazy answer, don't worry."

But there were no crazy answers. There's just a lot of talk about how folks help out and make sure everybody's OK. Wilma said what all the others said: "We're a family here. This is our home. We don't ever want to lose our spot on the map."

She thanked me for coming by and said to stop in next time I'm in town.

Then Lois told me there was one more thing we had to do before I left. She drove me over to the town bell.

"Everybody who comes here has to ring it."

I grabbed the long, thick rope and pulled hard. The bell rang and it felt good. So I rang it again. And then a third time.

Lois smiled. She knew exactly how I felt.

No comment by Rush? No way
October 13, 2003

I'm still trying to understand how somebody as morally incorruptible and virtuous as Bill Bennett was caught gambling away millions. And I still can't believe a family man like Arnold Schwarzenegger admits he "behaved badly" and apologized after a half-dozen women accused him of groping them.

Now I'm reading: "Conservative commentator Rush Limbaugh is being investigated for allegedly buying thousands of prescription painkillers from a black-market drug ring."

Think about it.

Rush Limbaugh accused of buying drugs from some woman at a Palm Beach gas station? Rush addicted to OxyContin, the stuff affectionately known as Hillbilly Heroin?

No way.

This is a guy who makes hundreds of millions of dollars lecturing the rest of us on why we should be law-abiding citizens, why we should fight corruption — in government, in the media.

He's the first — and loudest — to speak up when there's hypocrisy in this country. He's America's self-proclaimed guardian of truth and justice. Our go-to guy when we need the straight story on all that's right and good about America and the world.

Limbaugh buying drugs illegally? Not possible.

I'm thinking this has got to be the liberal media dumping on this poor guy when he's down. This all comes out the morning after his resignation for making racially insensitive comments on national TV. Rush Limbaugh being racially insensitive? And backing down?

Anyway, I start reading this drug story, and I can't wait to get past all the accusations so I can hear Limbaugh's vicious comeback. His two-fisted attack on the left. His rant about how his enemies are lying. I keep reading, and I finally come to his reaction. It said: "Limbaugh had no comment."

Limbaugh had no comment? Not possible. Limbaugh always has a comment. It's what he's about.

Now I'm thinking it's just part of the media's left-wing agenda to cover up his real response. Then I notice the story I'm reading is from the Washington Times — probably the most conservative daily newspaper in the country. These guys make Fox News look fair and balanced.

So I go to a better source. I go to rushlimbaugh.com. This is where I'll get the real story. No spin.

And there — on top of the site — is his defense:

"I am unaware of any investigation by any authority involving me. No government representative has contacted me directly or indirectly. If my assistance is required, I will, of course, cooperate fully."

This is the tough-talking, get-in your face Rush Limbaugh?

At the very least, I assumed he'd say, "It's not true. Go to hell." Or something like, "Is it true? That depends on what the meaning of is is."

But, "I am unaware of any investigation. . ." just doesn't cut it. That's the kind of thing you'd hear from some wimpy Democrat.

So there's only one way to get at the truth. I turn on the "Rush Limbaugh Show," and while I'm waiting for it to start, I can almost hear his take on the accusations:

"It's just more big government. They've got nothing better to do. No better way to waste your tax dollars than investigating innocent people."

Or how about something very Rush-like, something cute and clever: "The Clinton years were so relentlessly painful it was impossible to get through that time clean and sober."

I tune in, and there's no Rush Limbaugh. He's taking the day off. Talk about coincidence. There's some guy from California filling in. He's also a tough, no-nonsense type. Now I'm wondering how he's going to deal with the Rush stuff. And he opens with a line about how "only Rush can speak for Rush." So let's spend three hours discussing the telemarketing situation.

I thought about channel surfing, checking out the other news of the day. But I decided to pass. I was afraid I'd come across some story about how the White House was compromising national security by leaking information. Or something equally ridiculous.

'Come Be Our Alleged Guest'
February 4, 2004

I'm moping around the house the other night paralyzed by PCS — post-caucus syndrome. It was pretty bad. It got to the point where I was fantasizing about seeing Peter Jennings eating lasagna at Centro. And hearing Dave Barry mocking a place called A Dong. And listening to Mary Matalin talking — with a straight face — about how hot her husband is.

I miss that stuff. I want to see Greta and Tucker around town every night, not just once every four years.

Then I started to wonder what it would take to jump-start this state, to create something here that would make it a 24/7 place.

Sure, the Iowa Primate Learning Sanctuary will help. But I'm thinking we need something sexy and exciting, something sexier than the new library and even more exciting than the Pappajohn Higher Education Center.

So I'm sitting there thinking and on the table in front of me is the Register and the headline says: "Judge moves Peterson trial." It was a story about the murder case against Scott Peterson and how it was being moved from Modesto to San Mateo County.

I start reading and at one point the story said:

"Four counties had offered to host the trial: Alameda, San Mateo and Santa Clara in Northern California and Orange. San Mateo's tourism bureau sent a letter to the judge."

Tourism bureau going after a murder trial? It worked. They got it. I kept reading.

"Anne LeClair, president and chief executive of the San Mateo County Convention and Visitors Bureau, said her office was 'screaming with great excitement' upon hearing the news. Restaurants, hotels, car rental services and other businesses could see an influx of $8 million to $16 million, she said.

" 'There's just under 500 media people in attendance for the trial,' she said. 'They'll be staying for three, four or five months. The economic impact is tremendous.' "

As much as $16 million and 500 media people?

Now I'm thinking about the possibilities. Celebrity trials —

Peterson, Kobe Bryant, Martha Stewart, Michael Jackson, Rosie O'Donnell, Robert Blake, Winona Ryder. We're talking about one of the few growth industries to sprout up during the Bush administration.

That could be Iowa's niche. Where can you find a more fair-minded, down-to-earth jury pool, people who know what it means to put your hand on the Bible and swear to tell nothing but the truth.

There could be some problems. It would be tough for Michael Jackson to be tried by a jury of his peers. But that's not about Iowa, that's about Michael.

So is this a good idea?

I called Greg Edwards at the Greater Des Moines Convention and Visitors Bureau, and he didn't seem like the type who'd be "screaming with great excitement" at the idea of a high-profile murder trial in Des Moines. But he's not closed-minded. He thought about it and started coming around — "It's certainly outside the box. But, you know, the Martha Stewart trial would be awesome."

Edwards began to see the possibilities, he was getting worked up. He hadn't been this pumped since he landed the American Dairy Goat Association's convention. The guy was rockin'.

"Maybe we can take the 'Change Your View' slogan and tweak it a bit. How about 'Change Your Venue?'"

He got it. Now how do you sell something like this?

I talked with Kim Sporrer, an exec at a Clive marketing company. I asked about it, and she had a very thoughtful, responsible — and totally uptight — reaction: "We know that commercializing something that shouldn't be commercial isn't very favorable. But if such a campaign were actually launched in Iowa, the parties and communities would have to be sensitive to the judicial proceedings and all those who may be victims of a crime."

But then Sporrer got with the program and offered up a few thoughts. She suggested a play on the Iowa Tourism slogan "Come Be Our Guest."

How about "Come Be Our Alleged Guest?"

Good. Then it got even better: "Due Process? Do Iowa!"

All this great stuff from only two calls. So now I'm thinking that if we handle this right, we won't need the caucuses.

He'll go *anywhere* for a story
February 18, 2004

The thing I love about the news business is that you just never know how your day is going to play out. You get up in the morning and go to work expecting to cover the city council, and you find yourself running out to cover a double homicide. You might be interviewing a future president, or you might be in Algona interviewing the guy who owns the world's largest Cheeto.

So you've got to be loose, flexible. Not too judgmental and willing to go with the flow.

I was thinking about that yesterday morning while I was crawling through a 40-foot colon. I was thinking about that while I was looking around and trying to detect the differences between Crohn's disease and diverticulosis. I was looking at the polyps and hemorrhoids. I was looking at the various stages of cancer.

And I was trying to figure out how the hell I'd ended up here.

I'm a 30-year veteran of the business. I've interviewed world leaders and Nobel Prize winners, Mafia dons and Hall of Fame ballplayers — from Anthony "Tony Pro" Provenzano to Mickey Mantle. I've had coffee with Ronald Reagan and tea with Yitzhak Rabin.

I've stood at ground zero in New York City, and I've toured the Taj Mahal.

Now I'm trying to work my way through this damn colon, and it's not easy. Just crawling in was tough. Crawling out was going to be a lot harder. The long-term psychological effects could be devastating.

But that's the thing about the news business. You've got to be willing to go where the action is. And Tuesday, the action was in the lobby of Iowa Methodist Medical Center. The action was in and around this tube known as the Colossal Colon.

So there I was. And I wasn't alone.

A small crowd had gathered — people were fascinated by this thing. It wasn't possible to walk through that atrium without stopping and staring.

I stood by the door and listened to people as they walked in:

"What is that thing?"

"Oh, my God. Will you just look at that?"

"It's a WHAT???"

"I'm gonna need a throw-up bag."

"I've been around a lot of these over the years, but I've never been inside one. Hope this is the last time."

Two out of every three people used the word "gross," and the crude, silly jokes just kept coming. Several people asked if I was writing a "behind the scenes" piece about this.

There was stuff about "Secretary of State Colon Bowel," and it got a lot worse.

Pati Berger is a nurse, and she works with folks who have colorectal cancer. She says the jokes serve a purpose.

"Colon cancer can be very embarrassing to talk about, and people use humor to try to make it more comfortable. It usually ends up being crude humor. People feel they need that to get their point across. It's not a bad thing as long as people talk, as long as we raise awareness. That's what this is doing."

She was talking, and two little kids jumped inside the colon and raced through — rolling around, giggling. An older couple hobbled by, saw what the kids were up to, and — after the initial look of shock — laughed. The guy said he was tempted to "kick off the shoes, toss the cane and hop in with them."

A couple of young nursing students crawled in, and so did 66-year-old Mary Vaughn. She came and brought a bunch of friends with her.

"My daughter has been fighting colon cancer for three years, and I just had to see this for myself. I wanted my friends to come to help raise awareness, spread the word," she said.

So how did this thing end up here?

It was Shelley Anderson's idea. She's a cancer nurse, saw it in a trade magazine and read about how it was built by Molly McMaster, a woman who found out she had colon cancer when she was 23. McMaster started this national awareness crusade — skating from New York to Colorado, carrying the Olympic torch in 2002, running the New York City Marathon.

A 24-year-old woman whom McMaster met along the way died of colon cancer, so — in her memory — McMaster built the Colossal Colon. She got it on NBC's "Today" show and then took it on tour. Anderson heard about that, made a few calls, and now the exhibit is in Des Moines.

It'll be here until Thursday. And it's doing what Anderson hoped it would.

"Look at this. There are not too many people who can see it and not smile, not do a double-take. It gets people talking. It makes you wonder."

Which made sense. It had me wondering why the hell I was crawling through a colon.

'Passion' is awash in violence
February 25, 2004

It's tough to get people's attention these days. So you have to know what you're doing, and how far to push it.

You do the halftime show at the Super Bowl, show a little flesh, and you might get a quick mention on the news, a blurb in the paper. But pull out a breast, and you get a full-blown federal investigation.

A little prime-time peck on the cheek between Britney and Madonna won't even get a mention. But some tongue action between those two becomes one of the defining moments of the year.

You want to make a movie about religion and get a little buzz? Take Charlton Heston, dress him up like Moses and hand him the Ten Commandments.

You want to make a movie about religion and make it a national talking point during an election year? You want it to knock Janet and Britney off the front page?

If that's what you want, then you've got to market this right. Try months of hype, showing the movie only to a select few — from Rush Limbaugh to Pope John Paul II. That'll get people talking, calling your movie everything from brilliant to anti-Semitic.

Then trot out some kitschy little souvenirs, like T-shirts, books and large black nails on leather strings with Bible quotes on them. And make sure you've got the movie logo on a NASCAR entry.

Then, when the hype starts to get real old and tired, it's time to actually release the film.

This is where you've really got to deliver. It's got to be excessive, over the top, unlike anything anybody's ever seen on screen.

On that front, Mel Gibson delivers.

"The Passion of the Christ" is unique — good and bad.

It's a powerful look at the last 12 hours of Christ's life, and it shows the level of suffering. It does a good job of humanizing him, taking him down off the pedestal.

It shows him hanging around with his pals — the apostles — talking about God at the Last Supper, going through the consecration.

It shows him as a kid running around, falling, being gathered up in the safety of his mother's arms.

It shows him as a carpenter, making a table for a rich guy, sweating over the details, sharing a few laughs with his mom — who's not convinced this table is going to work.

Those moments in his life are all done in flashbacks and quick bites, and it's an interesting insight into Christ.

On the down side, "The Passion of the Christ" is too much Hollywood and way too much blood. It gives new meaning to how we think of on-screen violence.

Blood and violence have always been part of the mix in Christianity. The crucifix — the symbol at the heart of it all — is violent by definition.

If you went to Catholic school — or if you had an old Italian grandmother — you probably grew up looking at the image of Christ with blood dripping down his face from the crown of thorns, flowing from the holes in his hands and feet. So you expect some of that.

But this takes it to a new level.

Early in the film there's a fight and a guy gets his ear cut off. Blood all over the place. Then you've got a suicide. A bunch of little children gang up on a guy to beat him. At one point there's a large, rotting carcass — with close-ups of the animal's bug-infested face and stomach.

Once Christ is captured, the blood flow is nonstop. It runs for about the last 90 minutes of the two-hour film. He's beaten repeatedly with chains, sticks and fists. Over and over and over. The chains keep ripping away at his bloody flesh.

He's kicked, and they spit on him. He drags the cross, and they beat him the whole time. His blood is everywhere. You get close-ups of it pouring out of his eyes and out of his mouth. They keep beating him, throwing him to the ground and beating him some more.

Then you've got the scene where they finally nail him to the cross — with close-ups of the nails being driven into his hands and feet. Slowly. One blow at a time. Over and over. Relentless. It draws you in. It's got that same kind of compelling feel as the Janet and Madonna schtick.

So you sit and stare, the film ends and the room is silent — except for a few folks weeping softly. Nobody moves for about two minutes. Nobody can.

At last, there's comfort for tails of woe
June 30, 2004

When you're in this business, the news releases are nonstop. Everybody wants to get your attention — people on the left, people on the right, John Kerry.

You get the important stuff — political info from groups like Vegan Lesbians for Bush. Mostly, you get junk from these liberal crybabies looking for help.

But you have to sift through each item carefully, because every once in a while you get something that needs immediate attention. Something that's real news. The kind of thing people care about.

Like this announcement from the Surgery Center of Des Moines:

"BUTTOCK IMPLANTS NOW AVAILABLE
IN DES MOINES:
Local doctor first to offer them in the region."

Talk about shocking. You could have knocked me over with a deep-fried corn dog. I honestly hadn't realized it was a problem. And the folks I work with — journalists, all very well-informed — hadn't realized it either.

I showed the press release to one astute colleague, and his response was: "(Butt) implants around here? Isn't that like selling sand in the desert?"

Crass, but to the point.

This was big news. I called the doctor, Gene Cherny, and he agreed to talk about it. He asked me to meet him at the surgery center, in the cafeteria. I got there, and the meal of the day — and I'm serious — was macaroni with a side of mashed potatoes.

Now, wouldn't four or five plates of that stuff be a cheaper, less painful way to deal with the problem of a small behind?

I asked Cherny, and he answered with a straight face. He talked about how some folks lose a lot of weight — hundreds of pounds with gastric bypass — and they end up with this loose, flabby skin. They need an implant to round things out.

Some folks just want a more sculptured, attractive derriere. Cherny talked about how the idea of aesthetics is changing as we become a more multicultural society.

"Fuller lips, fuller breasts, fuller buttocks. That's attractive now. Fifteen years ago, I was doing lip reduction on African-American women. Not anymore. Now it's just the opposite. That's the look."

I started to ask Cherny if he'd heard of Mary-Kate Olsen, Lara Flynn Boyle or Uma Thurman, but the guy was on a roll. He talked about a return to the era when sex bombs were voluptuous women like Marilyn Monroe and Jayne Mansfield.

"Marilyn Monroe was probably a size 14 or 16. Today, that would be considered fat."

He said he has a waiting list of a dozen people wanting bigger bottoms. Nationally, this surgery was up 400 percent last year, and one-third of the patients were men.

It costs about $7,000, and I asked Cherny whether an HMO would pick up the tab.

Again with a straight face: "Forget it. They won't even cover heart attacks."

He said you'll need about two or three weeks to recover, and you have to stay off your back. So it probably wouldn't be a good idea to get butt and breast implants at the same time.

He talked about his practice — "a good mix of breast, face, nose, other body parts." And he talked about his own experience with plastic surgery.

"I had drooping skin on my face, so I had liposuction. I feel so much better about myself."

I thought about reaching over and giving him a little pinch on his new cheek, but I had work to do. What I needed was a real person. Someone who is actually having this surgery. Someone to put a face on this, so to speak.

Cherny made a quick call, and within minutes I was sitting across the table from Brenda Rowe, a 41-year-old nurse at the surgery center. She's 5 feet 2, 100 pounds, and she's getting the implants this fall.

Why?

"So I'll feel better. I just want to look good. I don't want to be some little old lady with a flat butt in elastic pants. I want roundness. I'm excited. I can't wait to go out dancing."

This wasn't always a problem. Back in high school, she "was full-figured."

So what happened?

"Everything happened — age, time, kids, gravity, men."

Rowe was wearing a long nurse's jacket so I couldn't really assess the extent of the problem. I thought a moment and decided we knew each other well enough to get personal. I asked, and she turned around and lifted her coat.

She wasn't that small, but I decided to let it go.

Lowdown on Bigfoot's demise
escapes Iowa columnist!

January 10, 2005

I took some time off, came back to work the other day and was eager to see what I'd missed. I opened my mail, and someone had sent me a front-page article from the Weekly World News headlined:
TWO-HEADED BIGFOOT SHOT BY IOWA COP.

There were exclusive photos of the cop gunning down the 8-foot creature, a cornfield in the background.

Also in the envelope was a note from a guy wanting to know how "The Des Moines Register, the Newspaper Iowa Depends Upon," could have missed this.

Reasonable question. I suspect we were too busy worrying about things like soda cans and tsunamis.

So I look at the magazine, and I see that's not all we missed.

We didn't have anything on this one:
AL-QAIDA PLANS TO DROP GAY BOMBS

Talk about the Bush administration's worst nightmare.

Then there was this one:
14% OF U.S. BRIDES ARE TRANSSEXUALS

A new study reveals there's a better than 1-in-10 chance that your wife or girlfriend was once a man!

That would certainly explain a lot.

I was sad to see we also missed the story about **DIVORCED PARENTS BATTLE TO SPLIT TWO-HEADED CHILD.**

But I was letting myself get distracted. I had to focus on this local story.

The piece said this happened in rural Iowa, about 60 miles outside Great Bend. It said the cops pumped at least 40 bullets into the creature's chest. 40?

So I'm thinking we could at least have done a story on how the cops are wasting tax dollars.

An angry scientist was quoted saying the cops acted "callously," and an animal-rights activist was even more angry, saying the police were "out of control" and calling them "a bunch of cowboys."

The article went on to say that Iowa authorities refused to discuss the incident, but an unidentified police source dismissed the activists and scientists as "eggheads."

Eggheads? That is so Iowa.

At that point I wanted to get in the car and go out to the Great Bend area, talk with some folks, maybe get lucky and interview a few witnesses. So I put the magazine down, checked the map, and I found there was no Great Bend in Iowa. Not even a Good Bend.

I wasn't going to let myself get discouraged. I called the Iowa Department of Public Safety, and the woman who answered the phone asked what I was calling about. I told her I wanted to know about the Bigfoot shooting near Great Bend and — after a moment of silence — she said she'd have someone get back to me.

It took a while, but eventually I got a call from Capt. Pat Hoye of the Iowa State Patrol. He was familiar with the story — "I saw it on the rack when I was going through the checkout line at Wal-Mart."

But he knew nothing about the actual incident.

"I'll be honest with you, as a high-ranking officer with the state I would have thought I'd have known. But I didn't."

I pressed him a bit, and the best I could get from Hoye was some speculation "that maybe it had something to do with RAGBRAI. I've seen more than a few two-headed monsters on that bike ride."

So there's no Great Bend, and the top cops don't know about this.

I needed a different perspective. I checked with Robert Shumaker, the man in charge of the Great Ape Trust of Iowa. Shumaker is an internationally recognized authority on primates, a man who has devoted his life to the study of this subject.

I called and asked if the Bigfoot shooting had caused a buzz among the primate crowd. The doctor claimed not to know what I was talking about.

"I wish I did know about it. I'd be curious to see even a one-headed Bigfoot shot by the cops. In any state."

There was an element of sarcasm in his voice. He seemed eager to get off the phone. So I let it go.

It was time to go to the source. I called the Weekly World News and asked to speak to Mike Foster, the guy who wrote the article.

I was told there is no Mike Foster. "That's just a pen name."

I told the woman where I was calling from, what I wanted and asked to speak to the paper's editor.

I was told "that is not possible."

End of discussion.

So I just gave up and got back to that story about how there's a 1-in-10 chance that your wife or girlfriend was once a man!

There's got to be an Iowa angle on that one.

Bringing home the bacon
with prosciutto plant

January 17, 2005

Herb Eckhouse is one of the first folks I met when I moved to Des Moines. I was impressed with the guy:

Harvard graduate, Pioneer executive who ran operations in Russia, France, Italy and Japan. A world traveler who has walked the streets of Bangalore, and cruised the canals of Venice.

He's a family man — married 25 years and the father of three extremely gifted children.

He's one of those guys whose input I seek. I value his insights and respect his opinions.

Then, about a year ago, we were talking and Herb mentioned that he was going to build a factory in Norwalk and manufacture prosciutto.

My first reaction was to get in his face and say: "Hey, goomba, where I come from it's not 'pro-shoo toe.' It's 'pro-zhoot.' So get it right."

My next reaction was to say: "A prosciutto factory in rural Iowa? What the hell are you talking about?"

Then there was the whole thing about this Jewish guy from Des Moines selling pork to Italian chefs and shopkeepers in New York and Jersey, Chicago and Vegas.

But I didn't even go there. I just figured I'd back off and wait until Herb came to his senses, realized this was crazy and found work as a consultant.

That was a year ago.

Thursday I was walking the halls of La Quercia, the 9,900-square-foot prosciutto factory on a hill at the south edge of Norwalk. So how did this happen?

This goes back to the years when Herb worked in Italy for Pioneer. He lived in Parma, a place where prosciutto is a $2 billion-a-year business. He loved the stuff. When he moved back to Iowa he got to thinking: "We produce all these commodities like corn, beans and pork and then we ship it out. Why not keep it here?"

He left Pioneer in 2000 and has spent the past four years fantasizing about owning a prosciutto factory.

Now he's ready. The grand opening is a week from today and Herb has invited everyone who has touched his life — from Lt. Gov. Sally Pederson to Rabbi David Kaufman.

Pederson said she'll be there.

Herb's looking to produce a few hundred thousand pounds of prosciutto a year — using Iowa pork.

And he'll have about seven employees — a labor boom in Norwalk, a town of about 7,000.

That got me wondering about how this deal is playing out with the locals.

I went downtown to Rudy's Bar and Grill on Main Street and talked to Bob Ross, the bartender. I asked how much he was hearing about the factory, are folks excited, what's the buzz at the bar?

Blank stare.

Then he remembered.

"Oh, you mean that place where they're going to make sausage or ham or something? Don't hear much, but it's a new business and that's good."

Some folks at the bar heard that and said it'll be good to have Norwalk famous for something besides baton twirlers. I didn't get it.

While they were explaining, Marty Bussanmas came in and grabbed a table for lunch. He's a trucker from Norwalk. I asked about the factory and I asked Marty if he'd ever eaten prosciutto.

"I think I have, but I won't swear to it."

Pause.

"No wait, that was portobello. That's not meat. I don't know that I've ever had that stuff."

But he'll try anything if it shows up on Rudy's menu.

Across the street and down the block I found the Norwalk Hardware Store. It was empty but the owner waved me in to his back office.

I walked in and the place smelled like my Aunt Millie's apartment on a Sunday — meatballs, heavy on the garlic. On the desk was a bag with prosciutto, salami, copacolla and some cheeses.

I'm wondering if this is some kind of setup, but it turns out this guy is Domonick Cimino and he grew up on the south side of Des Moines. He just got back from Graziano's and he's having lunch.

Nobody has to tell Cimino the difference between portobello and prosciutto.

He laughs and says: "I'm just hoping I can get some free samples."

Then he gets serious.

"We need business in this town and I'm excited about having this place here."

But he's not as excited as Herb Eckhouse — a Harvard grad, a world traveler, a family man, a corporate executive, a man who will be remembered as that guy who opened the prosciutto factory in Iowa.

"So I'm talkin' to this guy . . ."

Chapter 5: New York/Personal

By Rekha Basu
Columnist/*The Des Moines Register*

Some of my friends were intimidated the first time they met Rob. They saw the black leather jacket, the sarcasm, the fast-talking tough-guy confidence.

Then they got to know him, found the soft inner core, and wondered how they'd misjudged.

Rob's New York is a place where the hard edges can conceal the heart for only so long. He may have grown up in "the borough of last resort," but that perception others had of the Bronx was lost on him.

As he put it, "We didn't know we weren't supposed to feel good about ourselves. We thought we were to be envied."

The Rob I fell in love with is energized by urban chaos but shattered to learn a child has no

201

Christmas gifts to look forward to. Slices through political hypocrisy with paring-knife precision, but is undone by a stranger's pain, a son's departure for college.

Meets challenges head-on, never looking back — swearing off alcohol and cigarettes with one giant step where others might take 12.

And spreads laughter even through the toughest times, because life is too damn short not to.

So long, Uncle Bill
September 16, 1996

Bill Monroe's death last week wasn't a great shock. It had been expected. For years. And years.

The first time I heard Monroe was at death's door was in 1975 when he canceled a gig in upstate New York claiming poor health. And then a few years later I heard he had terminal cancer — not true — and it was going to kill him any minute.

And ever since then, there's been talk that "Uncle Bill ain't got but a little time left in this ol' world."

But he kept on touring, playing one-nighters at a pace that made him a legend in an industry where too many of the great ones died on the road.

Monroe died in bed. He would have been 85 last Friday.

He was one of a few musicians who could claim ownership of a musical form. In recent times, only Bob Marley and Muddy Waters come to mind.

And even those two didn't invent the genre. Monroe did. In fact, the music was named for his home state, Kentucky, the Blue Grass State.

Sometime between his birth in 1911 and his debut at the Grand Old Opry in 1939, Monroe perfected bluegrass, a hard-driving sound created by a combination of fiddle, banjo, mandolin, guitar and bass.

It was — it's been said — folk music in overdrive.

I first heard that sound in the late 1950s when I was about 8 or 9. For some reason my grandfather — a construction worker who came to the United States from Calabria in the '20s — liked bluegrass. It may have been, like baseball, his connection to America. He called it "cowboy music," and I will not attempt in print to show you how it sounds when pronounced with a thick Italian accent.

And so I'd sit with him, and we'd listen to Bill Monroe and His Bluegrass Boys on the big old Philco radio in my grandmother's kitchen, tapping along with "Blue Moon of Kentucky" or "Little Cabin Home on the Hill."

I didn't hear much about Monroe after my grandfather died in 1963. But when I rediscovered his music in the '70s, I read about all those years when his bands were a proving ground for acoustic musicians — Earl Scruggs, Lester Flatt, Mac Wiseman, Peter Rowan, Vassar Clements, Jimmy Martin.

Playing with Monroe was a necessary credential in the brotherhood of bluegrass. Through the '70s and early '80s, I'd heard him play at about a half-dozen festivals. And then — in the summer of 1983 — I was working at a newspaper in New York City. An editor walked into the newsroom and asked, somewhat hopelessly, "Any of you guys know anything at all about bluegrass music?"

Yeah, I told him, I knew enough not to call it bluegrass music. It's just plain bluegrass.

He handed me a picture of Bill Monroe and went into a long-winded story about how he was playing in town that week and some editor higher up the line wanted us to interview Monroe — this guy kept calling him Malone — and write about how traditional country music was becoming so popular.

A few nights later, I found myself sitting in a dingy dressing room at Manhattan's Lone Star Cafe waiting for an American legend. I'd been in the news business about 10 years then, and I'd interviewed three U.S. presidents, the former prime minister of Britain, the future prime minister of Israel, a handful of governors, a bushel of mayors and a couple of Miss Americas.

But none of the politicians had a message as honest and straightforward as Monroe's and — so far as I could tell — none of the beauty queens could hit those high notes while playing the mandolin and buck dancing.

When Monroe walked into the room, he seemed somewhat frail and tired, walking a bit slow and stoop-shouldered. He sat in a straight-backed wooden chair across from me, and before I could ask my first question, he asked his.

"Where you from, son?"

I told him I grew up right there in the city.

And he talked for some 15 minutes about rural life just after the turn of the century, poverty, his health problems as a child. I was thoroughly fascinated.

He loved baseball, traveling and farming. And from there, he segued into talking about his music. He kept calling it "the people's music."

When we wrapped up the interview, I wondered to myself how this old guy was going to drag himself up, get dressed and go out and play to the 500 or so people that had packed into that club.

I went out and took my seat in the audience and waited.

The lights went down and the announcer said, "please welcome Bill Monroe and His Blue Grass Boys," and out leading the pack — in a freshly pressed suit, white shirt and tie, large white cowboy hat — was Monroe, just vaguely resembling the frail guy I'd talked to backstage.

He walked to the mike, tipped his hat, lifted the mandolin, and ripped into "Rawhide," a rollicking instrumental that served as his signature tune.

For an hour or so he played, he sang, he danced.

He was Bill Monroe.

Rob Borsellino

1963: A Thanksgiving of sorrow
Novemer 22, 1997

It was sixth period, English, and I got the pass and walked down the hall to the boys' bathroom for a cigarette. I was about three drags into my Marlboro when Ralphie Lattarulo came busting in, yelling something about the president getting shot.

"Whaddya talkin' about shot? Who shot him?" I asked, trying to act only half-interested, waiting for what I figured would be a punch line.

"Some guy in Texas whacked Kennedy about an hour ago," Ralphie said. "Spano (the gym teacher) said he got a call from his sister who said they broke into the soaps to announce it. It's all over the TV."

I was still sort of thinking, maybe hoping, I was being set up for something. But just in case, I threw the rest of the cigarette in the toilet and headed out into the hall.

Right across from the bathroom was Miss Illovar's room. She was the tall, blond math teacher with the beautiful face that most of the boys at Junior High School 135 dreamed about at least three times a week.

She was there in front of me, sitting at her desk, her head in her hands, tears everywhere. I started to ask her a dumb question. I started to ask her if it was true that somebody killed the president.

Teachers in that part of New York City, at that time, did not cry in front of the kids. So I knew Ralphie was right.

Within minutes the bells were going off, the principal was on the PA telling us to go back to our homerooms and then we were dismissed for the day.

I walked home through the same two miles of streets I walked every day. But that day people — grown men and women, kids and cops and shopkeepers and bus drivers and delivery guys — were crying.

Strangers hugged.

Black and white and Hispanic — people who normally didn't have the time of day for one another were offering comfort where they could.

About a block from our apartment I saw my mother coming home early from her factory job. She threw her arms around me and cried uncontrollably. We got in the elevator, rode to the second floor, went into the apartment and turned on the tube without saying a word.

The next three days, as I remember them, were a blur of tears, and sadness, anger, disbelief: Jack Ruby shooting Lee Harvey Oswald on live

TV, Lyndon Johnson sworn in, Jackie in the veil, John Jr. saluting his father's casket, Bobby and Teddy and the Kennedy sisters all in black.

I sat in front of the tube all day and I hung out with my friends at night. We talked about the assassination in the unsophisticated way we talked about everything in those days. We made crude jokes about the beautiful Jackie being left alone and we laughed about the nefarious Richard Nixon guiding the finger that pulled the trigger.

But even we were wise enough to realize something had changed, that a line had been crossed and there was no returning to the lives we were living before Friday, Nov. 22, 1963.

Thirty-four years have passed since those bullets were fired and, after all this time, a guy who was president for a little more than 1,000 days can still command center stage.

With the release of Sy Hersh's book on Kennedy, "The Dark Side of Camelot" — and the emphasis on his sexual escapades and mob connections — the long-dead president is back on the cover of Time and occupying prime real estate in the New Yorker and the Sunday New York Times.

Every sketchy detail of his brief time in the White House is being picked over on the morning shows and talk radio.

Fair enough. You put yourself out there in public and you're up for grabs.

But at this time of year I don't think about who Kennedy slept with or whether he was mobbed up or if he put his hatred of Fidel Castro ahead of his country's security.

What I see is Connie Illovar crying at her desk and my mother leaving work early and probably losing five bucks she could have used.

I see the rough-edged folks in that working-class neighborhood crying and comforting one another on a bright autumn afternoon.

I remember a Thanksgiving when people in this country felt mostly sorrow, as if there was little to be thankful for.

Some years after the assassination I read a magazine article about that weekend. In the piece there was a description of a conversation between writer Mary McGrory and Daniel Patrick Moynihan.

As I recall it, McGrory — sensing the all-consuming sadness around them — said to Moynihan: "We'll never laugh again."

To which Moynihan said: "Heavens, Mary, we'll laugh again. We just will never be young again."

'Pvt. Ryan' reminds him of what war did to Danny

August 4, 1998

Danny Vellone came home from Korea in the summer of '53 and spent the next 35 years trying to get over the war. He finally died in the winter of '88 — in a veterans hospital — and those of us who loved him felt a sense of relief.

He never married, couldn't hold a job for more than a few months, couldn't stay sober for more than a few days, and never had his own place — he slept on the couch in his mother's living room for almost his entire adult life. And he never talked about what happened to him in the service.

Never. No matter how much he had to drink.

Danny — his real name was Dominick — was my mother's brother, my uncle. And you couldn't have designed a man less suited to the atrocities of combat. In our neighborhood — where sensitive meant weak — he was among the few gentle and soft-spoken men.

But after the war, the alcohol made him violent and abusive, and it was a rare night when he wasn't drinking.

I went to see "Saving Private Ryan" a week ago and I haven't been able to get the movie or Danny out of my mind. I've been thinking about a conversation we had late in the summer of '68, a few days after I received a letter from the draft board telling me to come down and take a physical.

I was 19, out of high school, not in college, single and ripe for the service. This was the period of the so-called Tet Offensive and the U.S. was throwing planeloads of young boys at the North Vietnamese. They were sending them back in body bags. I knew four guys from the neighborhood who were killed. I was not a particularly political kid, but I was beginning to think this whole Vietnam deal might not be a good thing.

And I had an out.

I was the only child of a widow and — at least on paper — was the sole support of the family. But I still had some crazy notion that it was my responsibility to go in the service. It was as if you couldn't really call yourself a man until you did.

All my life one old guy or another was telling me I was a punk kid and "The Army will make a man outta ya."

I had always believed them. Now I wasn't sure.

So one night after work I went over to my grandmother's house and sat down at the kitchen table with my uncle and — for the first time — I got him to talk to me about his war.

We sat there well past midnight, smoking Luckies and drinking quarts of Rheingold, a watery brew that was cheap.

He said a lot of things to me about what he saw and what he did in Korea. But the lines that stayed with me were: "It's not like in the movies. This was real blood. These guys didn't get up again. They were dead."

He talked about charging up snow-covered hills and watching guys in front of him, beside him and behind him get cut down by gunfire — some running a few steps even after they had their heads severed from their bodies or after they were virtually cut in half by a blast.

He talked about having to pull dog tags off dead kids — the same kids he had been sharing a smoke and a laugh with an hour earlier — and then having to stack those bodies like a cord of wood.

And in the years since then, he said, he stayed awake nights wondering why he lived and all those other guys didn't.

Then — on the verge of tears, but not quite crying — he said he was still angry because people never understood what the Korean vets went through. The World War II guys were heroes — fighting for God and country. But the government didn't even have the decency to call Korea a war. About 140,000 Americans dead or wounded, and they were calling it a conflict or a police action.

And he said he could see this Vietnam business was going the same way.

As things turned out, the decision was taken out of my hands — I got number 360 in this country's first draft lottery, effectively ending any chance I had of being sent to Vietnam.

I called Danny to tell him the news. He said it was about time one of us caught a break and he was glad it was me.

And then he said: "Somebody must be looking out for you."

Clinton managed to confess
using vague terms
August 19, 1998

Listening to Bill Clinton go through his very public act of contrition the other night, two things came to mind.

First: I'm thinking we might need a national day of atonement — something like a Yom Kippur that would include the goyim. It would be an excellent opportunity for each of us — once a year — to make a public confession for all our indiscretions in the prior 12 months.

It would have a wonderful healing effect. It would level the playing field between us common sinners and all the saints who vent their spleen on talk radio.

And — if the national landscape is any barometer — our poll numbers won't suffer.

Second: I'm thinking, on the confession front, Clinton got off easy. Real easy. All he had to do was go before the world and admit to "a relationship with Ms. Lewinsky that was not appropriate."

I used to have to go mouth to ear every Saturday night with Father Christopher, pastor of the Immaculate Conception Church — with only a small piece of plastic separating us in the confessional. And, as pastor, he knew the voice of just about every adult and child who went to the church.

With Father Christopher, there was none of this "inappropriate relationship" nonsense. You had to tell him what you did. When we tried to couch our behavior in vague terms – "I had impure thoughts and actions, father" — he wanted to know, in detail, what exactly we were talking about, as if he didn't know.

If you stole, he wanted to know what you stole, why and what you did with it. He did not offer "transactional immunity." There were no subpoenas to be dodged and no deals to be struck. You showed up at church, without benefit of counsel.

You did not blame Kenneth Starr or Satan.

And when it was over, the punishment was swift and certain — you received your penance.

"Son, I want you to say five 'Our Fathers' and 10 'Hail Marys.' Now say the 'Act of Contrition.' And Robert, behave yourself this week."

Then he would mumble something in Latin and I would try to detect some connection between the penance and the behavior. Like, would using the Lord's name in vain and stealing yield more penance than just stealing? Exactly how much would it cost me to worship a few false gods while coveting my neighbors' goods?

I could never get a fix on how that worked.

Many a night I wanted to demand to know why the week before — when my behavior was clearly much worse — my penance was the same, or less. But you didn't argue with Father Christopher. He seemed to have the power to bring a plague of locusts down on your house.

So Tuesday — with confession in the air — I tried again to get a handle on penance. I called Monsignor Frank Bognanno at St. Augustin's in Des Moines and asked if there's a priest's handbook that tells them how to dole out penance.

No, he said, but there are guidelines. He had to go back in his mind 33 years to seminary training.

"You want to assign a penance that will be medicinal. You want something that will help the person. If they confess to something that is of a very serious nature, it might be unwise to give them serious penance because they already feel so bad about what they did.

"On the other hand, you may have the impression that this person would like to do something demanding because they want to demonstrate their sincerity and penitence."

OK monsignor, let's take this a step further. Based on President Clinton's statement Monday night, if he came into your confessional and unburdened himself, what would you consider fair penance?

"From what he said (Monday) night, I couldn't even tell you what he did. It's as if someone came in and said they were guilty of misconduct. My question" — said Monsignor Bognanno, sounding very much like Father Christopher — "would be, could you be a little more specific?"

In home run race, he's silently rooting for Maris

September 8, 1998

All summer long, I've been living this lie. I've been making believe I want Mark McGwire or Sammy Sosa to break the home run record. I've done this because my 12-year-old is really into it, and I didn't have the heart to tell him I'd have been a lot happier if the two of them hit 60 apiece, got jungle rot and went on the disabled list for the rest of the season.

But I've played along, checking the papers with him, surfing the Net, watching ESPN every night, feigning excitement when Sosa hit one and McGwire answered with two.

I did it because I was 12 once, and I remember a few things about what that was like.

It was the summer of '61, and Roger Maris and Mickey Mantle were chasing Babe Ruth's 1927 record. There was no Net to surf and no ESPN to watch. If the game wasn't on TV — and if we missed the radio sports updates — we'd have to go down to the corner newsstand at night and wait for the big black Daily News truck to pull up and drop off the next day's paper.

We'd rip the paper out of the bundle — the stand owner would be cursing us in a strange combination of Yiddish and Lower East Side — and turn to the back page for our sports fix.

Then we'd argue.

Mantle was a genuine hero — an all-around ballplayer who could hit .300, smack 50 homers, steal bases and bunt if he had to. He could play center field in the tradition of Joe DiMaggio. He played hurt. And he was a lifelong Yankee.

Maris was a .260 hitter who came over from Cleveland and Kansas City and would probably be gone soon. But he was having a good year, and at least he was a Yankee. So either way, the record would stay in New York, where it belonged.

The record was like some sort of heirloom that had been in the family for generations. It belonged to us — like DiMaggio's 56-game hitting streak and Don Larsen's perfect game in the '56 series and the 14 pennants in 16 years. These weren't just baseball records. They were Yankee records. Our records. The home run record was always our record.

Ruth set it in 1920 with 54, broke it the next year with 59 and then he broke it again in '27 with 60.

Then, in 1961, it was going to be broken one more time. By a Yankee.

That was very important to a 12-year-old. I didn't know it then, but that was the last summer when baseball would have that kind of importance in my life.

I was going from elementary school into seventh grade — junior high — and I was on the verge of discovering girls and some other stuff that could also be harmful if you overindulged.

But that all came later. I was totally focused on the record, and I must have gone to 20 games that season. When either of those guys would come to bat, Yankee Stadium would be dead silent. The hawkers would stop hawking; folks heading out for refreshments would just stop where they were and wait.

When Mantle went down in mid-September with the flu, Maris was in it alone. I wanted him to break the record, and when he did — on Oct. 1, the last day of the season — I felt like I'd accomplished something. And I knew I'd never forget the feeling of that summer-long chase for the record.

Meanwhile, there were all these old guys — a lot of them sportswriters — moaning about how Mantle and Maris together weren't good enough to carry the Babe's jock. I didn't get it. It was an exciting summer to be following baseball. The Yankees had a 25-game winner and six guys with more than 20 home runs. And they were battling the Tigers for the pennant until September.

But all these old guys could think about was keeping alive an event that — as far as I was concerned — happened right after the pilgrims landed at Plymouth Rock.

I suspect in a few years baseball won't seem quite as important to my kid as it does today. So I've played along. I don't want him looking back on this summer and remembering his old man as some cranky guy who was hissing and moaning about McGwire needing all those strength pills to break the record. Which reminds me — did I mention that Maris didn't need drugs to set the record?

No Pulitzer, but a new way of looking at Christmas season

December 24, 1998

This one's for those folks out there who just want to pull the covers over their heads and pray for Christmas to go away. I can relate. I felt that way all through my teens and well into my 20s. Then I met an interesting kid and he helped turn me around.

It happened in the late '70s at the Kingston Daily Freeman — my first newspaper job. Kingston is in New York's Hudson Valley, about 90 miles north of Manhattan, and the 20-person newsroom was an odd collection of misfits, alcoholics, aging journalists and reckless young bucks looking to make a name for themselves. The features editor had a breakdown one morning and disappeared into the state mental health grinder. The sports editor ended up behind bars on a manslaughter rap.

The publisher was a brilliant loner, barely 30, who later bought himself a tiny island off the coast of Connecticut — his house is the only thing on the island — and retired.

The editor was a street-smart woman from the blue-collar Massachusetts town of Lawrence who later went off to the island of Malta to start a newspaper.

She ran the Freeman in the post-Watergate era, when every reporter was certain a Pulitzer Prize was behind every closed door in every City Hall in the country. The Freeman staff was infected with that disease. In a three-year period, the paper's constant hounding drove the mayor, the sheriff and the chairman of the county legislature into retirement.

The editor decided we needed something to show the community we had a heart. So she started a Christmas fund. She went to the county welfare office and got the names of families in need who would be willing to have their hard-luck stories plastered on the front page — with photos. The money would go into a pool and would be doled out to all families, not just those who agreed to speak with us. Then each of the paper's reporters was expected to knock out one of these tear-jerkers every week between Thanksgiving and Christmas Eve, making sure there was one in the paper every day.

And like everything else at the Freeman, this became a competitive exercise among the staff. We'd try our damnedest to write the saddest, most heart-rending story. After work, we'd have a few beers and a few laughs and argue over who had written the most maudlin piece. Late in the season, I was sure I'd locked up first place. I interviewed a father and son living in a shelter and they only had one coat between them.

My story ran under a 6-column banner headline — "Father and Son Share Overcoat." The outpouring from the community was exceptional. So was the response from my colleagues, most of it punctuated with that sick newsroom humor: "Hey, Pop, can I borrow the coat tonight? I've got a hot date."

I was about to claim victory when, a few days before Christmas, a reporter named Rick Remsnyder came into the newsroom with a tale to tell. We gathered around his desk and Remsnyder — a quiet guy who last I heard was writing for Golf Digest — seemed shaken.

He'd just come from the home of an elderly couple who lived in a two-story walk-up on the seedy side of town. And they were raising their 8-year-old grandson, a kid who I believe was named Ricky.

The only sign of Christmas in the apartment was an anemic plastic tree that they'd found on the street, dragged home and propped up in a corner. The only sign that a child lived there was some overused toys strewn about the living room floor. They were the kind of toys they give out at the fast-food places when you buy kid meals.

The couple didn't have much to say, but Ricky did. He said he'd have a happy Christmas if his grandma could get a robe and if Grandpa could have warm slippers.

"What about you?" Remsnyder asked.

The kid said he didn't need anything. But he was going to wrap up his old toys and put them under the tree so he'd have something to open on Christmas morning.

We stood around Remsnyder's desk and tried not to let each other see the tears.

The story ran, and the community response was just what you'd expect. For weeks after Christmas, folks were sending gifts and money.

There was other fallout. That was the last time we handled the Christmas Fund as an exercise for our amusement. And closer to home, not a Christmas goes by when I don't think about that kid.

Remembering Joe D. — the heart and soul of a dynasty

March 9, 1999

I always felt like I owed something to Joe DiMaggio. This was not some intellectual exercise. It was pure emotion.

In the 1950s, in the New York City of my childhood, the pecking order went something like this: Manhattan was the class act of the five boroughs — the glamour of Broadway, the high-end Upper East Side, the cutting-edge hipness of the Village.

Brooklyn was that colorful offbeat place of movie fame. If you were from Brooklyn, you were tough and talked funny and you rooted for that lovable bunch of losers called the Dodgers.

Queens? Staten Island? They might as well have been part of Jersey or Long Island. They were gray places that nobody I knew had ever been to.

And the Bronx was the borough of last resort. The dumping ground for those blacks and whites of every ethnic stripe who just couldn't seem to get with the program in the New World.

But growing up in the Bronx, we didn't know we weren't supposed to feel good about ourselves. In fact, we were actually an arrogant bunch. We thought we were to be envied. We had something no place else on Earth had: the New York Yankees.

From April through October, they were only a 15-cent subway ride away.

During the first 16 years of my life, the Yankees won the pennant 14 times. So I grew up expecting to win. Nobody I hung out with went through life feeling they'd be lucky to come in second. Or finish in the top 10.

We grew up in the company of the Yankee dynasty.

And the heart and soul of that dynasty was Joe DiMaggio — a guy whose skills on the ballfield cast a long elegant shadow over that teeming borough and the folks who lived there.

Years after DiMaggio was out of the game, kids would go to the stadium with their fathers and grandfathers and watch Mantle make a great catch in center or see Maris hit home runs into the upper deck or Berra stroke liners to every corner of that vast ballpark, and the reaction from the adult was always something along the lines of: "You think that's good? You shoulda seen Joe D. play the game."

Joe D.

It worked on several levels. People would talk about him like he was a member of the family. But he was also revered. He was a god in a time and place that needed heroes.

It went beyond baseball. He was a very private man in a very public city. A class act in a town that was prone to crude behavior on a grand scale. He married Marilyn Monroe — bringing together the sex appeal and glitz of Hollywood and the wholesome image of the national pastime.

And in our family — and a lot of families like it — there was also the Italian thing. Like Sinatra, Joe D. was one of us. In some circles, where ethnic pride was often confused with personal accomplishment, that was very powerful.

But it wasn't until years later that I really understood the reach of DiMaggio's mystique. In the late '60s, among the social upheaval, there was Paul Simon's metaphor: "Where have you gone, Joe DiMaggio?" Simon wanted to know where the heroes had gone. He said it all by asking about DiMaggio.

You grow up and move away from the Bronx, you go off to college and meet other guys who tell you they have the same reaction to DiMaggio.

You move to Des Moines and you run into a guy like Pete Leonetti, a former Yankee farm prospect now in his 70s. Weeks ago — as Joe D. lies dying — Leonetti says: "I pray for him every day."

And you know what he means.

You ask Leonetti if he ever met DiMaggio, and he says no, but he saw him in a Chicago train station almost 60 years ago. He still remembers that feeling.

"There were about 200 people, and I go and look at what's going on and there's Joe DiMaggio. In person. I looked at him and, Rob, it was like I was looking at the Lord. It's something I can't explain."

That's OK, Pete. You don't have to.

Memories of the Bronx still alive
after 35 years
October 26, 1999

In the summer of '64, the Beatles and the Stones were edging the Four Seasons and Dion off the charts. Guys' hair was getting longer, girls' skirts were getting shorter, the Yankees were heading for their 14th pennant in 16 years. Kennedy was dead, Johnson was in the White House, and most Americans couldn't find Vietnam on a map of Asia.

I was 15 and living in a public housing project in the Bronx. That summer the guys I ran with — a loose-knit group of nine or 10 — spent days and nights hanging out in Bronx Park. Our base was a 15-foot cliff surrounded on three sides by woods. The fourth side jutted out over the Bronx River Parkway.

In later times we might have been called a street gang. But — as those things go — we were pretty tame. Fists were the preferred weapon of combat. A tire iron or a chain might be needed to get you through a tough part of the projects, but that was rare. An occasional knife would be flashed, usually to send a message.

Cigarettes were the vice of choice and on weekends we might bribe some local drunk to buy us a few six-packs of Rheingold or some other watery beer. On special occasions — birthdays, holidays — one of the guys could be counted on to steal a gallon of cheap wine from his old man.

When you talked about drugs you were talking about heroin. Pot was still something that junkies smoked.

Once in a while we'd venture out to the movies or a dance or to the pool room. Mostly we'd hang out on that rock and talk trash. We called that spot the Cove.

One afternoon a couple of us went up to the hardware store on the avenue and — while the owner's back was turned — helped ourselves to a hammer and chisel. Fifteen minutes later we were back at the Cove, carving our names in the rock.

Paul's name was on top. Then, in no particular order, Dougie and Mike, Russell, Gene and Bobby, Ralph, Jerry and Joey were chipped into the stone. If we'd thought about it, it was the only way any of us expected to leave our mark on the world. When summer ended, we pretty much abandoned the Cove.

And in the next few years the group splintered. Some of us got into motorcycles, started hanging out at the neighborhood bars and married young. Others headed downtown to the Village and got swept up in all that the '60s are known for. Gene, Russell and Jerry went into the service. Ralph went to college. Dougie went to prison.

Last week I was back in the Bronx hanging out with Gene and — for the first time in 35 years — we went down to the park and out to the Cove. Our names were still there. I had to rub my fingers across the rock to make sure I was really seeing them.

I stood on the cliff and thought about the way it all turned out. For the most part we did OK for ourselves. Among us we've got a truck driver, a guy who does research for a drug company, a journalist and a couple of small-business owners. Russell survived homelessness — he lived under a Queens bridge for a few years — and now works for the city as a painter.

Mike and his brother Dougie are both dead — Mike from a heart attack, Dougie from cirrhosis of the liver. We've moved to Long Island, and Jersey, Connecticut, Brooklyn and Yonkers. Gene stayed in the Bronx. One of the guys is in exile in a place called Iowa.

Everybody's been married at least once, and we've all got kids. Several of us are in recovery from drugs or alcohol or both. There's been a fair amount of tragedy in each of our lives.

I found all this out last Sunday when we got together for the first time since the days of the Cove.

If you measure things in dollars — who's got the biggest house, the most toys — some made out better than others. But we didn't measure that way — not then and not now. We got together, looked around the room and saw the same guys who carved their names in the rock on a summer afternoon 35 years ago.

Mob's gone prime time, leaving the old school behind

January 20, 2000

The mob guy in charge of our neighborhood was Angelo. Out of respect, they called him Don Angelo. He was a short, fat, gray-haired man who wore shiny suits that smelled of a sickly combination of basil and mothballs.

This was pre-Godfather days, but Don Angelo already had it down — the slow talk, the ambling walk.

On the organized-crime front, this neighborhood was not prime real estate. For the most part, it was nickel-and-dime stuff — loansharking, protection, numbers, prostitution. Nobody was getting rich here. Nobody was getting whacked. Don Angelo's job was to keep things in order, keep everybody in line. They didn't want a lot of free-lance hoods skimming off the top.

His base of operation was a little grocery store and coffee shop a few blocks from Our Lady of Grace Church. All day long, folks were in and out of that shop, looking for favors, borrowing money, making loan payments, just making sure they were on the guy's good side.

Occasionally, I'd go in there with one of my grandparents to buy something, and Don Angelo would be sitting at a back table, shooting the breeze in broken English, cursing in Italian, insisting that one of the teen-age girls come over and sit on his lap. Sometimes he'd throw the little kids some change and say, "Goa buy youself icy creama." So we'd take the money and — quietly among ourselves — make fun of the way the old guy talked.

We meant no disrespect. We were kids.

I didn't understand what Don Angelo was about until he died. There was an outpouring like I'd never seen. Limos and Cadillacs lined the streets for about five blocks in both directions around the funeral home. The church was filled with flowers and street-level wiseguys from all over the city. The talk was that Angelo was one of the last old-school dons. He ruled by reason, not muscle.

People talked about it in hushed tones, looking over their shoulders. To a little kid, this was all very exciting. It was all very mysterious.

But now, 40 or so years down the road, there's no mystery. The mob's gone Hollywood. We've had "The Godfather" times three, "Goodfellas," "Married to the Mob," "Analyze This" and a bunch of others.

The mob's gone literary. We've had books from Joe Valachi, Sammy Gravano and some lesser lights — insiders looking at La Cosa Nostra. We've got Gravano doing a *New York Times* piece on the death of Mario Puzo.

And now the mob's gone prime time: We've got the *Sopranos*.

Tony Soprano, his family, his friends — Pavarti and Livia, Big Pussy, Paulie and Silvio, Carmela and the rest — are staring out at you from *Time* and *Newsweek*. They made the editorial page of the *Sunday New York Times* and the cover of *The Des Moines Register's* TV guide.

There's a life-size poster of Tony in the window at the mall. He wants you to buy his CD.

The word on the show — the big selling point — is that the characters are real. The other night, I tuned in to find out.

One minute into it they were playing Sinatra's "It Was a Very Good Year." That worked. Then the wife was pulling a lasagna out of the oven, and Tony was sitting there with what looked like a St. Christopher medal dangling from his fat neck. Tony — talking about his mother — says: "She's dead to me."

All of that rang true.

But then Tony goes outside to catch a quick smoke because he doesn't want the wife and kids to see him. He talks with his sister about "personal growth," and his wife heats the pasta in the microwave. Later, one of the hoods smacks his girlfriend in a bar and — in front of the guys — she smacks him back.

And he doesn't kill her.

None of that makes sense. Particularly the last part.

The whole time I'm watching the show, I'm trying to picture Don Angelo pitching his new movie, his book, his CD. Or having an anxiety attack or sneaking a cigarette so the wife doesn't see him.

I try to imagine Don Angelo sitting around with the guys and talking about "impulse control" and "personal growth." And I'm thinking that he couldn't have cut it in this 21st-century mob. His accent would have killed him at the box office.

Scrambling to watch some good guys on the court

March 30, 2000

By late last week I realized how far this had gone. I was in a beachfront town 1,000 miles south of here. The sun was down, the moon was high, music ruled the night — from mariachi and Marley to Santana and Limp Bizkit.

The aroma of fresh fish on an open fire floated from the waterfront cafes, mixing easily with the smell of sea water. This was the break I'd been looking for. This was the chance to let the stress wash off, spend some time with the wife and kids, away from the aggravation of deadlines, e-mail, voice mail and everything else. No editor coming up and asking "Whaddaya got for tomorrow?"

Perfect. So what am I doing? I'm going from bar to restaurant, from coffee shop to cabaret — along the beach, in the town — looking for a place that's got cable or a dish so I can watch the ISU-UCLA game.

I'm asking around and getting a lot of blank stares. Spanish is the language of choice, and I'm pretty much done after "por favor" and "gracias." I'm using body language. Shooting phantom free throws and saying — in a tortured Spanish accent — "basketball?"

Not even a blank stare.

But I press on because this somehow feels important, even if I'm not sure why.

I have never watched a college basketball game on TV. I've been to one ISU game — in '96 — and maybe four games at Drake. Until a month ago the only thing I knew about the ISU basketball team was that the coach makes close to $1 million a year in a state where most school teachers top out below $40,000. Part of it is by design: I secretly prided myself on not knowing anything about college basketball.

Go to a party sometime and casually ask: "Which one is Johnny Orr? Is he the goofy bald guy that does the car commercials or the one that's leading the Bulls into the toilet?" It's a good conversation starter, particularly in Ames.

But most of this ignorance is cultural, historical and geographic. I did not grow up with college ball. I grew up with the Yankees and that was it. Even pro basketball didn't show up much. After Frazier, Bradley, Reed and the rest of the '69 Knicks retired, I didn't pay much mind to the game. In my neighborhood the black kids played basketball and the white kids played baseball. It was no more complicated than that.

And anything below the pros was like watching Little League. Who took this stuff seriously?

Then I moved to the Midwest, and here I am — ignoring the beauty around me — looking for a place to watch a college basketball game.

This newfound interest in the Cyclones has its roots in a group of kids I met earlier this month. The Johnston Dragons are a dozen or so teens with all kinds of health problems — autism, spina bifida, Down's syndrome. They're the state Special Olympics champs, and one evening last year they went to Ames to meet and play ball with the ISU men's team.

The Cyclones had no real obligation to meet with these kids. It was just a request from a parent. But every guy on the team showed up. Fizer and Tinsley and Rancik, Johnson and Nurse — all of them were there. And for two hours this college team that was on its way to national prominence made time to play ball and hang out with these kids.

Marilyn Bauer's twin sons are Dragons, and she described what it meant to the team:

"For some of these children, it was the highlight of their lives. The Cyclones spent two hours playing with us. They picked up on which kids had the most severe disabilities, and they were lifting them up and letting them dunk the ball. It was fantastic. You have no idea how much this meant to these kids. And I think the Cyclones had fun. It's the only time I've seen Marcus Fizer smile on the basketball court. He's so serious."

So last Thursday I'm looking to see these ISU guys in their finest hour — on national TV, beating a tough team. It didn't work out. I couldn't find the game.

But maybe the ISU basketball team's finest hour had nothing to do with the Sweet 16 or the Elite 8. Maybe it had more to do with what these guys are about when they're not caught in the glare of the national spotlight.

Manhattan's own Des Moines
April 2, 2000

New York, N.Y. — It's late on a Thursday night, and I'm prowling the Lower East Side in search of a coffeehouse called Des Moines. No joke. Some guy from Iowa owns the place.

The problem for the moment is that the temperature is in the low 30s and the thin leather jacket I'm wearing isn't cutting it. And — to drive home the point — New Yorkers are overreacting. People are in ankle-length wool coats and down parkas, knit hats, gloved hands deep in their pockets. They're ambling along this little piece of real estate in the southeast corner of Manhattan, the place known as Alphabet City.

It's a neighborhood in transition, with a lot of street life and a lot of rough edges. Fliers in store windows warn that there was a rape attempt and six armed robberies on the street a week ago.

For years, the homeless and the working poor shared these streets with writers and actors, artists and dancers, filmmakers, all kinds of creative types. But now the bankers, diplomats and their friends are moving in. Apartments that were selling for $150,000 in '95 are going for three and four times that amount.

And when these uptown folks move in, they need support services — latte and arugula, fresh pasta and sushi. Walk a few blocks and you go past the Polish coffee shop, the East Village Farm, a bunch of 12-by-8 storefronts that have become three-table Thai restaurants and one-chair hair salons.

At the corner of Third and Avenue A, you pass a cafe where the sign touts coffee and chai, bagels, organic doughnuts and juice made with everything from apples and oranges to beets, ginger and parsley. Folks slip into the coffeehouse and grab one of the 20 or so tables. Others pull up a barstool. Some flop on the couch by the picture window.

This is it: Des Moines.

On a shelf behind the coffee bar is one of those kitschy white plates that says "Iowa — The Hawkeye State," with pictures of corn, the state capitol, an eastern goldfinch and Fort Dodge. Nearby is a bound copy of "The Historical Pages from *The Des Moines Register and Tribune*."

But that's about it for an Iowa presence. No stickers that say "Is This Heaven?" and no "Go 'Clones" signs. There's not even a mug shot of Bob Ray on the wall.

At a long table in the middle of the room, six women — four with crew cuts, two with hats — are talking about the film school at NYU. One table over, two guys with laptops and lattes, heads down, are working. Around the room a few others are reading newspapers and novels. A blond guy with dreadlocks rolls in on a skateboard, goes to the bar and gets in line behind a guy in a suit. An older guy at the coffee bar — sort of a well-dressed homeless type — is talking quietly to himself.

Iggy Pop is a regular and, when she's in town, Patti Smith comes in for the doughnuts.

The music is a mix of rock, techno-pop and country. The B-52's and Propellerheads follow Patsy Cline and Hank Williams.

Since it's Thursday night, Betsy Thomson made the two-hour trip from her Bucks County home in the Pennsylvania countryside and set up at a corner table. Two nights a week she's at Des Moines reading tarot cards — $25 for about 20 minutes.

"I'm an intuitive counselor. I read karmic energy and auric fields. I get guidance from birds. I listen to the land. Mostly what people want to know about are relationships and careers. Then comes health and emotional needs. This is New York, so people want to talk about where they live and where they're moving to."

Thomson — with close-cropped blond hair, seven earrings, three necklaces and a few chains — grew up on a Pennsylvania farm. The family raised corn and soybeans.

She likes working at Des Moines because of "the positive energy. It's down-home, cozy, smoke-free. A lot of cafes, they throw the coffee at you. Here they're sweet, genuine. That's Tim. That's his Iowa background."

She's talking about Tim McCoy, the owner of the place. Ask about McCoy at the bar and the woman working the counter — Sarah from Montana — says he'll be around in the morning.

"You'll love him. Everybody does. He's so warm and open. When he's not here there's an emptiness."

By 7 the next morning, McCoy is behind the counter. In between the bagels and skinny lattes, he talks about his Iowa roots. His father sold farm equipment and the family bounced from small town to smaller town — Sigourney, De Witt, Estherville, Grand Mound, Superior. At some stops he had just three kids in his class. By the time Tim was in high school, the family had crossed the Minnesota border to Blue Earth. Then it was on to college in Wisconsin.

"One day these friends of mine were driving to New York, and they asked if I wanted to go. I really wanted to go to California, but the car was heading east. That was in 1979. I got here with $16, and I fell in love with the place."

Work was easy to come by. He cut trees in Armonk — north of the Bronx — then sold cookies on a street corner. He was the nanny for a rabbi's two boys and later taught third, fourth and fifth grade in Queens.

For a while he worked as personal chef for a drug dealer and then he tended bar in a Tribeca club owned by cops and some low-level mob guys. He was a prop master and art director for MTV, VH1 and the BBC and ended up with a little face time in a k.d. lang video.

About 15 years ago, he moved to Alphabet City and in the early '90s he started managing coffee bars — "one place was so dirty even the roaches died." He opened Des Moines about a year ago.

Why Des Moines?

"Everyone has the sense that Iowans are trustworthy, honest, hard-working. I wanted that associated with my place. The other thing is, Iowans in New York hear about this place and they want to come in and talk."

McCoy talks and one of his regulars — Laurel Touby from Miami — jumps in: "You don't find this atmosphere in other places in the city. Tim's spirit makes this more of a community. This place is like an anchor store in the mall. It pulls everything together."

For two days I hang around Des Moines and talk to folks from Philadelphia, Cleveland, Austin, Seattle and just about every place in between — not one of them is from Iowa and not one has ever been there.

But I keep hearing about Tim McCoy's "small-town charm." And I hear about how folks are attracted to the guy and his shop because "he's got Iowa values." Ask McCoy about that and he smiles, shrugs, but he doesn't laugh it off.

"I guess there's something to that. You've been to Iowa. It's not like here, but that's not a bad thing."

And looking at the line of folks waiting for coffee at Des Moines, it's not bad for business.

A moving sight; Rocker brings New York together

July 4, 2000

New York, N.Y. — After months of hype and hysteria, everybody's eyes and attention were on the visitors' bullpen. The gate opened, and a few dozen cops came out and stood along the left field line. Within seconds John Rocker was running toward the mound, awash in the curses being sent by a crowd of about 50,000.

What followed was pretty standard stuff. One half inning, three batters, one strikeout and two weak infield grounders.

But John Rocker's return to New York the other night didn't have a whole lot to do with baseball. It was about race and about marketing. It was about the media and gays and immigrants and single parents. It had a lot to do with a city full of people who can't agree on anything. They argue over Rick versus Hillary, and they argue over a Springsteen concert because he's singing about the cops' shooting at Amadou Diallo 41 times.

But on the Rocker front there seemed to be little disagreement. The "Rocker Sucks" T-shirt was the preferred mode of attire. It wasn't all crude. Some folks got clever.

A sporting goods store took out a full-page newspaper ad with an unflattering photo of Rocker under a line that said "Show Compassion to a Troubled Soul," urging folks to be kind to "our angry prodigal son."

The Daily News had a front-page banner headline calling the pitcher a wimp. That was followed by eight pages of Rocker stories.

Scattered around inside the paper was the news of Elian's return to Cuba, the Supreme Court's striking down the Nebraska abortion law and the court saying it was not OK to be a gay scout leader. The papers even buried Darva Conger's getting naked for Playboy.

This goes back six months to a Sports Illustrated interview where the Braves reliever was describing his contempt for the city and the people who call it home.

He said to the reporter: "Imagine having to take the 7 train, looking like you're (in) Beirut next to some kid with purple hair, next to some queer with AIDS, right next to some dude who got out of jail for the fourth time, right next to some 20-year-old mom with four kids."

There was more: "The biggest thing I don't like about New York are the foreigners."

So Thursday night Rocker was coming back to play in New York for the first time, and I had tickets to the game. I took the kids. We rode the 7 train out to Shea. Outside the stadium we were greeted by a mob of guys carrying signs that said things like "I Hate RocKKKer," "The Ku Klux Kloser" and "Rocker I Want to Eat Your Liver."

A Fox News crew was whipping up the crowd, getting folks to chant "Rocker Sucks." I was almost moved to tears when I saw my 10-year-old at the front of the crowd — his 13-year-old brother behind him — chanting along. I couldn't wait to tell my wife and the grandfolks that the kids were on national TV.

Inside the stadium I ran into Larry P. — "Don't put my name in the paper; I'll get in trouble." He's worked security at Shea for 23 years, "and I ain't never seen this kinda cops around here. Don't put me in the paper. Where'd you say you're from?" On this night, Larry's job was to keep folks away from the Braves bullpen. Not a big problem.

"This is just people havin' fun with the guy. Nobody'll get hurt or nothin'."

Then he threw out a little street philosophy.

"The thing is, he should understand that you can't talk about people that way and not get them all worked up."

I was thinking about that while we rode the 7 train back to Manhattan after the game. I looked around the car, and it was thick with people of every shape, color, size, background — folks who seemed to have little in common. What struck me was how the city pulled together on this one. Even in this town where bigotry is no stranger, people got it.

Certain art just requires a certain frame of mind
July 13, 2000

I've seen the Mona Lisa and Picasso's Guernica. I've gazed up at Michelangelo's handiwork in the Sistine Chapel, and I've been through rooms full of Rembrandts and Monets. I've looked at the finest tribal art India has to offer, and I've been in the Guggenheim and the Met at least a dozen times.

And none of it has gotten through to me. On the art front, I just don't get it. That's not to say there isn't hope. When I was a kid the walls of my room were thick with Yankees photos. These were pictures clipped from newspapers, magazines, yearbooks and hung with Scotch tape. So when I think about that now I'm impressed with how sophisticated I've gotten.

These days, my walls hold framed and autographed photos of Mantle and DiMaggio, Berra, Larsen and Rizzuto.

And I've branched out into pop culture.

I've got an original poster from the '69 Woodstock Festival and one from a recent Dylan concert. I've even got a Marley print that I bought on a Jamaican beach in a previous life.

I bring this up because I was invited to an art gallery this week and — even though I knew I couldn't do the place justice — I went. What caught my attention was the location. I hear the word art, and I think of a paint-splattered garret in the West Village. Or a storefront gallery in Soho. Or even a loft in the shadow of the Iowa State Capitol.

This place is on the 18th floor of the Financial Center in downtown Des Moines — down the hall from a law office, above Wells Fargo and right below financier John Pappajohn.

But this is not about space. It's about art.

I walk through the door of the Steven Vail Galleries and the first thing to catch my eye is a 60-by-60 painting of a nude woman. Not to be crude about it, but it's basically a crotch shot. The little info tag says this is Gabriella and she was painted by Bob Stanley in 1997. It's on the block for $22,000 — an obscene amount when you figure a ball autographed by The Babe goes for only $5,000.

I walk on. A few feet over is Andrea, a similarly positioned, $22,000 Bob Stanley nude. She's not far from Suzanna. And Suzanna is near Samantha.

In between these women are abstract pieces by a guy named Jan Frank. To the untrained eye — that being my myopic vision — these 60-by-50s are no more than drippings on canvas. But Karolyn Sherwood, my guide on this tour, said these were also naked women.

"These are young female nudes who might hang out (with Frank) for a few hours and leave and then he paints what he feels. It's not 'Hold still and I'll paint you.' It's more lyrical."

Sherwood's role in this operation is to find local collectors and hook them up with paintings they like. Steven Vail is the big picture guy. His job is to broker the Rauschenbergs and the Warhols, the Rothkos and Pollocks, the museum-quality stuff. He's been at it about 10 years. He started when he was at Drake, not long after he graduated from Valley High.

"I was restless in college. Couldn't sit still. I started selling prints and posters out of my car. Then it just got out of hand."

For a few years he was partner in a gallery on Southwest Fifth. In December he opened this place. He said it's not easy selling six-figure art in this market, but there's an upside.

"We're not in the limelight here, obviously. But there are a lot of people who like that. There are people who are willing to come here and do business because they want a quiet process."

As for doing business in the Financial Center, Vail and Sherwood say they're aiming for a certain mind-set. Both use the term "downtown mentality." She says they're looking for the collector, not the impulse buyer.

"We're not selling art that matches your sofa. We don't sell landscapes. We're at a different level."

I think about that as I head out the door and I pass Gabriella, Samantha and the others. I'm thinking about how DiMaggio and Mantle — even Dylan — go well with my sofa.

Mets fan makes first trip to clamorous New York

October 24, 2000

At about 7 Saturday night I was on the corner of 161st and River — out past the left field wall at Yankee Stadium.

In front of me were a few hundred kids from four Jersey high school marching bands. They were banging loud enough to drown out the subway, getting ready to play at the opening game of the World Series. Off to my left was a gaggle of New York City cops in a variety of shapes, sizes, colors. One of the cops had stuffed herself into a sweater and pants outfit worthy of Jennifer Lopez. Another one had his long dreadlocks pulled back into a large bun.

Not far from that bunch was a woman holding a Chihuahua. The dog was wearing a custom-made Yankees uniform. Near the woman was a guy — he looked about 65 — telling a cop how he had his ticket ripped off. He was fighting back tears. His son stood next to him, his fists clenched. There was a sadness that touched everybody who watched that little bit of street drama.

One of the folks watching — one of the folks touched — was Troy Plummer of Des Moines, a Mets fan making his first trip to New York. Plummer, 31, works in admissions at Grand View. He won a radio contest and got tickets for the first two games at the Stadium. This meant going into the Bronx, one of the largest, toughest slums in the country. It's a place best-known for crime and drugs, hookers, violence and the New York Yankees. It's a place I used to call home.

Plummer was taking it in. In this neighborhood famous for poverty he passed a clothing shop selling Phat Farm sweaters for $102. He was walking past sports bars where a small Coke went for $5, beers were $8 and a double Stoly and tonic went for $16. There were lines to get into those places.

Plummer got to see an interesting mix of celebrities — Puff Daddy and Jesse Jackson, Chris Rock and Sarah Jessica Parker, Billy Joel and Penny Marshall. And he got to see folks who were prancing around, wanting him and everybody else to believe they were celebrities.

He walked past a ticketless pack of women who drove three hours from upstate New York, got to the Stadium at about noon —

"So I'm talkin' to this guy . . ."

eight hours before the first pitch — just to see the crowds and feel the excitement. They planned to be back home in Albany in time to watch the game on TV.

On one corner he met Jessie Foyla, an 85-year-old Phillies fan who hasn't missed a Series in 36 years. She was wearing a floor-length cape made with the ticket stubs from the games she's gone to. The oldest was from '64, the Yanks and Cards. It sold for $8 — about one-tenth the price of a cheap seat this year.

Plummer pressed on and found his seat out in left field. He sat near Yankee fans who were praying with men on base — "Please God, just a base hit" — and he talked with guys who drove in from Ohio to catch one game.

He sat near Herb Weidner, an old Brooklyn Dodgers fan who skipped high school and went to the Polo Grounds that October '51 afternoon when Ralph Branca threw the pitch to Bobby Thomson.

"In a lot of ways that was the high point of my life," said Weidner. "But the Dodgers lost. That still hurts. The worst part was that at the time I couldn't tell anybody I was there because I was supposed to be in school."

Plummer was taking videos and stills, peeking through binoculars. At times he was looking like a wide-eyed kid. Then, less than 48 hours after getting off the plane at LaGuardia, he was back at the airport heading home to Iowa. So what did he think about the city and everything around him?

He laughed and said he was still shaking his head over the cop in the dreadlocks.

"I can't get over that guy's hair. A cop. That just blows me away."

That's it? Anything else impress you?

"I noticed that New York women swear a lot more than I'm used to. Even the pretty women."

Then, after a little more thought, he said: "I guess the big thing is, I found the people to be a lot nicer than I expected, a lot tamer."

And that was after Clemens threw the bat at Piazza.

He waives right to remain silent . . . no more liquor

November 7, 2000

It was 2 in the morning, the road was dark, deserted, and he was having a hard time driving. He briefly strayed over the yellow line, into the other lane. He swung back as quick as he could, but it was too late. First he saw the red lights, and then he saw the squad car behind him. He pulled over.

He politely answered the police officer's question: "Yes, officer. I've been drinking." He took a Breathalyzer and blew a .17, well over the .10 limit. The cop asked him to step out of the car.

He was a newspaper executive in his mid-30s, a player in the community. The governor and mayor would take his calls. They knew he liked nothing better than a story about some politician or some self-important business-type screwing up, getting nailed for something like drunken driving. A decade earlier he'd hounded a city council president out of office with a week's worth of stories about the guy getting behind the wheel after a night of partying.

That series got him some attention. It helped make his newspaper career.

Now here he was — in a suit and tie — on the roadside being arrested in the middle of the night. He got out of the car, turned around to have the handcuffs slapped on. He listened to his rights being read. He should have resented this small-town cop — a kid of maybe 21 — pushing him around. There should have been some anger here, maybe even some embarrassment. But what he was feeling was an odd sense of relief. It was like a weight had been lifted. The secret was out. Let's go on from here.

For the past couple of years he knew his drinking was out of control. He'd been keeping a bottle in the car, slipping out of the office a few times a day to take hit of vodka or a shot of Jack Daniels. It was nothing to spend three or four hours at the bar after work — three or four times a week — and then go home and have a couple of drinks.

He'd go out to dinner with his girlfriend, they'd order a bottle of wine, she'd have a glass or two and he'd polish it off. He'd sort of slipped into this mode in the 12 or so years since college. Everybody drank, everybody got high. But more and more he was spending time drinking alone.

It was different when he was living in the city. After a night of drinking he'd jump on the subway, grab a cab. Now he was living upstate and he was driving a lot. He knew it was only a matter of time before he got busted. He hoped it would come before he did some permanent damage, killed somebody or killed himself.

This was it.

He was booked, photographed, stuck in the town lock-up for an hour or so. Then the cops drove him home and told him where he could get his car the next morning. On the counter in his apartment was a quart of vodka — Stolichnaya. He'd bought the bottle on his way home from work, drank three or four shots and then went out to dinner with friends. More drinks before dinner, some wine with the meal and a little time at the bar before driving home.

Then the arrest.

He stared at the vodka for a minute. He picked up the bottle, took a long hit and poured the rest down the drain, saying: "I am done with this stuff." He tossed the empty bottle in the garbage. It was like something out of an Italian opera — overly dramatic, done for effect. He had to laugh at himself. But it was going to be his last drink and he wanted to remember it.

And he did. That was May 29, 1985 — a date that's become one of those road-markers, as important as his birthday, his anniversary, the date his father died.

In the 15 years since that night, he's written more stories about politicians and others getting busted for drunken driving. And every time he writes one of those — or reads one of them — he gets this image in his head. It's late at night on a deserted road and there are red lights. He's standing there in handcuffs, a fresh-faced cop telling him he has the right to remain silent.

You still don't have to accept things as they are

December 7, 2000

It was about 11 at night and I couldn't sleep. Unusual in those days. This was back in December 1980 and I was the morning editor at the Kingston Daily Freeman, a small paper in New York's Hudson Valley. The paper came out at noon so I had to be up at 5 and at work by 6.

And now it was 11 and I couldn't sleep. I was sitting at the kitchen table thumbing through a magazine when the phone rang. Friends knew I kept crazy hours, but they wouldn't call that late just to chat. This had the feel of one of those 3 in the morning calls.

It was Neal Allen, a reporter at the paper. There was news breaking on the wires. John Lennon was shot to death outside the Dakota in Manhattan. Neal wanted me to know so I wouldn't walk into this story cold in the morning.

I thanked him and flipped on the tube. Crowds were gathering at the Dakota, people were already bringing flowers and cards, piling them outside the fence.

There was a lot of confusion, all kinds of speculation about why it happened, how it happened. There was talk about a fan gone mad. A guy who idolized Lennon losing it, pulling out a gun and emptying it into John while Yoko Ono stood and watched. All kinds of police brass and politicians were coming forward to weigh in. Everybody had something to say, a little tidbit about Lennon and his time in the city, a theory about why he was killed.

After a few minutes it all started running together. It was just background noise. I really didn't care who shot him or why. It didn't matter. John Lennon was dead and — almost immediately — it felt like something had changed.

I shut off the TV and went down to the office to get started on the next day's paper. It didn't help. That dark cloud hung around for weeks, ruining Christmas and everything else. It seemed like everybody had a Beatles story, all this coming of age stuff. Everybody wanted to talk about how John Lennon touched their lives — with his music, his politics, his humor, his style.

Even now, 20 years after those bullets were pumped into his

body, Lennon's still getting through to people, he's still some sort of symbol, a reminder of what can happen if you refuse to accept things as they are.

And personally, I still feel like I owe the guy something.

Back in the early '60s — pre-Beatles — I ran with the greaser crowd, guys who loved Dion, the Four Seasons, Bobby Darin. Life was pretty well laid out:

Finish high school — or quit at 16 — and go in the service for a few years. Come home, get a good union job, get married, live in the old neighborhood for a while and in a few years — if you're lucky — move from the Bronx to the Promised Land: Long Island or Jersey.

To the extent that I thought about it, I pretty much bought into that. And then the Beatles came along and I was totally hooked on the music — even if I was suspicious of this whole deal with the hair and the accents. Around that time, the winter of '64, only one guy from the neighborhood was cutting against the grain. Genaro Satriano went to the High School of Art and Design in Manhattan. Naturally he was looked at with suspicion. You know what kind of people go to those schools. And he loved the Beatles. So we started spending a lot of time together.

We even ventured out of the Bronx, heading down to the Village on weekends, walking through Washington Square Park and listening to the folkies jamming around the fountain, singing "The Times They are A Changin'." There were poetry readings. I met guys and gals who were different from the kids I grew up with. These folks were planning on going to college. And some of them weren't even Jewish.

I started reading — "Catcher in the Rye," "Stranger in a Strange Land." Within a year nothing was the same. And at the bottom of it all, holding everything together, was the music — Dylan and the Beatles, and Lennon in particular.

I didn't really think about it much until the night John Lennon was shot.

It sounds corny, but Iowa has kinda grown on me

December 23, 2000

Eight years ago this week I came to Des Moines for the first time and I felt — and acted — like I was on some sort of fact-finding mission. I was thinking about moving here and I wanted to know what these Iowans were all about: what they wore, what they ate, who they admired and why.

And — most important — I wanted to make sure that no matter how long I hung around, none of that rubbed off on me. So I moved here and I was constantly on the lookout for any sign that I was getting soft, losing it, becoming an Iowan. I kept my New York plates, I kept my accent and I kept my attitude. Nobody was going to look at me, listen to me and wonder whether maybe I was from Strawberry Point or What Cheer.

This is how bad it got: Not long after I moved here I was visiting a friend out in San Francisco. He introduced me to some folks and said: "This is Rob. He's from Iowa." I lost it. I got in his face and said: "I'm NOT from Iowa. I'm just living there. Temporarily. Short term."

He got the message and I don't think I've heard from him since. I felt bad, but I was obsessed. I had to make this work.

Now as I close out my Iowa phase, as I write my last column for *The Des Moines Register* and head back to the Eastern time zone, I see that I've failed miserably. I've let this town get to me. I leave here a changed man. I've traded in my short leather bomber jacket for a hooded down coat and I drive an SUV. I no longer yell obscenities at the radio when the guy is talking about the price of May beans, June hogs, July corn.

It's been at least two years since I've given another driver the finger. When the TV weather guy says it'll be "warming up to 12 degrees by this weekend," I know he's serious. I understand that when someone compliments a woman who's wearing reindeer earrings — with a red nose that lights up — they're not being sarcastic.

I realize that when properly garnished, Jell-O salad can be a very articulate culinary statement. And I'm no longer asking myself: "Why the hell is it pronounced nuh-VAY-duh and MAA-drid?"

After eight years I've come to terms with the fact that people in this state can elect one of the most conservative, mundane members of the U.S. Senate, a guy who lives in the background. Then they go to the polls a few years later and elect his counterpart — a left-wing quote meister, a guy who couldn't find the background with a road map.

I've stopped wondering how Tom Vilsack and Terry Branstad both get approval ratings in the 70 percent range. I've come to appreciate that when readers in Lamoni and Knoxville call to tell me they liked something that I've written and want me to stop by for coffee when I'm in the area, they mean it.

I've come to understand that it's possible for folks in an entire community — a neighborhood, a town, a city, a state — to look out for each other. Living in Iowa has taught me that not everybody is angling to get something for themselves. It took me a while to appreciate that, to be able to relax and let my guard down — a bit.

This is not the kind of thing I could have written four or five years ago. And maybe it's something I won't ever feel comfortable writing again. But for now, I feel like it's OK to admit this place has gotten to me in all the right ways.

So I've changed, and over the past few years I've come to recognize this change.

But I didn't appreciate how far I'd come until last month when I was down in Fort Lauderdale meeting with my new employers. One of the editors introduced me to a group of reporters, saying: "This is Rob. He's from Iowa." I let it go. I decided if they think I'm from Iowa, that's not a bad thing.

But later, when that editor had his back turned, I gave him the finger — just for old times' sake.

Attack leaves scar on my hometown
September 29, 2001

I got back from New York late Sunday night and a friend called from Iowa to see how I was, what it was like in the city. I told her it was very sad, but I was OK, glad to be home. I let it go at that.

Later I felt bad, I felt like I lied to her. I should have said that for the first time in eight days I didn't feel as if I was on the verge of tears, I wasn't surrounded by people who have been damaged in ways they might never understand.

And I should have at least tried to describe what I saw and felt that first night, when I got off the plane and grabbed a cab into Manhattan.

The cabbie was talking non-stop about what a bad week he was having, but when we reached the bridge he got real quiet and just pointed out the window. I looked to my left, down the East River and saw nothing but smoke where the World Trade Center used to be. I couldn't take my eyes off it, and I still can't get it out of my mind. That smoke-filled hole in the skyline is about as articulate as you can be if you want to tell somebody what's happened to New York City.

That was on Sept. 16. For the next seven days I walked around the city — my hometown — and found a sad, at times threatening, mix of the familiar and the unknown. I went down to Wall Street, not far from where I used to work, and had to show my ID at three check-points over four blocks.

Lower Manhattan was a maze of police barricades and road-blocks. The cops were in full battle gear, and the National Guard — camouflage, helmets, some gas masks — looked like an occupying force in a war-torn city. Smoke and ash shared the air space with patriotic music. Everything I saw and heard seemed exaggerated, but what hit me the hardest was the mood of the folks around me. I was expecting to see New Yorkers heading out to work in the morning — fast-paced, no time for pleasantries, keep your head down and get where you're going. What I found were slow-moving people looking straight ahead through sad, tired eyes, some crying.

Coming out of the subway by City Hall a guy brushed up against me and apologized — twice. And I found myself telling him several times that it was OK, don't worry. We both understood what was going on.

I walked past street vendors — the ones selling $5 wallets and bootlegged CDs — and they were branching out into flags and "God Bless America" buttons. Next to them were folks hawking the tabloids with front-page mugs of Osama bin Laden and the headline: "Wanted Dead or Alive."

Also on the rack was a weekly newspaper with a front page showing a World Trade Center postcard and the headline "Wish You Were Here." I passed an Italian restaurant on Chambers and Broadway with a "Declare War on Afghanistan" sign in the window.

I heard two women talking on Wall Street, one asking the other: "How many people did you lose?" I talked with a building manager four blocks from Ground Zero who was on the roof when the second plane hit and was thrown about 10 feet by the blast. He felt the heat.

I ate lunch in a pizza place where the owner was talking about how many of his customers were killed. I talked with dozens of people who lost hundreds of friends.

I walked into a union hall and found some folks gathered around a lunch table, some newspapers spread out in front of them. Guys reading the paper. It's what you'd expect to see in mid-September when the Yankees are up by 12, Clemens is 20 and 1, and the Mets are making a late run in the NL East.

But these guys were a long way from the sports pages. They were looking at a photo package of the dead. They found five or six co-workers. Another 20 are still missing.

And even if these guys had turned to sports, they'd have been reading stories about how nobody's got it in them to go to a ballgame and cheer. Not when 6,000 people are buried under that rubble downtown. I should have laid that all out for my friend when she called. But I couldn't find the words.

Humility easily trumps Big Apple's brashness

September 12, 2002

New York, N.Y. — When a city of 8 million people falls silent, it's a powerful moment, particularly in a place where people pride themselves on being loud and in your face. Where defiance and arrogance are worn like badges of honor. And where showing your patriotism — as one guy put it — is "like telling people how much you love your wife. Who cares? Keep it to yourself."

But Wednesday was different. This was a different New York. A mellower place, even humble at times. It was a day to honor heroes and remember the dead. There was a sense of cohesion, coming together. You could see it on the streets uptown where folks were walking arm-in-arm, holding hands, hugging their kids a bit tighter, wearing shirts that paid tribute to the fallen.

You could see it on the subway where it looked like every third person was wearing a flag — on a hat, a shirt, a scarf, on a bag or a tie.

And you could see it long before the sun came up. It started about 1 in the morning in the outer banks of the five boroughs where drummers and bagpipers marched all through the night, getting to ground zero about 8 in the morning.

You could see it in Greenwich Village, where folks at an all-night peace rally — complete with Father Daniel Berrigan and holistic massages — condemned America's actions, but praised the cops, firefighters and victims of 9/11.

Another place you could see the difference was at Rockefeller Plaza, where a photo exhibit — "Faces of Ground Zero," 85 portraits, each 9 feet tall — had people in tears as they walked along. These were pictures of survivors, of cops and firefighters, ministers, office workers, anybody who jumped in and helped with the rescue and the cleanup.

And you could see it across the street, along Sixth Avenue, where a 9/11 quilt exhibit covered six continents and showed the works of artists such as Jenny Hearn from South Africa and Jane Sassaman from Ames, who studied textile design at the University of Iowa. You don't usually see quilts getting that kind of attention, drawing crowds in midtown Manhattan. But like everything else about this city on Wednesday, this was different.

It was still New York. It wasn't as if folks were walking around hugging strangers, smiling and saying, "Have a nice day." In Union Square Park, Buddhist monks sat, prayed, chanted and softly banged their drums in the shadow of posters showing the names of the thousands who died a year ago.

If there was one place you could feel the impact, see the differences and sense a profound change in New York City, it was at ground zero. As you approached in the morning, there were no vendors selling T-shirts, key chains, cigarette lighters and other 9/11 junk. In their place were little prayer stands where folks gathered to hold hands and seek a few moments of peace. People were handing out pamphlets titled "Strategies for Coping."

Get closer to ground zero, and there were thousands of folks who lost family and friends at the World Trade Center. They were lined up waiting to get in and place flowers and other mementos at the site. They'd be hearing Gov. George Pataki read the Gettysburg Address and former Mayor Rudy Giuliani begin reading the names of the nearly 3,000 people who died in the attack.

As those family members walked along, each was given an orchid lei — 4,000 sent by the state of Hawaii. Many of these folks wore photos and pins showing the people they lost. Some children wore T-shirts that said things like: "In Memory of My Cousin Paul" and "My Daddy Died a Hero."

That was ground zero. Another place where the 9/11 impact was exceptionally powerful was at a firehouse in the Park Slope section of Brooklyn, Squad Company 1. These folks got one of the first calls a year ago. It was time for shift change, but they stayed on the job. Some even came in from home. It cost them. This company lost 12 men that day, killed when the south tower collapsed.

One of the dead was Capt. Michael Esposito, who left his parents, five brothers, a wife and two sons. They all showed up at the firehouse Wednesday to take part in a ceremony. They banded together at 10:29, the time of the second moment of silence, the time the second tower fell.

When the vigil was over, 16-year-old Andrew Esposito talked about his dad, about 9/11 and about the kind of year he's had. "I grew up a lot. I just look at life differently now. But I'm not angry anymore. I really miss Dad, but I've got to get on with my life. What else can I do?"

That was another thing that came across in New York. A lot of folks talked about the need to let go and move on. Not that anybody expects things to ever be the same.

Soul Searching — New York Style
October 18, 2002

It's been about 25 years since I moved out of my mother's apartment, but my room is intact, just like I left it — the bed and the bookshelf, the closet, the desk.

Over the years I've been in and out of there hundreds of times. I've looked in that closet, found the old Nehru shirt I wore once, the sandals I bought on a SoHo street corner and a shiny off-white suit that looked like it was lifted from John Travolta's locker. There was the guitar — a hollow red Gibson — and a set of bongo drums.

I've rifled through that bookshelf, pulling out the stack of Vonnegut paperbacks, some Hemingway, what looks like a virgin copy of "Catch 22." On the top shelf there's a pile of old yellow newspapers — the Kingston Daily Freeman from '76, my first job. And on the bottom shelf there's the box of 45s, from Dion and Bobby Darin — "The Wanderer," "Mack the Knife" — to the Beatles and the Byrds. There's even a copy of "Winchester Cathedral." Must have been a gift from a cousin out on Long Island.

So I've been through all that more than once. But I've never really ventured into the desk. I've never been real high on this "down memory lane" shtick. Then the other night I was back in the apartment with time on my hands, and I started going through the drawers. In the top one I found the business cards from my bands — the Fifth Generation and the Funkshin. Those were high school years, one rock 'n' roll, one rhythm and blues.

Then there was Carol and the Jubilettes, that first year out of high school when I was trying to make a living. This was serious. Three chick singers, two guy dancers and six musicians — that was 10 African-Americans and a white guy on lead guitar. We played the Harlem Cultural Festival, all kinds of bars in the south Bronx, and we played the Village Gate, a lower Manhattan jazz club that looked real good on my resume.

I kept going through the drawers and found my high school yearbook, class of '67. The guys all trying to look like a cross between James Dean and Keith Richards.

And then there were the girls with their puffed-up beehives, makeup by the pound.

Thumb through the book, look at the pictures, and under each one the student talked about ambition. It was a lot funnier if you knew these folks. Like Gene Gallo saying he wanted to be a neurosurgeon and Ralph Bianca hoping to become a wine taster and fresh air inspector. And me? My only goal in life was to meet Bob Dylan. That's what passed for ambition back then. I closed the yearbook, marveling at how clever I was for a kid of only 17.

One more drawer, on the bottom. Under a bunch of papers I found something I'd forgotten about. I found "The Bridge." This was the high school poetry book. On Page 33 I found my poem. I wrote it when I was about 16 and going through the kind of changes everybody goes through around then. I was in transition, having gone from Catholic school to public, from being a kid to trying to act grown up. But I wasn't quite there.

And that poem — called Soul Searching-New York Style — was a stark reminder:

Somewhere in this world lies the answer
The words which will show me the light
Before I die I must rise up to seek them
I believe I'll be leaving tonight
I've waited too long to be troubled
By the song the clergy all sing
I've listened to them for two decades
And they've never told me a thing
I may be wrong in my doubting
Of what the clergy all preach
But first I must learn to believe in myself
Or heaven I'll never reach
And at last I've discovered the reason
Clearly the light I can see
Although I may doubt I believe in God
God has always believed in me.

I put the book down and slowly closed the drawer. I was feeling a combination of embarrassment and pride. And I was surprised at how little things have changed in the years since I wrote that.

In the city that doesn't sleep . . .

August 20, 2003

Vacation time in New York City.

You're walking in the South Bronx, and some guy in cutoffs and a do-rag knocks into you, growls and tells you to "Watch where the (heck) ya goin'." You immediately check your wallet to make sure he didn't pick your pocket. You're walking on Fifth Avenue and some guy in an Armani suit knocks into you, smiles and says, "Pardon me, sir." You immediately check your wallet to make sure he didn't pick your pocket.

Some woman comes out of a SoHo gallery and she's wearing a see-through skirt and a thong. It's impolite to stare. And it's impolite to ignore someone so desperate for attention. It's a tough call on short notice.

You go into a midtown bagel shop and it's run by Muslims. You go into a grocery store on the lower East Side and the guy in the yarmulke is speaking Korean.

You're waiting for a bus in Harlem, feeling like you couldn't be any further from the Heartland. Then you look across the street and notice the billboard that says: "Go Ahead, Make My Pork Chop." It's an ad for the Des Moines-based National Pork Board.

You're going out to dinner and you can't figure out what to eat — Ethiopian, Turkish, Malaysian. You pick Indian and then you have to decide if you're going to do Punjabi or Bengali. Now you're thinking you might just stay home and eat cheap, get a $22 pizza — $25 with fresh tomatoes and basil.

You're walking in the East Village and you meet some woman running for Democratic district leader, and it turns out she was your wife's favorite teacher in high school. And she's also the daughter of Harold Stassen, the former Minnesota governor who ran for president so many times that he became a metaphor for hopelessness.

You go to a hip-hop dance club in the West Village, get there at 9 and have to wait two hours for the music to start.

You take the kids to a game at Yankee Stadium and it would have been cheaper to send them to ISU for a semester.

You go to a dinner party — some friend of the in-laws — and you find yourself in an upper West Side penthouse overlooking the

Hudson River. It turns out the host is a writer, the guy who writes the scripts for Ken Burns — "Civil War" and "Baseball," "Jazz" and "Mark Twain." And his next-door neighbor is Chris Columbus, the guy who produced the Harry Potter films and directed "Home Alone," "Mrs. Doubtfire" and a bunch of other stuff.

Then there's the New York City news.

There's the Queens firehouse that was closed down because the place was overrun by rats. There's the Brooklyn councilman who was shot to death by his political opponent. There's the multi-billion dollar hole in the city budget. There's the two drunks beating up a Sikh because — with his turban — he looked like Osama bin Laden.

But the story that gets your attention is the one about Jean Marie Graziano, the Staten Island defense lawyer banned from visiting her clients in jail because she was caught "interacting intimately" with one of the inmates, a murder and racketeering suspect named Frank "Frankie Fap" Fappiano. And the headline on the story? "La Cozy Nostra." Cute.

Then there's the simple things. Go up to the Bronx to visit your mother, get to the apartment building and find out the buzzer system isn't working and you don't have your cell phone and can't call to tell her to let you in. So you go stand under her second-floor window and scream her name a half-dozen times. She doesn't hear you, but her downstairs neighbor does. So the neighbor bangs on the heating pipes with a broom handle to get your mother's attention — it saves a phone call. Your mother comes to the window and throws down the keys, but they fall short and end up in the bushes on the other side of the fence. So you climb the fence, rifle around, find the keys, climb back over the fence and let yourself into the building. And the elevator's broken so you have to walk up.

But it's worth the effort. You're greeted with a hug, a kiss, a smile and the kind of in-your-face honesty that makes the mother-son relationship so special:

"When the hell did you get so gray . . . Your hair's starting to fall out . . . You're getting a belly."

Now it's been about two weeks and you're ready to leave. You've done it all, seen it all. Then there's a blackout and the city gets real interesting.

Home to a strange country
October 22, 2003

In those early years I was never much of a traveler. Vacation usually meant a week at some funky beach on the coast of Maine. Or a road trip to some exotic cultural shrine, like Graceland or Cooperstown.

International travel?

Maybe fly to San Diego, rent a car, drive over the border and spend some time doing those things that make Tijuana worth visiting.

But that's changed. Now I'm hooked, and I've been on the road a lot lately — business and pleasure, boredom, mid-life crisis. And I'm seeing these patterns. I'm getting a sense of how being in these different places feeds into your mind-set. How it sometimes changes you — long and short term.

I get off a plane in California — San Francisco, L.A. — and there's this self-conscious hipness. Everybody wants to be noticed, so you've got to play into it or get lost in the crowd. I'm suddenly thinking that maybe some blonde streaks in with the brown and gray might not be a bad idea.

In New York I get energized by the chaos. I feel this need to get out in front. I've got to be the first one down to the baggage claim, just for the hell of it. I've got to cut some guy off to be first in line for a cab — even if there are a dozen cabs lined up. And the longer I'm there, the crazier it gets.

Then there's the big picture, the world view, the places beyond Tijuana, the places that are even more exotic than Graceland.

There's India — where my wife is from. I get there and feel an overpowering sense of spirituality. It's in the air. The comfort level, the sense of security, is like nothing I've ever felt. I never thought I'd have fun and a few laughs while hanging out at 15th-century tombs. Or feel a sense of peace and isolation in a place where there are 1 billion other people. But that's India.

And that brings me around to Italy, a place that — for me — has a strange sense of familiarity.

Familiar because I grew up with grandparents from Palermo and Calabria, and with friends named Nunzio and Bianca. Strange because I haven't spent much time in Italy, but it feels like home. I don't know the place, but I can get around. I can't speak the language, but I can recognize it, I can make my point.

I know when to get in somebody's face and I know when to back off. You just have to listen, pick up the signals, the little nuances. If a guy is gesturing like he's going to strangle you if you don't shut up and leave him alone, it's time to chill. Don't cut him off. Smile politely and keep moving.

This is all on my mind because I just spent a week in Trevignano Romano. It's a lakeside village about a half-hour north of Rome. I was there on personal business, and there wasn't much time to play.

But I did slip away for a few afternoons to wander around aimlessly and take it all in.

It was interesting to see a 30-foot statue of Jesus — the halo lights up at night — out in front of City Hall. On one edge of town there's a grotto and fountain, with the Virgin Mary in the middle. There were large wooden crosses everywhere — in the pharmacy, the bank, the real estate office, the coffee shop.

I'd walk those streets and see the laundry hanging from the apartment windows, the little garden in front of the grocery store, the grapevines around the schoolhouse, the Christmas wreaths draping the post office. I'd just hang back and hear folks speaking Italian — men and women, kids who are learning to talk, old folks who can barely remember how to talk. They'd all be waving their arms, yelling to make sure they were understood — even if they were just giving you directions to the hardware store.

I'd meet people named Angelina and Luigi, Giovanna and Cosmo.

And it felt, looked and sounded comfortable, natural. I got myself one of those Italian guy haircuts — longer in the back, short on the top — and I was even starting to pick up the language. It all made sense.

By the end of the week, the only thing I couldn't figure out was why guys like Giuseppe Borsellino would give this up — the fresh mozzarella, the cobblestone streets — to go live in a tenement and eat Chef Boyardee ravioli.

'60s pop culture writer has a few more stories to tell

May 17, 2004

The other day my phone rang, and it was Al Aronowitz. I was in shock. More than 20 years had gone by since we last talked, and I couldn't believe he was still alive. I had dozens of questions, but I just opened with:

"How the hell did you find me in Des Moines?"

One-word answer: "Google."

Not only is he still alive, but he's gone high-tech.

We haven't been in touch, but there were still times over the years when I'd thought about Al. When I pick up a book about '60s music, the first thing I do is turn to the back, check the index and see if there's any mention of Al Aronowitz.

If he's in there, then I know the book was well-researched and it's got some excellent detail and eyewitness accounts.

Al, now 76, was the pop culture columnist at the New York Post in the 1960s, "the godfather of rock journalism." He was one of the few reporters who took this stuff seriously, so most of the time he was the only one on the scene. If you were a musician, an artist, a writer, a poet or any kind of hipster wannabe, a mention in Al's column meant you had reached a new level. His person-to-person style set the tone for other writers in that period. It's a tone that continues into this century.

He was working the Village bars and Bowery clubs back when folks like John Sebastian and John Hammond were still passing the hat after every set. He had access. John Lennon and Allen Ginsberg would take his calls.

One of the defining moments in his career came in the early '60s when he was hired to write a piece for the Saturday Evening Post. There was a buzz in New York about this guy who was playing down in the West Village, singing Woody Guthrie-type "protest songs."

The magazine asked Aronowitz to interview Bob Dylan. The two connected and became friends.

Within months, Dylan's career took off, and Al got some of the credit. So that helped.

But the thing he's most remembered for happened on Aug. 28, 1964. That's the night Al took Dylan over to the Hotel Delmonico on Manhattan's Park Avenue and introduced him to the Beatles.

And — thanks to Al's stash — that was the night the Beatles first smoked pot. So whatever else he did with his life, Al was the guy who mixed Dylan, dope and the Beatles.

Some folks have gone on to write about that night and say it changed culture and affected world consciousness. As Al has described it, "I was just a proud and happy shadchen, a Jewish matchmaker, dancing at the princely wedding I arranged."

But the dancing didn't go on forever. The '60s didn't last, the Beatles broke up, Dylan moved on and Al fell deeper into a crippling hole of drugs and alcohol. That led to other problems — personal, professional. By the late '70s his writing career fell apart, and by the early '80s he was barely hanging on.

He was very angry, but mostly at himself. He realized he blew it big time. He couldn't get anything published. Lennon was dead, Ginsberg was old news and nobody was taking his calls. He was a charity case, living in a friend's house in upstate New York, the town of Woodstock.

Around that time, I was also living in Woodstock and working at a local newspaper. Al read something I wrote, liked it and called to invite me to his place for a drink. I ran over and could not believe that I was sitting with Al Aronowitz, the guy I grew up reading. This was the guy who could write about dinner with Mick and Keith, or hanging with the Band at the Isle of Wight Festival. There was the whole Beatles-Dylan deal and hundreds of smaller stories.

I also couldn't believe the shape he was in — he could barely walk and talk, and he had a hard time breathing. I'd go by his place a few times a week, listen to his stories and leave thinking it was the last time I'd ever see him.

But he hung on.

At some point, Al moved to Jersey, I ended up in Iowa, and we lost touch.

Then last week he called. He wanted to let me know he was sending me his new book — "Bob Dylan and the Beatles." It's a look back, a 600-page collection of columns, essays, random thoughts and photos — Al with George Harrison, with Dylan, John and Yoko. And photos of Al with some long forgotten '60s icons like Albert Grossman, Bobby Neuwirth and Dr. John.

It's a unique insight into a defining period in American history.

It's a sad look at how high you can fly and how far you can fall.

It's a powerful reminder of why I still pick up those '60s music books, turn to the back and see if there's any mention of Al Aronowitz.

Weaning myself away from Fox News
July 21, 2004

I've got this Fox News problem. I'm hooked.

I've always thought it was kind of a personal thing, sort of like a victimless crime. I'd only watch it in my room with the door closed or when I was home alone. I never talked about it in public and — most important — I never took it seriously.

But then it got ugly.

The other night my wife and I came home unexpectedly and we caught our kids — two boys under the age of 18 — watching Sean Hannity.

Naturally my wife was pretty upset. She grabbed the remote, switched to Iowa Public Television and then got in my face and blamed me for the children's behavior.

"What next, Rob? Are they going to be quoting Cal Thomas? Or picketing Planned Parenthood?"

My first instinct was to get back in her face and tell her to shut up, call her a left-wing nut case who is weak on defense and refuses to acknowledge that the Bush tax cuts are fueling an economic recovery that will benefit all Americans, not just the wealthy.

But I decided to back off. I promised her I'd try to deal with my problem, an addiction that goes back four years, back to the 2000 Iowa caucuses. It started with a call from a producer in New York, a guy from a show called "The O'Reilly Factor."

I'd heard about the show, but hadn't really watched it.

They wanted my take on the GOP race and they were offering me national attention.

I grabbed it.

I went on and this guy Bill O'Reilly introduced me as some respected authority on the ins and outs of Republican politics. I laughed and he was put off. We got past that and I talked about the potential for Gary Bauer to actually finish ahead of Alan Keyes. I think he was impressed.

Then the segment ended and within minutes my phone started ringing.

Ronnie Schwartz called from Florida wanting to know if I was the same Bobby Borsellino he grew up with. He was surprised that the kid who couldn't have picked President Eisenhower out of a lineup was now on TV pontificating on the finer points of the American political process.

Robert Kleinrock called from California. He was asking the same questions. There were about a half-dozen other calls from my past.

Then folks around Des Moines started weighing in. A lot of people watched that show.

So I started watching.

It pulled me in. It was more compelling to hear O'Reilly yelling at some liberal whose father was killed in the World Trade Center than it was to hear Larry King interviewing some porter who once carried Princess Di's bags at Heathrow.

I could watch folks like Newt Gingrich and Ollie North — disgraced Republicans who were driven from public view in the '90s — being reborn as respected authorities with valued opinions.

I could hear Bill "Roll 'Em" Bennett lecturing me about morality and family values.

Then there was Geraldo. Even if he hadn't been thrown out of Iraq I'd still say he was one of the true stars of the war.

So while I channel-surfed, I'd make it a point to check out Fox News. It was fun.

And — like I said — I didn't take it seriously. It's TV schtick. It's entertainment.

But as I begin to wean myself off this stuff I've come to realize that not everybody is laughing. Some people actually take this network seriously. They really believe Fox News is fair and balanced.

I've come to realize that some folks who watch it don't know that the guy running the show — Roger Ailes — was a top campaign consultant for Ronald Reagan and George H.W. Bush.

I've seen polls that show over 65 percent of the folks who get their news from Fox still believe there's a link between Iraq and 9/11.

I've seen "Outfoxed," the Robert Greenwald documentary where former Fox employees explain how their bosses would reward them for putting a right-wing slant on a story. They talk about the daily memos telling them how to frame information — and it was always pro-Republican.

So I go through all that and now I'm thinking maybe — for the kids' sake — I shouldn't pull back. Maybe I should keep watching Fox News and see what they're up to.

I think about that and I hear the words of Don Vito Corleone: "Keep your friends close, but your enemies closer."

That's something I want my kids to understand.

From strollers and T-ball to schedules and dorm halls

August 25, 2004

It was a Sunday morning, I walked into the kitchen to grab some coffee and my wife was standing there smiling.

She told me she was pregnant.

This was great. We hugged, sat and talked about our hopes and dreams, had a few laughs, some tears of joy.

I drank my coffee.

Then a couple of days later, I started to obsess about what it would be like when the kid turns 18 and goes off to college.

Now I'm finding out.

Last week he turned 18. This week we're heading east to drop him off at school.

It's a good thing. He's going off to college, not prison. So I'm smiling, upbeat, telling myself it's a blessing. I'm showing an interest in his schedule and making sure he has the proper sheets for the bed in his dorm.

Inside I'm a wreck. I'm closing out this chapter in my life, but I'm not ready to let go.

The problem is that I'm just getting with the program.

It took 18 years, and I finally realize it's not the end of the world if he leaves a half-eaten piece of pizza on the computer keyboard.

It's not a problem if he turns on every light in the house and all three TVs, and then goes outside and shoots hoops in the driveway.

He left the phone tucked into the couch in the basement?

A week's worth of dirty laundry under his bed instead of in the hamper?

Forgot to tell me about a parent-teacher conference that starts in 15 minutes?

What's the big deal? You think yelling and slamming doors is going to make things better?

Cut him some slack. He's a kid.

In the past year or two I've gotten to a point where I understand that. I've calmed down. I've learned to live with the dirty laundry, the lights and the pizza.

I'm even willing to admit that I've changed.

If you had asked me 18 years ago I'd have been lying if I had said I'd rather see my kid play T-ball than go see the Yankees and Red Sox at the stadium.

If I had to pick, back then I'd go see Bruce Springsteen at Madison Square Garden a lot faster than I'd go hear the Callanan Middle School choir.

Now?

I can still go see the Yankees and Springsteen, but my kid isn't playing T-ball anymore.

So I spend a lot of time looking back at what I could have done differently.

I wish I'd made his childhood less like the "Simpsons" and more like "Ozzie and Harriet," less "Sopranos" and more "The Brady Brunch."

But this was a "learn as you go" deal.

So it took a while to get up to speed on things like strollers and car seats. We'd go out to dinner, and I'd have to be less interested in the menu than whether a particular restaurant was "kid-friendly."

The kid would cough, and I was sure he had some rare fatal illness. I'd go in his room at night to make sure he was still breathing — and I'd run into my wife who was doing the same thing.

Now he's leaving, and I'm struggling. But I'm not alone there.

I've been talking with other folks who've been through this. I've asked what it's like when one of your kids — the first one — goes off to college.

The reaction is pretty much the same:

"It's terrible. . . . It's heartbreaking. . . . Your baby is going away. . . . Your family is being torn apart. . . . Life will never be the same."

I should have expected to hear that.

What I didn't expect were the words of wisdom I got from my mother.

She suggested there's something to look forward to.

She said: "Being a grandparent is a hell of a lot more fun than raising kids."

Grandparent? Like I wasn't feeling old and depressed already.

Iowa delegates pitch in in Harlem
September 1, 2004

New York, N.Y. — You work in the city parks and rec department, and you see it all — from the drugs and violence, to the giddy kids on the swings and slides. Even an occasional wedding.

But Tuesday morning Mike Sahariam saw something he hasn't seen in almost 30 years on the job.

Something he couldn't have expected to see as head groundskeeper at Morningside Park in Harlem.

A bus carrying three dozen peppy Iowa Republicans pulled up to the gate, and these folks got off and got to work.

For three hours they cleaned the paths, scraped and repainted the benches and picnic tables, pulled weeds around the trees, hauled garbage.

They did all this while songs like "Jungle Boogie" and "Where is the Love?" were blaring in the background.

They worked around the 11-year-old playing basketball with his grandfather, and around the homeless types snuggled up near the handball courts.

Sahariam stood there, watched, shook his head and smiled.

"When I heard volunteers were coming, I just figured it would be kids, like, teenagers. That's what you usually get around here."

This time he got lawyers and lobbyists, engineers, a couple of farmers and a bunch of politicians.

He watched them get down on the ground, crawling under the benches to scrape off the old paint, making sure the job was done right.

He saw Leon Mosley, the head of the Iowa GOP, raking leaves and plowing small piles of dirt in 80-degree heat.

He saw state senators and reps from Marshalltown, Davenport and Keota helping each other shovel, sweep and cut grass.

He watched as the head of the United States Senate Finance Committee — Chuck Grassley, decked out in jeans and sneakers — filled wheelbarrows with mulch and pushed them around the park, making sure every tree had all that it needed.

Then there was the unannounced arrival of federal Interior Secretary Gale Norton, complete with an entourage of staff and press, and at least three security guards. She walked around shaking hands, thanking folks for coming and working, talking up the Bush administration.

But even with that, the event was surprisingly apolitical.

Some folks were wearing Bush-Cheney pins, hats and T-shirts, but there was little talk about politics. That was striking, given the atmosphere in this city as it hosts the Republican National Convention.

Besides, these people were working, trying to get done before it was time to leave.

Sahariam was impressed.

"These people didn't have to do this. They could have slept late and just gone out and enjoyed the city. But we are so grateful. We need the help. Where do you start? Who do you thank?"

One person Sahariam could thank was Isaiah McGee, a 25-year-old Drake grad student from Waukee. He was the Iowa connection to this Compassion Across America project. It's something the entire Republican Party is doing in and around New York this week.

Once it was decided that the convention delegates would do volunteer service in the city, McGee decided where the Iowans would end up.

They could have gone to a Bronx soup kitchen, a homeless shelter or hospital in Brooklyn, an old-age home in Queens or one of about two dozen other places.

But McGee picked Morningside.

"As an African-American, I guess I felt a certain connection to Harlem. I thought it would be a good place for all of us. It's a place none of us would have gone. So we get out and see something new."

Then he laughs and says: "Besides, we're Iowans. We've got expertise when it comes to working outdoors."

He says that, and Grassley comes grunting by with another wheelbarrow full of mulch.

A good line and an interesting image.

He finds holiness on road less traveled
April 4, 2005

The way my grandmother saw it, the pope was God on Earth. She mentioned him, and she did the sign of the cross. He was someone who could take a problem and make things right.

So it made sense that she'd look to him and talk about him on one of the stranger days of her life — the day I got married.

My grandmother was very traditional. A wedding involved church, a priest, a white gown, tuxedos.

There were a few glitches over the years. My uncle Joey married a Jew, and my uncle Ralph married a woman from Chile.

But this still involved gowns and tuxes, stuff my grandmother could relate to.

I got married on the lawn of my in-laws' house in the Catskill Mountains, in the town of Woodstock. About 100 people gathered on the grass.

The bride was wearing a red sari. There were women in salwar kameez, men in turbans. Sitar players wearing kurta pajamas.

There were readings from the New Testament, from the Sikh and Hindu holy books, and the two families exchanged garlands. A justice of the peace performed the ceremony.

My grandmother was almost 90. She sat and watched all this, and after I'd kissed the bride, she called me over and told me to sit down next to her. She knew my wife and I were leaving for Italy the next day, and she had an idea, a plan to make this marriage work in the eyes of God.

"Bobby, go see the pope when you're over there. Go to confession. Get him to bless you."

I told her I'd see what I could do.

A week later, I was in the Vatican, walking around St. Peter's. It was all about Michelangelo, art, history. It was also about faith, about being Catholic. I thought a lot about the pope, what my grandmother said, and I was thinking that maybe starting this marriage off with a blessing, a confession, wasn't a bad idea.

I didn't get to meet the pope, and now I regret it. But a few days later I wandered into a church in Pompeii, asking around for a priest who spoke English so I could do confession.

They found a priest for me — a cute little old Italian guy. He sat down next to me, asked my name, if I was married and then said: "Go ahead."

This wasn't what I was used to. Confession meant sitting in a dark booth, being anonymous.

On top of that, I hadn't been to confession in about 15 years, I'd just lived through the 1960s and '70s, and I'd broken most of the commandments.

Now I'm sitting there telling this guy everything. He's got his head down, he's nodding along, and I'm figuring my penance will involve saying nonstop Hail Marys and Our Fathers for at least three years.

I finish, the priest looks up at me and says: "Robert, do you love your family and friends?"

I said: "Yes, Father."

He asked: "Do you care about people? Do you try to be a good person?"

I said: "Yes, Father. I try."

He stared at me, shrugged and said: "So whata yuh worried about?"

I almost laughed, but that one line got me back in touch with what's really important. It put things in perspective. It's made a difference.

It showed me you could go to the Vatican to find holiness and wisdom.

Or you can find it in a small church on a back road.

"You're kidding, right?"

By Paul Anger
Editor/*The Des Moines Register*

In early November 2004, Rob Borsellino walked into Managing Editor Rick Tapscott's office. Rick and I put our conversation on hold and waited to be entertained.

Rob always had something interesting to say. Maybe a street-wise anecdote from his next column, maybe a joke he'd heard, maybe a deadpan jab about how he was sorry to interrupt yet another high-level meeting.

Rob has always liked to poke fun at his bosses, and at himself.

So when he leaned against Rick's glass window overlooking the newsroom and said he probably had Lou Gehrig's disease, or ALS, we waited for the punchline.

"You're kidding, right?" Rick finally asked.

Rob wasn't kidding.

We talked awkwardly for a while about how it couldn't be ALS, that it wasn't confirmed. But over the next few weeks, other possibilities were ruled out.

Rob kept his sense of humor: He told newsroom colleagues he wanted more respect out of them now, given his diagnosis.

He kept writing despite increasing fatigue and deepening symptoms.

As always, his columns were irresistible, irreverent, soulful, much like Rob himself. He wrote about Liberian refugees finding comfort in a Des Moines church, got to the bottom of a tabloid report headlined "Two-Headed Bigfoot Shot by Iowa Cop," told the story of how a millionaire developer bought furniture for a family that lost everything in a fire.

Between all the medical tests, Rob did what he always did – write about the human condition in Iowa.

And then, when he felt he was ready, it was time to write about his own condition.

I can kick the denial, not the disease
February 23, 2005

I was slurring my words, I was tired and I felt weak. Friends kept asking if I was drinking again. Finally, I went to see a doctor.

I figured I'd give him my $20 co-pay, get a scrip for some useless pills, then go home and wait until I felt better.

But the doctor ran some tests and was spooked by what he saw. He sent me to a second doctor — a nerve specialist.

That guy ran more tests and at the end of the session he's telling me I have some fatal, incurable, exotic-sounding disease — amyotrophic lateral sclerosis.

Also called Lou Gehrig's Disease.

Then he's telling me most people only live a few years with this.

It's been a few months, and since that day I've had several other doctors around the country tell me pretty much the same thing.

Each time I hear it I'm in denial. I find myself sitting there avoiding the important stuff:

I won't be there for my sons' weddings, and I won't see the grandkids.

What about a will and life insurance?

Do I want to live strapped up to some breathing machine and a voice box?

Instead, I'm listening to the doctor and thinking about what a lousy year I'm having.

First my hair is getting thinner, and I have these bags under my eyes. My 29-inch waist is up to 30 and growing. The Yankees lost, and the Republicans won.

Or I'm sitting there trying to think of some positive angle, trying to find some lines to lighten things up.

I'm toying with the name. At least it's called Lou Gehrig's Disease and not Steinbrenner Syndrome or Dizzy Dean Disorder.

And once the word gets out, folks I run into will be asking about my health instead of getting in my face about the Register's liberal bias.

Sometimes it works, it takes my mind off what's really going on.

But then I try to button a shirt or make a phone call sounding sober, and I'm slapped back down to reality.

It happens when I look at my night table and see the little glass angel Laurie Gallo sent me from the Bronx, the angel blessed by Father Grippo at St. Theresa's.

It happens when I wake up in the middle of the night and my wife's lying there awake, thinking about how we went from planning our life as empty nesters to worrying about survival.

Or I hear that I'm being remembered in a Sikh temple in New Delhi at a prayer service put together by my in-laws.

Or a friend of a friend e-mails about a miracle-worker, a shaman in Brazil who might be worth seeing.

A half-dozen people are net surfing every day, checking out stem-cell research in Beijing and hearing about those rare cases of folks who live with this for as long as 30 years.

The phone rings, and it's Neal in San Francisco, Joey in Jersey or D.J. down in Kansas, old friends, guys I haven't talked with in years. They heard, and show up in Des Moines a few days later.

I find myself talking with St. Jude, the patron saint of lost causes.

In the newsroom a guy I hardly know says: "If you or your family need anything, please tell me. I'm serious. Anything I can do."

Word has started getting around, and I'm hearing that from dozens of people. It's humbling.

I've gotten get-well cards from strangers, lunch and dinner invites from business types, and teary-eyed hugs from politicians.

Several folks asked when I was going to go public, when was I going to write about this.

I kept thinking: "When I have something to say."

Then the other night I was looking back over the past few months and realized there was a lot to be said.

And I was ready to say it.

"So I'm talkin' to this guy . . ."